Violence in the Service of Order:
The Religious Framework
for Sanctioned Killing
in Ancient Egypt

Kerry Muhlestein

BAR International Series 2299
2011

Published in 2016 by
BAR Publishing, Oxford

BAR International Series 2299

Violence in the Service of Order: The Religious Framework for Sanctioned Killing in Ancient Egypt

ISBN 978 1 4073 0876 0

© K Muhlestein and the Publisher 2011

The author's moral rights under the 1988 UK Copyright,
Designs and Patents Act are hereby expressly asserted.

All rights reserved. No part of this work may be copied, reproduced, stored,
sold, distributed, scanned, saved in any form of digital format or transmitted
in any form digitally, without the written permission of the Publisher.

BAR Publishing is the trading name of British Archaeological Reports (Oxford) Ltd.
British Archaeological Reports was first incorporated in 1974 to publish the BAR
Series, International and British. In 1992 Hadrian Books Ltd became part of the BAR
group. This volume was originally published by Archaeopress in conjunction with
British Archaeological Reports (Oxford) Ltd / Hadrian Books Ltd, the Series principal
publisher, in 2011. This present volume is published by BAR Publishing, 2016.

Printed in England

BAR titles are available from:

	BAR Publishing
	122 Banbury Rd, Oxford, OX2 7BP, UK
EMAIL	info@barpublishing.com
PHONE	+44 (0)1865 310431
FAX	+44 (0)1865 316916
	www.barpublishing.com

*To the wonderful lady
who brought order to my house and my life.
Thank you so much,
Julianne Muhlestein*

Table of Contents

Chronology vii

Acknowledgments ix

Abbreviations x

Chapter 1. The Act of Killing: An Introduction 1
    Focus 3
    The Terminology of Sacrifice 5
    Getting Past the Labels 7
    Method 8

Chapter 2. Death by Narmer and Others: The Archaic Period 9
    The Narmer Palette 9
    Enigmatic Labels 10
    Sacrificial Servant Burials 11

Chapter 3. Slaying under the Aegis of the God-King: The Old Kingdom 16
    Execution 17
    Execration Texts 18
    Other Forms of Ritual Slaying 20

Chapter 4. Sanctioned Killing in the Time Between: The First Intermediate Period 26
    Egyptian Inscriptional Curses 26
    The Threats of the First Intermediate Period 29
    A Royal Decree (Coptos Decree R) 30
    The Tomb of Ankhtifi 31
    The *Instructions for Merikare* 32
    Servant Burials 33

Chapter 5. Death by Drowning, Burning, and Flaying: The Middle Kingdom and Second Intermediate Period 34
    Sacrifices associated with Burials 34
    Death by Fire and Other Unpleasant Methods 37
    Miscellaneous Punishments 40
    Curses 40

    Ritual Slaying 41

    Funerary Literature 41

    Drowning in the Second Intermediate Period 42

Chapter 6. **The Slayings of the Great Pharaohs: Dynasty 18** 45

    Possible Examples of Ritual Slaying 45

    The Death Penalty 48

    Inscriptional Threats 50

    Funerary Literature 50

Chapter 7. **Instances of Intrigue: The Ramesside Era** 52

    Royal Inscriptions 52

    Various Capital Offenses 55

    Possible Examples of Ritual Slaying 57

    The Harem Conspiracy 57

    The Great Tomb Robberies 60

Chapter 8. **The Constancy of Killing Amidst Anarchy: Dynasties 21, 22, 25, and 26** 63

    Dynasty 21 63

    Dynasty 22 64

    Dynasty 25 65

    Dynasty 26 67

Chapter 9. **A Time to Kill: The Appropriateness of Violence** 70

    A Time to Kill 77

    A Reason to Kill 80

Chapter 10. **Foreigners and** *Isfet* 83

    Chaotic Foreigners 83

    The Smiting Scene 85

    Evidences for Smiting 88

Chapter 11. **Violent Myth in the Ritual of Return** 92

    Ritual and Return 92

    The Egyptian *Illud Tempus* 94

    The Egyptian Return 95

Chapter 12. **Those Who Are about to Die, We Abhor You** 99

List of Figures

Figure 2.1 – The Narmer Palette 10

Figure 2.2 – Label of Aha 10

Figure 3.1 – Scene from the Tomb of Mereruka 18

Figure 3.2 – An Execration Figure 19

Figure 3.3 – Cage found buried near Khufu's boats at Giza 21

Figure 3.4 – Relief of Tutankhamun boat with suspended prisoner 21

Figure 4.1 – Hekaib Sanctuary on Elephantine Island 29

Figure 5.1 – Strangling scene from Mentuherkhepeshef 35

Figure 5.2 – Relief from tomb of Mentuherkhepeshef, depicting the *tekenu*
on a sled 35

Figure 5.3 – Relief of *tekenu* sled and glyphs from the tomb of Mentuherkhepeshef 35

Figure 5.4 – Relief of *tekenu*, heart, hair, and foreleg glyphs from the tomb of
Mentuherkhepeshef 36

Figure 7.1 – Determinative depicting impalement 54

Figure 9.1a – Evidences of Violence by Period 71

Figure 9.1b – Evidences of Violence by Period as Learned from Textual Sources 71

Figure 9.2a – Evidences of Plausible Violence by Dynasty 71

Figure 9.2b – Evidences of Plausible Violence by Dynasty as Learned
from Textual Sources 71

Figure 9.3a – Evidences of Burning by Dynasty 72

Figure 9.3b – Evidences of Burning by Dynasty as Learned from Textual Sources 72

Figure 9.4a – Evidences of Decapitation by Dynasty 72

Figure 9.4b – Evidences of Decapitation by Dynasty as learned from textual sources 72

Figure 9.5a – Evidences of Killing in a Ritual Context by Dynasty 73

Figure 9.5b – Evidences of Ritual Killings by Dynasty as Learned
from Textual Sources 73

Figure 9.6a – Evidences of Impalement by Dynasty 73

Figure 9.6b – Evidences of Impalement by Dynasty as Learned
from Textual Sources 73

Figure 9.7a – Evidences of Killing Associated with Burial Practice by Dynasty 74

Figure 9.7b – Evidences of Killing Associated with Burial Practice
by Dynasty as Learned from Textual Sources 74

Figure 9.8a – Evidences of Formal Execution of Enemies by Dynasty 74

Figure 9.8b – Evidences of Formal Execution of Enemies by Dynasty as Learned
   from Textual Sources 74

Figure 9.9a – Evidences of Execution of those who Uprise by Dynasty 75

Figure 9.9b – Evidences of the Execution of those who Uprise
   by Dynasty as Learned from Textual Sources 75

Figure 9.10a – Evidences of Death for Damaging or Stealing State Property
   by Dynasty 75

Figure 9.10b – Evidences of Death for Damaging or Stealing State Property
   by Dynasty as Learned from Textual Sources 75

Figure 9.11a – Evidences for Death for Those Who are False in Office by Dynasty 76

Figure 9.11b – Evidences for Death for Those Who are False in Office
   by Dynasty as Learned from Textual Sources 76

Figure 9.12a – Evidences of Death for Murder by Dynasty 76

Figure 9.12b – Evidences of Death for Murder by Dynasty as Learned
   from Textual Sources 76

Figure 9.13 – Evidences for Pages in Breasted by Dynasty 77

Figure 9.14 – Evidences for Pages in Breasted by Dynasty 77

Figure 9.15 – Evidences for Number of Pages in Breasted by Dynasty 77

Figure 10.1 – Naqada Ware Smiting Scene 85

Figure 10.2 – Ring of Amenhotep II 89

List of Tables

Chapter 2: Archaic Period Evidence of Sanctioned Killing 15

Chapter 3: Old Kingdom Evidence of Sanctioned Killing 25

Chapter 4: First Intermediate Period Evidence of Sanctioned Killing 33

Chapter 5: Middle Kingdom and Second Intermediate Period Evidence
   of Sanctioned Killing 44

Chapter 6: Eighteenth Dynasty Evidence of Sanctioned Killing 51

Chapter 7: Ramesside Evidence of Sanctioned Killing 62

Chapter 8: Third Intermediate Period and Twenty-Sixth Dynasty Evidence
   of Sanctioned Killing 69

Chronology

Early Dynastic Period

Dynasty 1 ca. 3000–2800 BCE
  Narmer?
  Aha
  Djer
  Djet
  Den
  Anedjib
  Semerkhet
  Ka'a

Dynasty 2 ca. 2800–2650 BCE
  Hetepsekhemwy
  Raneb
  Ninetjer
  Weneg
  Sened
  Peribsen
  Khasekhemwy

Old Kingdom

Dynasty 3 ca. 2650–2600 BCE
  Nebka
  Djoser
  Sekhemkhet
  Khaba
  Huni

Dynasty 4 ca. 2600–2450 BCE
  Snefru
  Khufu
  Djedefra
  Khafre
  Menkaure
  Shepseskaf

Dynasty 5 ca. 2450–2350 BCE
  Userkaf
  Sahure
  Neferirkare
  Shepseskare
  Neferefre
  Niuserre
  Menkauhor
  Djedkare
  Unas

Dynasty 6 ca. 2350–2200 BCE
  Teti
  Userkare
  Pepy I
  Merenre I
  Pepy II
  Merenre II

First Intermediate Period

Dynasties 7–8 ca. 2200–2150 BCE
  Various ephemeral rulers

Dynasties 9–10 ca. 2150–2000 BCE
  Various rulers, including:
  Kety I
  Kety II
  Kety III
  Merikare

Dynasty 11 ca. 2100–1950 BCE
  Mentuhotep I
  Inyotef I
  Inyotef II
  Inyotef III
  Mentuhotep II (Nebhepetre)
  Mentuhotep III
  Mentuhotep IV

Middle Kingdom

Dynasty 12 ca. 1950–1750 BCE
  Amenemhet I
  Senusret I
  Amenemhet II
  Senusret II
  Senusret III
  Amenemhet III
  Amenemhet IV
  Sobeknefru

Second Intermediate Period

Dynasty 13 ca. 1750–1650 BCE
  Numerous rulers

Dynasty 14 ca. 1700–1650 BCE
  Minor kings

Dynasties 15–16 ca. 1650–1550 BCE
  Sheshi
  Yaqib-har
  Khiyan
  Apophis
  Khamudi

Dynasty 17 ca. 1650–1550 BCE
  Rahotep
  Inyotef V
  Sobekemsaf
  Senakhtenre
  Seqnenre
  Kamose

New Kingdom

Dynasty 18 ca. 1550–1300 BCE
  Ahmose
  Amenhotep I
  Thutmosis I
  Thutmosis II
  Hatshepsut
  Thutmosis III
  Amenhotep II
  Thutmosis IV
  Amenhotep III
  Amenhotep IV/Akhenaten
  Smenkhkare
  Tutankhamun
  Aya
  Horemheb

Dynasty 19 ca. 1300–1200 BCE
  Ramesses I
  Seti I
  Ramesses II
  Merneptah

Seti II
Siptah
Twosre

Dynasty 20 ca. 1200–1100 BCE
Sethnakht
Ramesses III
Ramesses IV
Ramesses V
Ramesses VI
Ramesses VII
Ramesses VIII
Ramesses IX
Ramesses X
Ramesses XI

Third Intermediate Period

Dynasty 21 ca. 1100–950 BCE
Smendes
Amenemnisu
Psusennes I
Amenemope
Osorkon the Elder
Siamun
Psusennes II

Dynasty 22 ca. 950–700 BCE
Sheshonq I
Osorkon I
Sheshonq II
Takelot I
Osorkon II
Takelot II
Sheshonq III
Pami
Sheshonq V
Osorkon IV

Dynasty 23 ca. 800–700 BCE
Pedubastis
Sheshonq IV
Osorkon III
Takelot III
Rudjamum
Peftjauawybast
Iuput II

Dynasty 24 ca. 750–700 BCE
Bakenrenef

Dynasty 25 ca. 700–650 BCE
Piankhy
Shabako
Shebitku
Taharka
Tantamani

Late Period

Dynasty 26 ca. 650–550 BCE
Nekho I
Psamtek I
Nekho II
Psamtek II
Apries
Amasis
Psamtek III

Dynasty 27 ca. 550–400 BCE
Dynasty 28 ca. 400 BCE
Dynasty 29 ca. 400–350 BCE
Dynasty 30 ca. 350–300 BCE

* Dates are approximate and rounded to the nearest half century

Acknowledgments

A work of this expanse and nature is not possible without the help of a great many people. The number of people who have contributed to this disquisition is great, and I am certain I will accidentally omit some who have made valuable contributions. I ask their forgiveness in advance. Of course I am forever indebted to Dr. Antonio Loprieno and Dr. Willeke Wendrich in particular, who have put in long hours of work and offered many invaluable aids. I would not be capable of doing this work were it not for their tutelage. I also would never have been able to wade my way through the myriad tasks that were a part of completing this without the help of Diane Abugheida and Anna Kaanga. Staff members of the UCLA library, especially those who work with interlibrary loans, have been unflagging in helping me procure more materials than any person has the right to request. Of particular help were A. Caitlin Lester and Reynoir I. I owe much gratitude to everyone at the BYU Religious Studies Center for editorial help, but I am most indebted to Beth Sutton, a truly gifted and motivating editor who has made this a much better work than it was when she first set eyes on it. Thankfully, the Ancient Near Eastern Studies program at BYU graciously provided funding for the illustrations. I am grateful for the gracious help I received from Harco Willems, Barry Kemp, John L. Foster, John Gee and Marcelo Campagno. My parents-in-law, Barry and JoAnn Larsen, have helped my family feel less neglected as I worked long hours. To all of these people I am grateful. Still, my greatest debt is to my family. Thanks go to my children, who provided many encouraging pictures and signs and who dutifully left their father's room so he could work. Most of all, I am eternally indebted to my wife. Without her encouragement, inspiration, and help, neither this work nor I would be.

Abbreviations

ARE	*Ancient Records of Egypt* by James H. Breasted
ASAE	Annales du service des antiquites de l'Egypte
BdE	Bibliothéque d'Étude
BES	Bulletin of the Egyptological Seminar, Brooklyn
CD	*A Concise Dictionary of Middle Egyptian*, by Raymond O. Faulkner
CdE	Chronique d'Egypte
DE	Discussions in Egyptology
GM	Göttinger Miszellen
JARCE	Journal of the American Research Center in Egypt
JEA	Journal of Egyptian Archaeology
JSSEA	Journal of the Society for the Study of Egyptian Antiquities
JNES	Journal of Near Eastern Studies
KRI	Kitchen Ramesside Inscriptions
LÄ	Lexicon der Ägyptologie (Lexicon of Egyptology)
LEM	Late Egyptian Miscellanies
MDAIK	Mitteilungen des Deutschen Archäologischen Instituts Abteilung Kairo
RdE	Revue d'Égyptologie
SAK	Studien zur altägyptischen Kultur
Urk.	Urkunden
Wb	Worterbuch
WZKM	Wiener Zeitschrift für die Kunde des Morgenlandes
ZAS	Zeitschrift für Ägyptische Sprache and Altertumskund

Chapter 1

THE ACT OF KILLING: AN INTRODUCTION

He will go to the fire of the king on the day of his fury. His Uraeus shall spit fire on their heads, annihilating their bodies and devouring their flesh, having become like Apophis on the morn of the New Year.

—*Tomb of Amenhotep, son of Hapu*

The sacred structure of Montu in Djerty had just been renovated and expanded; a priceless treasure of gold, silver, lapis lazuli, and other goods from around the known world had been buried in four bronze chests beneath the floor. The temple was renewed and rededicated but not without a price. Smoking on its ritual braziers were the ashes of human flesh. Surrounding the sacred precinct were vile foreigners' corpses, impaled upon stakes and rotting in the sun. Some had been beheaded, mercifully sparing them from the pain experienced by others who had been flayed. Thus, Senusret I boasted, he had reclaimed the temple and ritually restored it and the cosmos to Order. The smoke, the carrion, and the carcasses bore graphic and striking testimony: the king was more than willing to blaze out in white-hot fury while in the service of Order. He would brook no divergence and would spare no wrath in the discharge of this, his greatest duty.

But why? What made the king of such a cultured land engage in such wildly violent acts? How did this "Lord of Kindness," as Senusret I is described in the Tale of Sinue, burst into a "vengeful smasher of foreheads"?[1] To answer these questions, we must delve into the history of one of the grandest and most variegated cultures of the world. This is no easy task. Not only did the Egyptians generally leave no records explaining explicitly why they engaged in many practices, but also their civilization lasted for over three thousand years, during which time much of their practices and thoughts changed. Thus, attempting to trace Egypt's sanctioned violence over time becomes arduous.

Such a task is best accomplished with an important fact kept in mind: historians do not know as much as they think they do on this subject. I have taught history at three universities (Cal Poly–Pomona, UCLA, and Brigham Young University–Hawaii) and have worked with national world history organizations, including editing two world history textbooks and working with the AP World History exam. Through these experiences, I have known enough historians to realize that only the very best of us admit, even to ourselves, how much they do not know and are incapable of learning. Moreover, most Egyptologists have undergone no historical training. In addition, Egyptological issues often suffer from a lack of properly applied historical methodology.[2] As we examine the issue of Egyptian violence, we will combine the best tools of philological, archaeological, and historical disciplines, and we will question assumptions that either have not been thoroughly examined or have not been revisited in the light of new evidence. In many ways, this book tells not only the story of what the ancient Egyptians did but also the story of how Egyptologists have interpreted the evidence and how those interpretations are changing. Thus, we have the story and the story behind the story.

Modern scholars and readers are not the only ones who desire to turn back the pages of history. The ancient Egyptians themselves felt relentlessly compelled to move back in time. We find in their cultural mindset an urgent,

---

[1] Both are descriptions of Senusret I in the Tale of Sinuhe, P. Berlin 3022, lines 65–7, R. Koch, *Die Erzählung des Sinuhe*, BIAE 17, 1990.

[2] See Kerry Muhlestein, "Teaching Egyptian History: Some Discipline-Specific Pedagogical Notes," in *The Journal of Egyptian History*, 2, 2009, 173-231.

incessant, inescapable need to return to an earlier era—the era of Order. In Egyptian religious thought, the world was created in a perfect pristine state: a state of ideal cosmic, social, and physical Order. The Egyptian term for this Order is *Ma'at*. The time immediately after creation was the time before the gods separated themselves from the earth,[3] the time before strife came about.[4] All was as it should be. We will explore the interruption of Ma'at more fully later, but at the onset we must understand that, in the mind of the Egyptians, rebellion shattered this pristine state: the gods left mankind and Earth, strife was introduced, and Ma'at was largely lost. Chaos, or *Isfet*, appeared and gained a toehold in the world and inexorably strove to erase Ma'at from creation. All forms of rebellion were an echo of this earlier day and had to be eradicated with a burning fury that would destroy their ability to invite Chaos into this world or the next. Thus the Egyptians, especially their king, were driven to obstinately wrestle with time, unceasingly and unyieldingly endeavoring to return to the era of Order. The very life of the cosmos depended on their efforts. The king and his people relentlessly drove out Isfet and replaced it with Ma'at, striving to turn the world back to a bygone day.[5] They were their own type of historians.

Scholarship in Egyptology has focused a great deal on the concept of Ma'at—specifically on the importance ancient Egyptian religious thought placed on establishing and maintaining Ma'at and the forms this took.[6] This level of scholarly attention is justified, for Ma'at was an idea that affected innumerable aspects of Egyptian society. It is clear that such an all-encompassing concept would have an overarching effect on Egyptian society and that Egyptologists in turn would devote a great deal of study to it.

What is somewhat overlooked is the idea that to truly understand Ma'at, we must also understand its negative counterpart, Isfet—not the absence of, but the antithesis of, Ma'at.[7] Egyptologists have noted that from the earliest to the latest periods of ancient Egypt it was the duty of the state, specifically the king, to destroy Isfet and replace it with Ma'at.[8] One seminal text about the king's role addresses this subject: "Re has put the king on the land of the living for eternity and infinity so that he may judge mankind, so that he may satisfy the gods, so that he may bring about Ma'at, so that he may destroy Isfet."[9] Obviously the re-creation of Ma'at was intrinsically connected with the destruction of Isfet. Entire studies have been devoted to this interrelationship.[10] Elsewhere the extirpation of Isfet and its relationship to upholding Ma'at has received attention only in passing, as a parenthetical aspect of other topics. The method of upholding Ma'at has received the majority of academic ink.

As for the topic of destroying Isfet, several studies have dealt with certain aspects but only in passing. For example, much has been written about the perception of enemies as Isfet's minions and the ensuing necessity of their destruction.[11] Scholarly attention has also been given to punishment for crimes, accompanied by brief forays into the implications of such punishment for the containment of Isfet.[12] The issue of human sacrifice in ancient Egypt has also been discussed, along with its implications of Isfet's ritual destruction.[13]

---

[3] Pyr. 1208 speaks of the time "when heaven was separated from earth, indeed, when the gods went to heaven" (*m wpt pt ir t3 m prt r=f ntrw ir pt*). Pyr. 1778 speaks of one who "keeps assuming the office of Atum of separating heaven from earth and the primeval waters" (*itt hrt itm n dsr pt ir t3 nnw*).
[4] Pyr. 1040 speaks of the time "before strife existed, before fear came about through the Horus Eye" (*n(i) hprt hnnw n(i) hprt snd pw hpr hr irt hrw*).
[5] See P. Leningrad 1116B, 69, as in Wolfgang Helck, *Die Prophezeihung des Nfr.tj*, Wiesbaden: O. Harrassowitz, 1970, p. 57, and *Urk.* 7, 27.
[6] See Jan Assman, *Ma'at: Gerechtigkeit und Unsterblichkeit im Alten Ägypten*, Munich: C.H. Beck, 1995; Erik Hornung, *Idea Into Image: Essays on Ancient Egyptian Thought*, trans. Elizabeth Bredeck, Princeton: Princeton University Press, 1992, pp. 131–46; Stephen Quirke, "Translating Ma'at", *JEA* 80, 1994, 219–31; and Terence DuQuesne, "I Know Ma'et: Counted, Complete, Enduring", *DE* 22, 1992, 79–89.
[7] Jan Assmann, *Ma'at*, pp. 213–14; DuQuesne, "I Know Ma'et: Counted, Complete, Enduring", 90; B.W.B. Garthoff, "Merenptah's Israel Stela: A Curious Case of Rites de Passage?", in Jacques H. Kamstra, H. Milde, and K. Wagtendonk Kampen (eds), *Funerary Symbols and Religion: Essays Dedicated to Professor M.S.H.G. Heerma van Voss on the Occasion of His Retirement from the Chair of the History of Ancient Religions at the University of Amsterdam*, The Netherlands: J.H. Kok, 1988, p. 25. See also Pyr. 265 for what is probably the earliest textual setting of the two concepts in direct opposition: "King N has put Ma'at in the place of Isfet." Ma'at is a large enough concept that no term signifies its exact opposite.
[8] See PT 265 in which the king "put Ma'at in the place of Isfet" *di.n N m3ʿt im=f m st isft*; Pyr. 1774–76, "the King put Ma'at in the place of Isfet" *dd N m3ʿt m st isft*; Eloquent Peasant B1.272 the king should "bring about Ma'at"; *Urk.* 7:27, "his majesty came to drive out Isfet *iit hm=f dr=f isft* . . . since he loves Ma'at so much. *ʿ3t n mrr=f m3ʿt*; and *Urk.* 4:2026 Tutankhamun has "driven Isfet out of both lands, and fixed Ma'at in its place" *dr.n=f isft ht t3wy m3ʿt mnti m st=s*.
[9] "The King as Sun Priest", as in Jan Assmann, *Der König als Sonnenpriester*, Glückstadt: J.J. Augustin, 1970, p. 19.
[10] Harry Smith, "Ma'et and Isfet", *The Bulletin of the Australian Centre for Egyptology* 5, 1994, 67–88; Assman devotes much of the second section of chapter 7 in *Ma'at* to this idea.
[11] G. Belova, "The Egyptians' Ideas of Hostile Encirclement", in *Proceedings of the Seventh International Congress of Egyptologists*, C. J. Eyre (ed.), Leuven: Peters, 1998; Clive Broadhurst, "Religious Considerations at Qadesh, and the Consequences for the Artistic Depiction of the Battle", in *Studies in Pharaonic Religion and Society in Honour of J. Gwyn Griffiths*, Alan B. Lloyd (ed.), London: The Egypt Exploration Society, 1992; Mario Liverani, *Prestige and Interest: International Relations in the Near East ca. 1600–1100 B.C.*, Padova: Sargon, 1990.
[12] See Ellen D. Bedell, "Criminal Law in the Egyptian Ramesside Period", unpublished dissertation, Brandeis University, 1973; Wolfgang Boochs, "Religöse Strafen", Ursula Verhoeven and Erhart Graefe (eds), in *Religion und Philosophie im Alten Ägypten*, Leuven: Peeters, 1991; David Lorton, "The Treatment of Criminals in Ancient Egypt", *Journal of the Economic and Social History of the Orient* 20, 1977; Joyce A. Tyldesley, *Judgment of the Pharaoh: Crime and Punishment in Ancient Egypt*, London: Weidenfeld & Nicolson, 2000; Renate Müller-Wollermann, *Vergehen und Strafen: zur Sanktionierung abweichenden Verhaltens im alten Ägypten*, Leiden: E.J. Brill, 2004. Laure Bazin, "Enquête sur les Lieux D'Exécution dans l'Égypte Ancienne," *Égypte, Afriqe et Orient* 35 (2004), 31-40, examines so few examples and jumps around so much in a 3000 year time period without regard to possible change over that time, that the conclusions are based on faulty methods.
[13] Nigel Davies, *Human Sacrifice in History and Today*, New York: William Morrow and Company, 1981; Alberto Ravinel Whitney Green, "The Role of Human Sacrifice in the Ancient Near East", unpublished dissertation, University of Michigan, 1973; J. Gwyn Griffiths, "Human Sacrifices in Egypt: The Classical Evidence", *ASAE* 48, 1948; J. Gwyn Griffiths, "The Tekenu, the Nubians and the Butic Burial", *Kush* 6, 1958, pp. 106–20; John G. Griffiths, "Menschenopfer", in *LÄ* 4, 64–65.

Violence in the Service of Order will examine the violent destruction of Isfet in ancient Egypt. This has not been done before. Among all of the worthwhile works mentioned above, none has concentrated on how its particular topic affected the expurgation of Isfet. To my knowledge, no scholar has published anything that outlines the various methods of destroying Isfet, or any other religious violence for that matter, and looks for commonalities and a religious framework. In other words, there has been no systematic program of exploring the methods by which Isfet was destroyed nor has there been an attempt to explore the role that violence played in the consubstantive establishment of Ma'at. Undoubtedly violence was an important servant of Order, but little has been written concerning how or why violence played this role. The current study will partially rectify this situation, though much work remains to be done. In the pages of this book, the reader will see how the ancient Egyptians used every means at their disposal to eradicate Isfet, since any degree of tolerance shown to Chaos could prove their complete undoing. Page after page will reveal the Egyptians' triumph as they continually turned back time, wiping out Chaos and restoring Order.

Although violence was used to destroy Isfet, religious violence was not reserved exclusively for this purpose. Because of the interconnections of the diametric pair, some forms of violence may not have destroyed Isfet but may have still contributed to establishing Ma'at. This disquisition will systematically explore the variety of violent means used to uphold Ma'at—whether indirectly by destroying Isfet, or directly by imposing the correct order demanded by Ma'at. This will enable us to arrive at a better understanding of religious violence, of Ma'at, of Isfet and its destruction, and of their interrelationship.

Focus

This book is hoped to be only the beginning of explorations of the ancient Egyptian notion of upholding Ma'at through violence. Because of the scope of the topic, this study will be limited to the most extreme measure of violence perpetrated in the service of Order: sanctioned killing. This study will explore incidents of killing actual people, texts that affirm the proper occasions for such killings, and the religious framework behind these actions. Myths,[14] mythical references,[15] depictions of the afterlife,[16] apotropaic architecture and images,[17] abstract descriptions of the king,[18] violent forms of punishment,[19] and literary motifs will only be considered as they shed light on the topic at hand. They are, of course, essential to a comprehensive understanding of the subject and deserve studies of their own.

We will examine the phenomenon of state-sponsored killing from the Early Dynastic Period to the end of the Twenty-sixth Dynasty (3000–550 BCE). These parameters have not been chosen randomly; they are pivotal points in Egyptian history. We will begin our study with the reign of King Narmer. Although his dynastic placement is debated, our study is not affected by it. Whether or not Narmer actually unified Egypt, it was the culture he represented that gained dominance within a united kingdom. Even with all of its regional differences, this culture is the most natural starting point for our disquisition. While we do not understand exactly when or by what process this largely homogenous culture was formed in the Nile Valley, by the beginning of the Early Dynastic Period it seems that the inhabitants of the Nile Valley and the Nile Delta had developed a concept of cultural community.[20]

Studying evidence before this period tells us more about several local cultures than about a pan-Egyptian society. This danger does not completely disappear in the Early Dynastic Period, for there were certainly local anomalies throughout Egyptian history. Yet, since we will examine only sanctioned killing, the existence of a centralized government over all of Egypt makes it probable that the sanctioned acts—seemingly endorsed by the ruling class—which we encounter are links in the nearly unbroken chain we call Pharaonic history.

The terminal era for this study—the Twenty-sixth Dynasty—was more difficult to determine. Law, punishment, sacrifice, and killing are matters easily influenced by foreign cultures.[21] Since Egypt, especially beginning with the Eighteenth and Nineteenth Dynasties, was increasingly influenced by foreign elements, any temporal terminus we draw will be somewhat artificial. For example, Dynasty 22 was ruled by Libyans; however, these were Libyans who had lived in Egypt for some time and had become quite acculturated; yet, how much of their original heritage they brought with them to the throne it is impossible to know.[22] Therefore, this period

---

[14] Erik Hornung, "Der Ägyptische Mythos von der Himmelskuh. Eine Ätiologie des Unvollkommen", *Orbis Biblicus et Orientalis*, Göttingen: University of Freiburg Vandenhoeck & Ruprecht, 1982.

[15] See PT 255, which contains references to the eye of Horus.

[16] See the depictions of decapitated souls in the Book of the Night, Fifth Hour.

[17] Some examples include scenes of the king crushing enemies under his feet at Abu Simbel and the tiles depicting enemies laid on the floor of Ramesses III's palace at Medinet Habu. The enemies were crushed under his feet every day as he walked.

[18] This is found in "The King as Sun Priest", as in Jan Assmann, *Der König als Sonnenpriester*.

[19] See Lorton, "The Treatment of Criminals in Ancient Egypt", 3–64.

[20] See John Baines, "Kingship, Definition of Culture, and Legitimation", in David O'Connor and David P. Silverman (eds), *Ancient Egyptian Kingship*, New York: E.J. Brill, 1995, pp. 3, 6, wherein kingship is said to develop nearly concomitantly with the state. See also John Baines, "Origins of Egyptian Kingship", in the same book, p. 102.

[21] For example, Smith, "Ma'at and Isfet", 87, contends that societal elements of Ma'at were heavily influenced in Hellenistic times. Other studies have seen a rise in sacrifice due to Semitic influence. See Griffiths, "Human Sacrifices in Egypt: The Classical Evidence", 423.

[22] See Kenneth Kitchen, "The Arrival of the Libyans in Late New Kingdom Egypt", in *Libya and Egypt, c1300–750 BC*, Anthony Leahy (ed.), London: SOAS Centre of Near and Middle Eastern Studies and The Society for Libyan Studies, 1990, pp. 23–24; see also the entire chapter, but especially pp. 103–9, of David O'Connor, "The Nature of the Tjemhu Libyan Society in the Later New Kingdom", in the same book.

could certainly constitute a fair ending point for any study. Similarly, the rulers of Dynasty 25 come from Kush (Nubia). Again, they were very Egyptianized,[23] but it is impossible to know the extent to which their treatment of criminals, enemies, and other persons deemed fit for death derived from Egyptian culture as opposed to Kushite culture. While anything attested in this dynasty that was consistent with those of previous dynasties likely represents a continuation of Egyptian culture, the guesswork involved in making this connection also makes a good case for ending our study before this dynasty. Dynasty 26, another Libyan dynasty, likewise presents a similar scenario, although these Libyan rulers made a conscious effort to rule in a manner similar to the Eighteenth and Nineteenth Dynasties.[24]

However, it is only after the Twenty-sixth Dynasty that we find Egypt being ruled by a wholly non-Egyptianized government that considered the country not a political entity but merely a small part of a larger empire. Even though Egypt was part of the Assyrian Empire during periods included in this study, the extent of self-government allowed to Egypt sets Assyrian domination apart from the periods succeeding the Twenty-sixth Dynasty. In contrast, the Persian Empire made Egypt a satrapy, relegating her to a wholly different role than she had played before and making her rulers less beholden to Egyptian tradition than previous foreign rulers had been. Certainly, Egyptian culture was still the dominant culture, probably even in most matters of state business. Still, this seems to be the most natural and logical place to draw our limiting line, for continuing beyond this point would necessitate a thorough study of Assyrian, Persian, Macedonian, and Roman cultures. Such an investigation is beyond the scope of this study. Therefore, while the concept of sanctioned killing in later periods deserves investigation, the current investigation will stop at the end of the Twenty-sixth Dynasty.

Related to the issue of temporal parameters is the use of chronological labels in Egyptological convention. There is a lack of *communis opinio* over which dynasties belong to the Early Dynastic Period as opposed to the Old Kingdom, or which should be part of the Middle Kingdom as opposed to which should be included in the Second Intermediate Period. Such concerns are not really relevant to this study. The labels and grouping presented herein will be determined by units that are cohesive concerning the topic of violence in the service of Order. For example, a burial practice that may have included religious violence seems to be a feature of Dynasties 1 and 2 but disappears thereafter. Therefore, these dynasties form a cohesive unit and will be examined together. The Egyptians of the First Intermediate Period may have carried on in violent traditions similar to those of preceding periods, but the nature of the evidence changes. For these dynasties, we must rely almost completely on tomb inscriptions for our information. Thus, the coherency of the unit comes not only from the period but also from the types of sources available. There is often an interplay between historical phenomena and the sources that bear witness of them, but, at times, societal changes influenced the sources, such as changing the topics deemed appropriate for inclusion in texts. This disquisition will divide its chapters according to periods that cohere, either in practice or in available sources.

These chronological concerns naturally segue into the question of a presentational method. The most entertaining way to cover our material would be topically. Our attention would be most easily held were we to first look at all examples of burning throughout Egyptian history, then delve into the incidents of drowning, beheading, and more. This is how I originally conceived of doing this work. Yet if we were to indulge ourselves in such a method, we would not be able to trace the chronological patterns; we would lose the historical sense we so need. The storyteller in me would like to treat our subject topically, but the historian in me would never let me sleep at night if I let the storyteller get away with this. To accomplish the goal of understanding the role violence played in the service of Order, we will examine sanctioned killing throughout time. This approach will allow us to see both patterns of consistency and patterns of change over time. Examining the ideology behind this killing will enable us to investigate whether the ideology remained the same over time or whether it evolved as its society changed. Of course, this research method has complications. When examining evidence for a certain violent killing, we will sometimes need to examine comparable acts in later periods to assess its likelihood in any period. For example, when investigating the possibility of killing associated with execration texts, we can only determine the probability of such events by examining what we know of this topic throughout time. Hence, when certain methods of killing are introduced, a discussion of the given method will follow. After a proper topic–contextual understanding of each method is thus obtained, the treatise will continue with its diachronic analysis, and each example of that method will be revisited in its proper historical context. This approach will necessitate some redundancy but will make it possible for the reader to make a much more accurate assessment of each act of killing. I trust that the readers of this volume are sufficiently patient and advanced that they will be able to both follow the story and avoid being derailed by repetitions. The stories encountered in each chapter are sufficiently intriguing to satiate the storyteller in us, while encountering stories in their proper historical context will also satisfy the historian within us.

Another matter of presentation must be addressed. In order to properly evaluate many possible cases of sanctioned killing, a detailed analysis must be employed. Many of these are quite technical in nature, and I must

---

[23] See Lázló Török, *The Kingdom of Kush: Handbook of the Napatan-Meroitic Civilization*, New York: E.J. Brill, 1997.
[24] Peter Der Mannuelian, *Living in the Past: Studies in Archaism of the Egyptian Twenty-Sixth Dynasty*, New York: Keagan Paul International, 1994; Anthony Spalinger, "The Concept of Monarchy during the Saite Epoch: An Essay of Synthesis", *Orientalia* 47, 1978; Antonio Loprieno, "Le Pharaon recostruit: La figure du roi dans la littérature égyptienne au Ier millénaire avant J.C.", *Bulletin De La Société Française d'égyptologie* 142, June 1998; and Baines, "Kingship, Definition of Culture", pp. 36–38.

often engage in scholarly debate, including the incumbent citation of others' ideas and the refutations and agreements that naturally follow discussing the ideas of others. Many will be quite interested in these technicalities, details, and debates. Others will be less so. In order to facilitate reading for both audiences, most of the lengthy scholarly debates have been put into shaded boxes. When many readers encounter a shaded box, a glance at the title will be sufficient. The box may be skipped, and the story line will happily continue. For those few who enjoy these technicalities, I hope you will find within the boxes a spirited yet cordial and stimulating debate. Either method may be profitably employed.

The Terminology of Sacrifice

I have often informed my history students of an important maxim to keep in mind when evaluating scholarship: the more a topic touches on scholars' religious and political viewpoints, the less they are able or willing to evaluate the evidence as objectively as possible. The same is equally true of topics that touch on subjects to which we have strong emotional reactions. These truisms have affected scholarly perspectives of Egyptian practice. This is doubly so because so many Westerners view themselves as cultural inheritors of Egypt. Because we dislike seeing what is abhorrent in our culture in those we perceive as our cultural ancestors, we often put on intellectual blinders, which prevent us from accurately assessing evidence. Hitherto, there has been a near consensus, with notable exceptions, that human sacrifice was not a part of ancient Egyptian society. This *communis opinio* has lost some ground recently, in part due to new discoveries.[25] Clarifications are thus in order as we attempt to understand what is meant by the term *human sacrifice*. Many Egyptologists have denied the existence of the practice, allowing for possible exceptions in the early history of Egypt. To illustrate, the British Museum's *Dictionary of Ancient Egypt* states, "There is no certain evidence of the practice of human sacrifice in Egypt from the Old Kingdom onwards."[26] Jean Yoyotte points out that Egyptologists dislike the idea that good Egyptian peoples could religiously kill their fellow beings.[27] Herodotus,[28] Mercer,[29] Kees,[30] Ward,[31] and Junker[32] all dismiss the possibility of human sacrifice in ancient Egypt. Yet Isocrates,[33] Willems,[34] Griffiths,[35] Green,[36] and others propose its existence. Why such a scholarly division?

According to Tierney, "Not wanting to know about human sacrifice is one of the dominant motifs of religious history—almost as dominant as its repeated performance."[37] Yet, ironically, the idea is also titillating, receiving attention in the popular media and bringing headlines to scholars who detail the phenomenon.[38] This binary attitude toward the investigation of human sacrifice may explain some of its mixed reception in Egyptological literature.

Such ambivalence is inevitable. This topic touches on the sanctity of human life, an idea that holds powerful sway over both human reason and emotion. Scholars cannot avoid filtering their research through the lens of their own experiences and values, and modern values crushingly condemn human sacrifice. Because as scholars we try to avoid retrojecting our values onto earlier cultures, we must be aware that our valuation of human life is perhaps unique in history. Our view of the sanctity of human life leads to questions unpursued previously in human society. As Paper writes, "Our questioning is unique, and its uniqueness reflects our society's uniqueness in regard to sacrifice. In my opinion, it is not merely probable but certain that this uniqueness determines both the kind of questions we can ask and the kind of answers we can give."[39] Furthermore, the symbolic nature of sacrifice complicates the issue: "Once one has made up one's mind that sacrifice is an institution essentially if not entirely symbolic, one can say anything whatsoever about it. It is a subject that lends itself to insubstantial theorizing."[40]

---

[25] See the discussion on the Mirgissa execration rite in chapter 5, the section on ritual slaying, or the discussion in chapter 2, the section on sacrificial servant burials. See also John Noble Wilford, "With Escorts to the Afterlife, Pharaohs Proved Their Power", *New York Times*, 16 March 2004, p. 16.

[26] See Ian Shaw and Paul Nicholson, *The Dictionary of Ancient Egypt*, London: British Museum Press, 1995, p. 134. Similarly, see Gertie Englund, "Offerings: An Overview", in *The Oxford Encyclopedia of Ancient Egypt* 2, Donald B. Redford (ed.), London: Oxford University Press, 2001, p. 568, in which Englund writes, "Human sacrifices were not part of ancient Egyptian religious rites yet a few prehistoric and early dynastic finds have been interpreted in that way by some scholars." Griffiths, "Menschenopfer", 64–65, is more open to the idea: "Human sacrifices, then, were not a constant or common feature of religious rites, but they occurred in certain areas, in some cases through foreign influence."

[27] See Jean Yoyotte, "Héra d' Héliopolis et le Sacrifice Humain", *Annuaire—Ecole pratique des hautes aetudes, Section-sciences religieuses* 89, 1980–81, 36. Yoyotte refutes the idea himself later, on page 39, writing that it is not reasonable to ask the Egyptian *a priori* to fit the modern idea of humanitarianism into their idea of morality and that we should instead expect that they would know several rites for ritualistic executions.

[28] Herodotus II, 45.

[29] Samuel A.B. Mercer, *The Religion of Ancient Egypt*, London: Luzac, 1949, p. 358.

[30] Hermann Kees, *Totenglauben aund Tenseitsvorstellungen der Alten Ägypter*, Berlin: Akademic Verlag, 1956, pp. 129–30.

[31] William Ward, "Review of Ceremonial Execution and Public Rewards", *JNES* 51, 1992, 152–5, 153.

[32] Hermann Junker, *Pyramidenzeit das Wesen der Altägyptischen Religion*, Einseideln: Bewziger, 1949, p. 51.

[33] See Isocrates, *Busiris*, cap. 10:26.

[34] Harco Willems, "Crime, Cult and Capital Punishment Mo'alla Inscription 8", *JEA* 76, 1990, 27–54.

[35] Griffiths, "Human Sacrifices in Egypt: The Classical Evidence", 418, in which Griffiths admits that before Greek influence it may have existed sporadically.

[36] Green, "The Role of Human Sacrifice in the Ancient Near East", pp. 220–88.

[37] Patrick Tierney, *The Highest Altar: The Story of Human Sacrifice*, New York: Viking Press, 1989, p. 10.

[38] Tierney, *The Highest Altar*, p. 22.

[39] Girard Paper, "Discussion", in Wlater Burkert, René Girard, and Jonathan Z. Smith (eds), *Violent Origins: Ritual Killing and Cultural Formation*, Stanford, CA: Stanford University Press, 1987, p. 109.

[40] René Girard, *Violence and the Sacred*, trans. Patrick Gregory, Baltimore: The Johns Hopkins University Press, 1972, p. 1.

Creating a theory about the nature and constitution of human sacrifice must proceed, as Burkert writes, on unsure footing:

> We can hardly expect a definite theory to emerge. If scientific theory means a limited number of propositions from which further statements can be deduced to be controlled by the data and thus falsified or corroborated, we must remember that in the humanities we are usually dealing with chance selections of data, especially in all fields of history, and even more, that our data are already interpretations, acquiring their meaning in a preconceived system of meaning. This is why theories ad libitum may be possible, forming the data, by choice and interpretation, into strange and striking configurations. Yet an absolutely objective scientific theory would not be gratifying as long as we endeavor to "understand" the phenomena, to assimilate them into our own outlook on life.[41]

Arriving at a theory of human sacrifice for ancient Egypt is more difficult than for many other cultures. One factor that impedes progress toward such a theory is the lack of data, especially from the earlier Egyptian periods. Often, even when we have archaeological information—such as the case of three generations of one family slain and buried together—we have no texts with which to interpret the data.

A related limiting element is the lack of attention the subject has received regarding ancient Egypt. For example, as Burkert attempts to develop a theory of sacrifice, he avoids Egypt: "Let us concentrate on the area of study with which most of us are familiar—namely, animal sacrifice in Jewish, Greek, and Roman religion, including its sublimation in Christian theology."[42] A lack of familiarity with Egyptian rites in the broader academic community, accompanied by a lack of easily interpretable data, has largely precluded the discussion of ancient Egypt's society in sacrificial theory.

This study is further hampered by an unequal understanding of different types of sacrifices. As Barta argues, a distinction should be made between daily offerings on which the gods and the dead subsisted and other types of sacrifices, such as those involved in festivals.[43] The daily offerings for the gods and the dead are fairly well documented and understood by Egyptologists. Large lists of sacrifices have been found, and we know much about the rites involved with this type of offering. In contrast, very little other than what materials were to be offered is known of the sacrifices involved in the numerous religious festivals celebrated in Egypt.[44] Breasted estimated that by the Ramesside Era, a religious festival may have been held, on average, once every three days.[45] The majority of sacrifices relevant to the current study would not fall within the system of daily subsistence offerings. Of greater interest are the daily offerings designed to have an apotropaic effect.[46] We know that some animals, such as goats and gazelles, could symbolize disorder and were sacrificed in an effort to destroy Isfet.[47] For example, Assmann writes that some sacrificial animals were identified with Chaos and were addressed in ritual as the enemies that slew the King, or Osiris.[48]

Such offerings—in conjunction with the intent to establish Ma'at which was part of the daily subsistence offering[49]—illustrate in ritual the intertwining of the upholding of Ma'at and the destruction of Isfet. However, the sacrifices associated with Isfet's destruction were not recorded as well as the daily subsistence offerings were, probably because recording a continuous extirpation of Isfet was a constant reminder of its existence. On the other hand, festivals often contained rituals that destroyed Isfet and thus had annihilative sacrifices.[50] These too are poorly documented. Part of the lack of evidence may stem from the strong Egyptian sense of decorum: sanctioned violence against Isfet may not have been fit for presentation in most contexts due to a proscription against picturing Isfet in most forms of discourse.[51]

While the actual offering of subsistence materials had to happen in a ritual context, since their presentation needed to affect multiple spheres, animals destined for this offering could be butchered in a slaughterhouse. In contrast, it is likely that victims who represented Isfet were killed as part of a rite. These sacrifices concerned the actual destruction of the victim, and thus the destruction had to be a part of the ritual in order for it to have transworldly effects. Furthermore, since part of the purpose of ritual is to make actual reality match ideal reality and since Isfet was a part of actual but not ideal reality, the destructive act of sacrifices concerning Isfet necessarily took place in a ritual setting.[52]

---

[41] Walter Burkert, "The Problem of Ritual Killing", in *Violent Origins: Ritual Killing and Cultural Formation*, p. 149.

[42] Burkert, "The Problem of Ritual Killing", p. 163.

[43] Winfrid Barta, *Die altägyptische Opferliste, von der Frühzeit bis zur griechisch-römischen Epoche*, Berlin: B. Hessling, 1963, and Englund, "Offerings: An Overview", p. 568.

[44] See the Medinet Habu Temple Calendar, which lists over forty-five festivals in the first 138 days of the year.

[45] *ARE* 4, 84.

[46] Stephen Thompson, "Cults: an Overview", in *The Oxford Encyclopedia of Ancient Egypt*, Redford (ed.), pp. 328–9. See also Rosalie David, *A Guide to the Religious Ritual at Abydos*, London: Aris & Phillips, 1981.

[47] Byron E. Shafer, "Temples, Priests, and Rituals: An Overview", in Bryon Shafer (ed.), *Religion in Ancient Egypt: Gods, Myths and Personal Practice*, Ithaca: Cornell University Press, 1991, p. 25; and Englund, "Offerings: An Overview", p. 567.

[48] Assmann, "Spruch 23 der Pyramidentexte und die Ächtung der Feinde Pharos", in Catherine Berger, Gisèle Clerc, and Nicolas-Christophe Grimal (eds), *Hommages à Jean Leclant*, Cairo: French Institute of Oriental Archeology, 1994, p. 52.

[49] Serge Sauneron, *The Priests of Ancient Egypt*, trans. David Lorton, Ithaca: Cornell University Press, 2000, p. 82.

[50] Dimitri Meeks and Christine Favard-Meeks, *Daily Life of the Egyptian Gods*, trans. G.M. Goshgarian, Ithaca: Cornell University Press, 1993, p. 191.

[51] David O'Connor, "Egypt's View of 'Others'", in John Tait (ed.), *Never Had the Like Occurred: Egypt's View of Its Past*, Portland: Cavendish, 2003, p. 157, and John Baines, "Society, Morality and Religious Practice", in Shafer, *Religion in Ancient Egypt*, pp. 137–47.

[52] See Ronald L. Grimes, *Beginnings in Ritual Studies*, Columbia, SC: University of South Carolina, 1995, p. 480.

As mentioned above, the subject of human sacrifice in ancient Egypt is hindered by a reluctance among Egyptologists to ascribe such practices to the society they study. A general application of this is seen in Eyre's discussion of the specific possibility of the practice of cannibalism:

> Moreover, the negative, primitive associations of cannibalism do not fit well with the romanticised vision of Egypt as a civilised 'High Culture'. Such assessment, however, reflects more of the preconceptions of traditional Western scholarship than the reality of ancient ideals or behaviour. . . . Egyptology has tended to idealise pharaonic Egypt as honorary 'us' rather than negative 'them'. From classical Greece onwards Egypt has been claimed as part of the heritage of the West. Only more recently has pharaonic Egypt seriously been claimed for the cultural heritage of modern Egypt, or seriously incorporated into the vision of a common African heritage. Scholarship that sees Egypt as High Culture has no room for the wild and primitive, so that the theme of cannibalism is shocking to its cultural assumptions.[53]

Another example of Egyptological hesitation in recognizing human sacrifice in ancient Egypt can be seen in Emily Teeter's statements from the *New York Times* that archaeological remains being interpreted as evidence for human sacrifice were "embarrassing for Egyptologists, who like to stress how relatively humane the ancient Egyptians were."[54]

Getting Past the Labels

Another factor that obfuscates the idea of human sacrifice in ancient Egypt is the problem of labeling. What one scholar may identify as *human sacrifice* another will label *capital punishment*. This confusion is somewhat inescapable when studying ancient Egyptian society because the lines with which we compartmentalize our own culture become blurred or nonexistent. Our idea of the separation of church and state is completely antithetical to the zeitgeist of ancient Egypt. Even the term *religion* has little, if any, meaning for ancient Egypt. To us, human sacrifice is inseparable from ritual and religion,[55] but for the ancient Egyptians these concepts were equally inseparable from politics, foreign relations, and matters of jurisprudence.

As an example of the labeling problem arising from these blurred lines, let us consider the scenarios of Senusret I at the Temple of Tod and of Prince Osorkon at Thebes. In the Middle Kingdom, Senusret I found a group of rebellious foreigners who he felt had desecrated the Temple at Tod. In response, he burned them on the altars of the temple. This act certainly contained an element of punishment for crimes and could thus be labeled *capital punishment*. Slaughter was also a familiar way of dealing with foreigners and could be labeled under the Egyptian program of foreigner containment. Yet, at the same time, its effects of cleansing the temple and the cultic setting of temple altars suggest that it could be considered an act of "human sacrifice."[56]

Further illustrating the labeling problem discussed above, Prince Osorkon of the Twenty-second Dynasty was forced to put down a rebellion in Thebes. After quelling the rebellion, he burned the perpetrators, stating specifically that he did so as if they were sacrificial goats or birds. The sacrifice took place at the time of the daily offering and was also affiliated with a certain festival. The execution of traitors is not uncommon and is often labeled *capital punishment*. Yet in this text, Osorkon undeniably intended there to be a sacrificial association for the deaths of these individuals. Both labels—*human sacrifice* and *capital punishment*—apply to this situation. The distinction between the two is not likely one an ancient Egyptian would have understood or made. Insisting that an act must be either capital punishment or human sacrifice artificially compartmentalizes modern standards that were foreign to Egyptian society. This is highlighted by the fact that Egyptian terms for executing are also used for other forms of killing; they did not make a semantic distinction.[57]

We will encounter many cases in which the incident under investigation can be found at the merging point of more than one category of study. While the use of labels other than *human sacrifice* is justified and useful in many lines of inquiry, such as investigations into Egyptian juridical procedure, the abandonment of any term denoting sacrifices involving humans can have serious ramifications. For example, Altenmüller's discussion of the Cannibal Hymn is affected by the avoidance of a human sacrifice label in Egyptological literature.[58] He assumes that there was no human sacrifice in the Old Kingdom and thus posits that the hymn may represent such barbaric rituals from earlier periods, but it does not represent such rituals at the time of the hymn's inclusion in the Pyramid Texts. Altenmüller's conclusions may be correct, but his reasoning is circular and is greatly affected by Egyptologists' unwillingness to label acts of killing as *human sacrifice*. As will be seen throughout this study, a great deal of circular reasoning has been employed and often a possible case of human sacrifice has been dismissed because of a tacit agreement that such a practice was not part of the ancient Egyptian character. This agreement comes only by dismissing all possible evidence. This situation cannot be perpetuated.

---

[53] Christopher Eyre, *The Cannibal Hymn: A Cultural and Literary Study*, Bolton: Liverpool University Press, 2002, pp. 153–4.
[54] Wilford, "With Escorts to the Afterlife, Pharaohs Proved Their Power", 16.
[55] Nigel Davies, *Human Sacrifice*, p. 15.

[56] For independently reached conclusions about the difficulty in distinguishing between execution and human sacrifice, see Renate Müller-Wollermann, *Vergehen und Strafen: Zur Sanktionierung abweichenden Verhaltens im alten Ägypten*, Leiden: E.J. Brill, 2004, p. 205.
[57] Müller-Wollermann, *Vergehen und Strafen*, p. 205.
[58] See a discussion on Altenmüller's article and the Cannibal Hymn in chapter 3.

Applying the term *human sacrifice* to ancient Egyptian practices is also problematic because our knowledge of Egyptian actions does not exist in a vacuum. It is impossible to read the phrase "human sacrifice" without recalling practices in other cultures that have the same label. Thus, in establishing a terminology of sacrifice, we must also be cognizant of gradations in human sacrifice. Practices such as the sacrifice of servant retainers or prisoners of war should not be considered on the same level as the ritual sacrifice of a human who was deemed of great value, such as a child. Still, many of these lower-level offerings are ritual sacrifices of human beings just the same. Regrettably, there are no terms that provide semantic distinctions for the gradations of human sacrifice.[59]

Equally regrettable is the semantic combination of human sacrifice containing differing levels of frequency and violence. For example, the term *human sacrifice* has been applied equally to the potential slaughter of a rebel[60] and to the rampant and relentless sacrifices of the ancient Aztecs.[61] While it would be best to create a definitive definition of *human sacrifice* and a terminology that pertains specifically to ancient Egypt, such an undertaking is beyond our scope. It is therefore preferable, within this context, to abandon the use of the term *human sacrifice*. It carries with it vagueness and connotations of the more severe human sacrifice in Carthaginian or Mesoamerican rites. For the purposes of this study, the term *ritual slaying* will be used to denote sacrifice of humans within an Egyptian context.

Method

With these goals and provisos in mind, we must now discuss a method for reconstructing slayings and the religiocultural perspectives on such killing. Not all sources of evidence are of commensurate value, nor is it equally easy to glean accuracy from them. In order to truly understand how the Egyptians put into action the concept of destroying Isfet and the religious framework that surrounded this action, we will examine every available piece of evidence, employing the method appropriate for each type of source. The potential fallacies and filters appropriate for each piece of evidence will be discussed individually. Yet we must be aware that the temporal and social gap, the lack of a modern continuity of culture from which to draw comparisons, and the piecemeal nature of the material with which we have to work create a patchwork of reliability across a broad spectrum of sources. While some items of evidence yield solid conclusions, others offer implications with varying degrees of opaqueness. Thus, we must admit that often we are unable to determine whether a particular practice happened. Instead, in this study, each possibility will be evaluated as to whether it is supported by *weak evidence*, *plausible evidence*, *strong evidence*, or *very strong evidence*. Such an evaluation is subjective and variable; however, the case will be carefully laid out for each example, and the reasons I have assigned one or another evaluation should be clear in every example. Each type or episode of violence examined in this disquisition will be categorized using one of these labels. While this is not completely satisfactory due to the very nature of our field, it is the bed in which we must lie.

Equipped with these ideas, let us try our hand at uncovering lost history. With the ancient Egyptians, we will attempt to return to an earlier day, working our way toward the time before time began.

---

[59] For a thorough discussion of this issue as connected with Greek rites, see Dennis D. Hughes, "Sacrifice and Ritual Killing: Terminology and Types", in *Human Sacrifice in Ancient Greece*, New York: Routledge, 1991, pp. 1–12. I encountered this discussion after arriving upon the term *ritual slaying*, only to find that in dealing with similar problems he employed the term *ritual killing*.

[60] Such is done by Green, "The Role of Human Sacrifice in the Ancient Near East", pp. 251–52.

[61] Elizabeth H. Boone (ed.), *Ritual Human Sacrifice in Mesoamerica*, Washington DC: Dumbarton Oaks, 1982.

Chapter 2

DEATH BY NARMER AND OTHERS: THE ARCHAIC PERIOD

Thirteenth Year of the reign of Netjerimu: First occurrence of the Feast Worship-of-Horus-of-Heaven. Hacking up of the city Shem-Ra. Hacking up of the city House-of-the-North.
—Palermo Stone

Djer sat, cold and proud, on a raised throne outside the niched wall of his palace. As son of the mighty Aha, he was the second king to rule over a united Egypt. He would let nothing stand in the way of the pressing need for the ritual he oversaw that day: the Receiving of the Two Lands. With all the splendor and pomp the powerful king could command, he looked on as a stately procession of nome representatives presented him their sacred standards and the goods of their lands. Then a bearded prisoner was brought forward, his arms bound behind his back. A priest knelt before this unlucky captive, carefully placing a bowl below the man's torso. Holding aloft a sacred flint knife, the priest waited for his king's approval and then suddenly plunged the knife deep into the chest of the bound victim, making sure that the flowing blood collected in the bowl. The Order of the realm had again been preserved through this violent ritual: Djer followed in the footsteps of his great father.

The Narmer Palette

Few pieces of Egyptian art have received so much attention as the famous Narmer Palette, discovered in the main deposit of the Hierakonpolis temple. Since its discovery, debate has swirled around the events depicted thereon. Does the palette depict the unification of Egypt in a picture of the semi-mythical Menes, who Egyptians believed brought the two lands of Egypt together into a unified, powerful whole? Might it commemorate the formation of the most stable and longest-lasting empire of all time? While many aspects of the palette have deservedly received a great deal of attention, only a few of them concern us. It is apparent that the artistic elements of the palette illustrate the aftermath of a battle Narmer has won.[1] On one side, Narmer is shown in what would become one of the most persistent and common motifs of royal Egyptian art: the smiting scene (see fig. 2.1). In this scene, Narmer grasps a subdued enemy leader by the hair. With the other arm Narmer raises a mace, threatening the imminent sacrifice of the prisoner. Whether smiting scenes represented a real sacrifice of prisoners will be dealt with substantially in a later chapter.

On the obverse side of the palette is an intriguing scene: Narmer and several attendants are surveying ten prisoners. These prisoners are bound and decapitated, each with his head placed neatly between his legs. Their tidy arrangement denotes that they are in a state of Order after being been conquered by the king. Symbols above the two rows of decapitated prisoners unfortunately cannot be interpreted with confidence.[2] One would wonder whether these enemies had been beheaded in battle,[3] but they are bound: it is unlikely that dead and

---

[1] It is not important to the current study if the unification of Egypt was actually depicted. For more on this issue, see Alan Schulman, "Narmer and the Unification of Egypt: A Revisionist View", *BES* 11, 1992, 85. While Whitney Davis, *Masking the Blow: The Scene of Prepresentation in Late Prehistoric Egyptian Art*, Berkeley: University of California, 1992, pp. 38–9, holds that looking for historical meaning in these types of palettes is a mistake because they are designed to mask as much as they depict, we cannot discount the fact that the mask also carries historical value because it reflects the mores and norms of the culture that created it.

[2] Barry J. Kemp, *Ancient Egypt: Anatomy of a Civilization*, New York: Routledge, 1989, p. 42. For an inconclusive attempt at interpretation, see Peter Kaplony, "Zu den beiden Harpunenzeichen der Narmerpalette", *ZÄS* 83, 1958, 76–8.

[3] This was done by William C. Hayes and the Metropolitan Museum of Art, *The Sceptre of Egypt*, New York: Harper, 1953, vol. 1, p. 31. See also Joachim Sliwa, "Some Remarks Concerning Victorious Ruler Representations in Egyptian Art", *Forschungen und Berichte*, 1964, vol. 16, p. 107, who believes it is a scene of Narmer inspecting the battle and counting the dead.

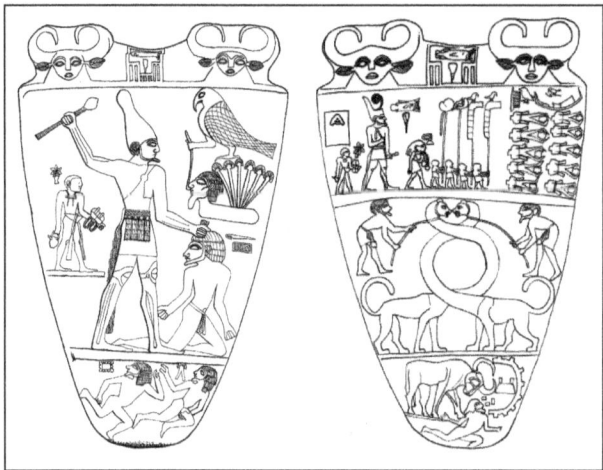

Figure 2.1 – The Narmer Palette

Figure 2.2 – Label of Aha

headless prisoners would later be tied in such a manner. We must assume that these men had been captured, subdued, and systematically beheaded.[4] Hence, the question is begged, does the depiction of beheaded, bound prisoners reflect an actual event, or is it an iconographic portrayal of Order being brought to a chaotic people?

There are valid arguments for both hypotheses. It is likely that the creators of a commemorative palette would want to demonstrate that Narmer had brought *Ma'at* to this band of *Isfet* representatives. After all, it was not uncommon to render chaotic representations impotent by showing them bound or mutilated. However, the artistic repertoire of the creator(s) of the palette included other ways of representing the subdual of chaotic elements. On the same palette, two unfettered and intact enemies are shown under the king's feet, and another is shown being gored by a bull. This favors the interpretation that the headless men represent men beheaded in an actual event,[5] though we cannot be certain of this interpretation. Even if the scene does not represent an actual event, we must acknowledge that the palette "presents decapitation as an element of the depicted world."[6] If the scene does actually depict slain prisoners, the nature of the formal setting and presentation of the scene make it strong evidence for ritual slaying.

Enigmatic Labels

Very enigmatic evidence of ritual slaying comes from Abydos Cemetary B in a label containing the *serekh* of Aha, first king of the First Dynasty.[7] Pictured thereon is a kneeling, bound prisoner faced by a kneeling man who holds a bowl-like object with one hand, and with the other hand, stabs the prisoner with what appears to be a knife (see fig. 2.2). Similarly, an ivory label from Saqqara bearing the name of Djer, second king of the First Dynasty, appears to record a slaying in connection with a religious event.[8] It is difficult to distinguish the figures, but in the top register, men are carrying a body to present to Horus, who is atop a *serekh* (a representation of the king). Directly to the right of this, another figure stabs a person with a knife, again holding a bowl-like object below the victim with his other hand. A similar scene may be depicted in the second register of the Palermo Stone, in association with Year Three of Djer.[9] These figures could signify some kind of ritual slaying, but we know very little of the context surrounding the events the scenes depict—though it is generally accepted that it is some kind of ritual of Receiving Upper and Lower Egypt.[10] Baud and Etienne argue strongly that these scenes are part of a royal ritual.[11] They also convincingly tie the rite to the slaying of Seth and the extirpation of his heart; thus, in the ritual of Receiving the Two Lands, the

---

[4] John Baines, "Origins of Egyptian Kingship", in David O'Connor and David P. Silverman (eds.), *Ancient Egyptian Kingship*, New York: E.J. Brill, 1995, p. 117, writes that they were either executed or killed in battle. See Alberto Ravinel Whitney Green, "The Role of Human Sacrifice in the Ancient Near East", PhD dissertation, University of Michigan, 1973, pp. 241–3, 283, for more discussion on this scene and its scholarly history.

[5] This was argued by Ellen D. Bedell, "Criminal Law in the Egyptian Ramesside Period", PhD dissertation, Brandeis University, 1973, p. 157.

[6] Davis, *Masking the Blow*, p. 41.

[7] William Matthews Flinders Petrie and Francis Llewellyn Griffith, *The Royal Tombs of the First Dynasty, 1900–1901*, London: Egypt Exploration Fund, 1900, vol. 2, pl. 3.

[8] See Walter B. Emery, *Archaic Egypt*, Harmondsworth: Penguin, 1972, pp. 59–60; see also Francesco Tiradritti (ed.), *Egyptian Treasures from the Egyptian Museum in Cairo*, New York: Abrams, 1999, pp. 30–1.

[9] Such is argued by Michel Baud and Marc Etienne, "Le vanneau et le couteau. Un rituel monarchique sacrificiel dans l'Ègypte de la Ire dynastie", in *Archèo-Nil*, 2000, vol. 10, pp. 66–7; see also Bernadette Menu, "Mise á mort cérémonielle et prélèvements royaux sous la 1ère Dynastie", in *Archèo-Nil*, 2001, vol. 11, pp. 172–5.

[10] See Peter Clayton, *Chronicle of the Pharaohs*, London: Thames and Hudson, 1994, p. 22. However, Emery, *Archaic Egypt*, pp. 59–60; and Green, "Human Sacrifice", pp. 225–6, are less hesitant to say that it does depict human sacrifice. For a discussion of the possibility of human sacrifice in ancient Egypt as depicted by the classical writers, see J. Gwyn Griffiths, "Human Sacrifices in Egypt: The Classical Evidence", *ASAE* 48, 1948, 409–23

[11] Baud and Etienne, "Le vanneau et le couteau. Un rituel monarchique sacrificiel dans l'Ègypte de la Ire dynastie", p. 59.

king ritually destroyed the enemies who could prevent the unification of these lands.[12]

Baud and Etienne also find reasonable parallels between this rite and what could be its textual preservation in the Cannibal Hymn.[13] Menu articulately argues that these labels represent part of a rite performed at the beginning of harvest and that labels of every ruler from Narmer to Den indicate that this ritual was performed regularly.[14] She opines that the suppression of revolts may have contributed the victims for such rites.[15] While her arguments are fundamentally sound, we must categorize them as based on plausible evidence. Recent archaeological finds from earlier periods, such as those at Adaima and Hierakonpolis, have also stimulated a small but growing body of scholarship convinced that these labels depict ritual slaughter.[16] That two rulers are depicted performing this rite suggests that the ritual was ongoing, but we cannot be sure.

Sacrificial Servant Burials

There has been a great deal of argument over whether a particular burial pattern found in many early-dynastic royal tombs represents a practice of *sacrificial servant burial*. This term is used in our context to mean burials in which people were killed expressly to be buried with their ruler to accompany him or her to the afterlife. The evidence comes from the large *mastabas*, or rectangular tombs, of the Early Dynastic Period, in which a large chamber was surrounded by numerous smaller chambers. In some cases, varying numbers of people were buried in many of these smaller chambers, and the architecture is such that archaeologists have concluded that all the people in the tomb were interred at once, just before the tomb was sealed shut. Possible reasons for this practice will be discussed below.

One of the earliest cases of possible sacrificial servant burials is found in Saqqara Tomb 3357, often identified with King Aha. This identification, however, is complicated by a scholarly controversy about the burial site of these early-dynastic kings. Notwithstanding, Saqqara Tomb 3357 does not contain the subsidiary graves we find in the tombs of most of Aha's dynastic successors. Moreover, the tomb has been so disturbed that it is difficult to draw any conclusions about the sequence of objects therein. Still, Emery and Saad, who reported on the excavation in 1949, were certain that the numerous fragments of human bones found in the subterranean chambers were part of the original interment.[17] Certainly much of this conclusion came because Emery and Saad saw a parallel between this tomb and those of Aha's successors. Still, both Emery and Petrie felt that the human bones found in the tomb were those of slaves who had been interred with the king.[18]

Debate: Ownership of Early-Dynastic Royal Tombs

Most of the rulers from this time period have a tomb associated with them at both Abydos and Saqqara. Scholarly opinion has swung from favoring one site or the other as the actual burial place of the kings, with the second site serving as a royal cenotaph.[19] Much of current opinion is that Abydos is probably the actual burial site of the king and the Saqqara tombs were burial sites for powerful courtiers.[20] Arguments against the northern tombs serving as cenotaphs, similar to the dual tombs of the Djoser complex, fail to account for the existence of sacrificial servant burials in both the northern and southern tombs in what seems to be an almost exclusively royal practice; however, no arguments have accounted for all of the data. For our purposes, it matters little which site the king was actually buried in, as the remains found represent a phenomenon associated with the ruling elite. Furthermore, if the secondary tomb, be it the northern or the southern tomb, is a cenotaph, it holds the same royal connotations as the actual tomb. The sacrificial burials to be discussed detract from the hypothesis that the Saqqara tombs were those of courtiers. Nevertheless, if these sacrificial burials are associated with courtiers, they still represent a form of sanctioned killing. Therefore, we need not concern ourselves with the issue of royal tomb versus cenotaph or courtier tomb.

There was no evidence originally found of sacrificial servant burial at Aha's Abydos tomb, Tomb B19, though more recent excavations have found many human bones in this tomb. Some skeletons of young men found in the tomb exhibited marks indicating that they did not die

---

[12] Baud and Etienne, "Le vanneau et le couteau. Un rituel monarchique sacrificiel dans l'Égypte de la Ire dynastie", pp. 62–3.
[13] Baud and Etienne, "Le vanneau et le couteau. Un rituel monarchique sacrificiel dans l'Égypte de la Ire dynastie", p. 63.
[14] Menu, "Mise á mort cérémonielle et prélèvements royaux sous la 1ère Dynastie", pp. 163–75.
[15] Menu, "Mise á mort cérémonielle et prélèvements royaux sous la 1ère Dynastie", p. 75.
[16] Éric Crubézy and Béatrix Midant-Reynes, "Les sacrifice humains à l'époque prédynastique: L'apport de la nécropole d'Adaïma", *Archèo-Nil*, 2000, vol. 10, 21–40.
[17] Walter B. Emery and Zaki Yusef Saad, *Excavations at Saqqara, 1937–1938. Hor-aha*, Cairo: Government Press, 1939, p. 77; David Wengrow, *The Archaeology of Early Egypt: Social Transformations in North-East Africa, 10,000 to 2650 BC*, New York: Cambridge University Press, 2006, pp. 226–8 questions the assumptions on which the debate is based and takes a nuanced approach.
[18] Walter B. Emery, *Great Tombs of the First Dynasty; Excavations at Saqqara*, Cairo: Govt. Press, 1949, vol. 1, pp. 1–4; Petrie, *Royal Tombs, II*, pp. 12–17. See also Green, "Human Sacrifice", pp. 221–2. For a brief report on recent excavations in this area see Günter Dreyer, "Recent Discoveries at Abydos Cemetery U", in *The Nile Delta in Transition; 4th–3rd Millennium B.C.*, Edwin CM van den Brink (ed.), Tel Aviv: R. Pinkhas, 1992, pp. 293–9.
[19] See Green, "Human Sacrifice", pp. 220–1, who cites scholarly opinion in 1973 as already having changed several times and who asserts that at that time most scholars believed that Saqqara was the actual burial site of the kings. See also Clayton, *Chronicle*, p. 21, who writes that Abydos is the accepted burial place and that the tombs of Saqqara are those of powerful nobles. See Nicolas-Christophe Grimal, *A History of Ancient Egypt*, Oxford: Blackwell, 1994, p. 49, who is one representative of the idea that Abydos was the royal burial site but that the Saqqara tombs were royal cenotaphs.
[20] Barry J. Kemp, "The Egyptian First dynasty Royal Cemetery", *Antiquity* 41, 1967, 22–32, made a pivotal and powerful argument for this case. See also David O'Connor, "The Earliest Pharaohs and The University Museum", *Expedition* 29, 1987, 28.

naturally.[21] Kemp lists 34 burials associated with this site.[22] Most recently, David O'Connor's excavations, guided by magnetic surveys, have determined that an unknown number of court officials, servants, and artisans were interred in graves separate from the king at his mortuary enclosure. Yet the wooden roofs of their graves were covered by a contiguous layer of mud plaster. O'Connor argues that "this makes a strong case that all these people died and were put in the graves at the same time."[23]

Saqqara Tomb 3471, linked to Aha's successor, Djer, contains no evidence of sacrificial servant burial.[24] However, his Abydos tomb, Tomb O, yielded 318 subsidiary graves, largely those of women; many of the graves bore crude stelae recording the names of the deceased.[25] Reisner, who studied the subsidiary graves, also determined which graves were probable and which were possible examples of sacrificial servant burial. He concluded that 63 graves were probably such examples, and an additional 99 possibly were, making for 162 total possible sacrificial servant burials—51 per cent of the total subsidiary graves.[26] Additionally, Kemp has demonstrated that large "funerary palaces" were connected with the royal tombs, and these palaces also contained subsidiary burials.[27] He associates a total of 269 burials with Djer's palace.[28] Until recently, we could not be certain that all of these burials occurred at the same time, though the excavators believed that those burials associated with the tomb did,[29] and Kemp felt that such was the case for the funerary-palace burials as well.[30] The most recent archaeological work has confirmed these ideas. Careful study has revealed that over two hundred of the subsidiary graves were covered by a contiguous, uninterrupted wooden roofing, leading O'Connor and his excavation team to conclude that the burials had to have been made at the same time as the king's.[31] Additionally, the stelae these servants were buried with assured them a continued existence in the afterlife;[32] the significance of these stelae will be addressed later in the chapter. It should also be noted that unless the tomb was reopened and resealed, an unlikely scenario, a bejeweled queen or princess was also interred with Djer.[33]

Djer's wife, Queen Merneith, is also connected with two tombs. The first, Tomb 3503 at Saqqara, contained 21 subsidiary burials symmetrically arranged below the superstructure.[34] These graves were found undisturbed, containing objects that symbolized the particular service each person had performed for the queen.[35] Again, we are unable to indisputably ascertain whether these burials were all performed simultaneously with the queen's. However, their position under the superstructure of the queen's grave makes this very likely. The other tomb with which Merneith is associated, Abydos Tomb Y, contained 41 subsidiary graves, all fashioned in a manner similar to those in her Saqqara tomb; some of the servants' graves contained stelae akin to those found in Djer's tomb, carrying with them the same connotations of continued life.[36] Reisner felt that 33 of these were probable cases of sacrificial servant burial, constituting 80 per cent of the total subsidiary burials.[37] Merneith's funerary palace contained the burials of eighty servants.[38]

The reign of Djet, the third king of the First Dynasty, witnessed the construction of three tombs containing subsidiary graves. Tomb 3504 at Saqqara contained, under the walls of the superstructure, a series of 62

---

[21] David O'Connor, "Abydos, Early Dynastic Funerary Enclosures", in Kathryn A. Bard (ed.), *Encyclopedia of the Archaeology of Ancient Egypt*, New York: Routledge, 1999, 94, after opining that presumably all first-dynasty tombs possessed subsidiary graves, writes that "Aha's subsidiary graves were perhaps adjacent to his enclosure, rather than surrounding." For more on this tomb see also Günter Dreyer, "Ein Siegel der frühzeitlichen Königsnekropole von Abydos", *MDAIK* 43, 1987, 42–3; and Werner Kaiser, "Zum Siegel mit frühen Königsnamen von Umm el-Qaab", *MDAIK* 43, 1987. Also see also Günter Dreyer, "Umm el-Qaab: Nachuntersuchungen im frühzeitlichen Königsfriedhof. 3/4. Vorbericht Mit Beiträgen von Joachim Boessneck und Angela von den Driesch und Stefan Klug", *MDAIK* 46, 1990, 81–9, for a report on numerous animal and human bones.
[22] Kemp, "First Dynasty Cemetery", p. 24.
[23] John Noble Wilford, "With Escorts to the Afterlife, Pharaohs Proved Their Power", *The New York Times*, 16 March 2004, Science—16. See also "Archaeologists Discover Evidence that Courtiers Were Sacrificed to Accompany Early Egyptian Kings into the Afterlife", Press Release from the Office of Public Affairs, New York University, March 16, 2004.
[24] Emery, *Great Tombs I*, Tomb 3471.
[25] Emery, *Archaic Egypt*, pp. 56–60, lists 338 tombs. A discrepancy between the numbers in original reports and those in Kemp's *Antiquity* article is common. Because Kemp's article reflects more recent research, the text of this study will include his numbers, but the varying numbers will appear in the notes. See also Dreyer, "Umm el-Qaab 3/4", 71–2; see also Werner Kaiser, "Zu den Königsgräbern der I. Dynastie in Umm el-Qaab", *MDAIK* 37, 1981, 251–2.
[26] These figures are from Hoffman's careful examination and analysis of Reisner's work, as reported in Michael A. Hoffman, *Egypt Before the Pharaohs*, New York: Knopf, 1984, p. 276. Hoffman's work is based on a careful study of George Andrew Reisner, *The Development of the Egyptian Tomb Down to the Accession of Cheops*, Cambridge, MA: Harvard University Press, 1936. Since Hoffman's work is more modern, applying the latest standards of scholarship to Reisner's (for his time) groundbreaking and progressive methodology, Hoffman will be cited in most instances instead of Reisner.
[27] See Barry J. Kemp, "Abydos and the Royal Tombs of the First Dynasty", *JEA* 52, 1966. See also Werner Kaiser and Günter Dreyer, "Umm el-Qaab. Nachuntersuchungen im frühzeitlichen Königsfriedhof. 2. Vorbericht", *MDAIK* 38, 1982, 241–60; and O'Connor, "Earliest Pharaohs", pp. 35–9, for a discussion on tomb development in Abydos during the early-dynastic era. See also Wengrow, *The Archaeology of Early Egypt*, 248.
[28] Kemp, "First Dynasty Cemetery", p. 24. See also Petrie, *Tombs of the Courtiers and Oxyrhynkhos*, London: British School of Archaeology in Egypt, 1925.
[29] Emery, *Archaic Egypt*, pp. 56–64. See also Petrie, *Royal Tombs I*, vol. 2, pl. 60 and 61; and Green, "Human Sacrifice", p. 225.
[30] For an example, see Kemp, "Abydos and the Royal Tombs", p. 16.
[31] Wilford, "With Escorts to the Afterlife, Pharaohs Proved Their Power", p. 16. See also NYU Press Release.
[32] See Richard Parkinson, *Cracking Codes. The Rosetta Stone and Decipherment*, Berkeley: University of California, 1999, pp. 140–2; and Manfred Lurker, *The Gods and Symbols of Ancient Egypt*, London: Thames and Hudson, 1974, pp. 7–8, for a discussion on the importance of preserving a name for continued existence in the post-mortal realm.
[33] Hoffman, *Egypt Before*, p. 279.
[34] Walter B. Emery, *Great Tombs of the First Dynasty*, London: Oxford University Press, 1958, vol. 2, 128–38, lists 20; see also Green, "Human Sacrifice", p. 223; and Clayton, *Chronicle*, p. 22.
[35] Emery, *Archaic Egypt*, pp. 66–8; and Green, "Human Sacrifice", pp. 223–4.
[36] Petrie, *Royal Tombs I*, pp. 10–11 and pl. 60 and 61.
[37] Hoffman, *Egypt Before*, p. 276.
[38] Petrie, *Tombs of Courtiers*; and Petrie, *Royal Tombs I*, Tomb Y, lists 77.

subsidiary graves. The roofs of these graves were timbers upon which the main superstructure rested, making the nearly inescapable conclusion that they were part of the original burial.[39] Abydos Tomb Z is also ascribed to Djet, around which 171 (174, according to Reisner) retainers had been buried.[40] Reisner estimated that 14 burials were probable sacrificial servant burials, with another 99 possibly being such, totaling 113, or 65 per cent, of the graves as possibly representing a sacrificial practice.[41] The nearby funerary palace included 154 servant burials.[42] The fact that the contemporary Saqqara tomb contained what were almost certainly sacrificial servant burials greatly increases the likelihood that Tomb Z also manifests of the same practice. Additionally, Giza Tomb V is associated with Djet and contained 52 (56, according to Reisner[43]) subsidiary graves.[44]

Saqqara Tomb 3506, from the reign of Den—son of Djer and Merneith and successor to Djet—contained a mere ten subsidiary burials, but due to their placement in the architecture, they were almost certainly buried at the same time as the king.[45] Den's southern structure, Abydos Tomb T, was not so modest, containing 133 burials.[46] Reisner felt that 40 of these were probable cases of sacrificial servant burial, and 83 others possibly were, making for 123 (92%) possible sacrifices.[47] Petrie felt that many of the positions of the skeletons implied at least partial consciousness at burial."[48] Again, while the Abydos structural remains do not conclude that servant and tomb owners were simultaneously buried like they were in the Saqqara tomb, if Den or his courtiers had engaged in sacrificial servant burials in the north, they would probably have done so in the south as well. Den may also have had a tomb at Giza, but some have contended that the mastaba belongs to a queen.[49] This Giza site also contained subsidiary burials. Three other Saqqara tombs—Tombs 3035, 3507, and 3036—are associated with Den but contain no subsidiary graves.[50]

Saqqara Tomb 3038, assigned to Anedjib, Den's successor, contains no evidence of sacrificial servant burial. Also at Saqqara and assigned to Anedjib is Tomb 3111, containing one subsidiary burial. On the other hand, Anedjib's tomb at Abydos, Tomb X, includes 64 interred servants.[51] However, the preservation of this tomb and its subsidiary graves is so poor it is impossible to ascertain through analysis of the architectural structure the likelihood that the bodies in the 64 graves were buried concomitantly with the king.[52] Reisner estimates that even with the poor state of preservation, 14 of those Abydos graves exhibit characteristics of sacrificial servant burials.[53] Because of the strong trend demonstrated both before and after the creation of this tomb, it is at least likely that they were so.

No tomb has been identified at Saqqara with the next ruler, Semerkhet; however, his Abydos tomb possesses significant evidence of sacrificial servant burial. The superstructure of Tomb U covers both the main burial chamber and all of the subsidiary graves in a way that made the excavators certain that these 64 burials occurred at the same time as the owner's burial.[54] Reisner concurred that all 64 tombs were sacrificial servant burials.[55] Wilkinson concludes that the tomb was a "proven instance of retainer sacrifice."[56]

The tomb of the next king, Ka'a—Abydos Tomb Q—used the same method of construction, enabling a sure conclusion that the 27 (26, according to Reisner, who felt all were examples of sacrificial practice) retainers interred there were all buried when the king was. Saqqara Tomb 3505, the last northern tomb with subsidiary burials, contained only one such grave.[57] Another tomb from Ka'a's reign, Saqqara Tomb 3500, is unassigned to an individual. This small tomb contained four subsidiary burials that were likely buried concomitantly with the owner of the tomb.[58]

The next tomb in which there is any sacrificial servant burial evidence is that of the last king of the Second Dynasty, Khasekhemwy. When it was excavated, the state of preservation in his Abydos Tomb 5 was poor, and it had been looted extensively. Nevertheless, it is apparent that it had contained between ten and fifteen subsidiary burials.[59] Reisner found two individuals that he

---

[39] Emery, *Great Tombs II*, 3 13; Emery, *Archaic Egypt*, 71–72; and Green, "Human Sacrifice", p. 223, 243.
[40] Petrie, *Royal Tombs I*, pp. 8–10, plates 61, 62, and 63; Emery, *Archaic Egypt*, 69–71; and Green, "Human Sacrifice", p. 226, list 174. See also Kaiser, Königsgräbern der I. Dynastie, 249–50.
[41] Hoffman, *Egypt Before*, p. 276.
[42] Petrie, *Royal Tombs I*, p. 69–71, lists 161.
[43] Hoffman, *Egypt Before*, p. 280.
[44] Kemp, "First Dynasty Royal Cemetery", p. 24.
[45] Emery, *Great Tombs I*, pp. 37–42; Emery, *Archaic Egypt*, pp. 73–80; and Green, "Human Sacrifice", pp. 224, 229.
[46] Petrie, *Royal Tombs I*, pp. 11–12 and plates 59; and Emery, *Archaic Egypt*, pp. 73–80, list 136; see also Green, "Human Sacrifice", 226; Günter Dreyer, "Umm el-Qaab: Nachuntersuchungen im frühzeitlichen Königsfriedhof. 5/6. Vorbericht Mit Beiträgen von Ulrich Hartung und Frauke Pumpenmeier", *MDAIK* 49, 1993, 57; and Dreyer, "Umm el-Qaab 3/4", pp. 71–82.
[47] Hoffman, *Egypt Before*, p. 276.
[48] Petrie, *Tombs and Courtiers*, p. 8.
[49] See Clayton, *Chronicle*, p. 24; and Emery, *Great Tombs II*, p. 140.
[50] Kemp, "First Dynasty Royal Cemetery", 24.

[51] Petrie, *Royal Tombs I*, pp. 14–15 and plates 61, 65, and 66; Dreyer, Umm el-Qaab 5/6, 57–61; and Green, "Human Sacrifice", p. 227.
[52] Emery, *Archaic Egypt*, pp. 80–4.
[53] Hoffman, *Egypt Before*, p. 276.
[54] Emery, *Archaic Egypt*, pp. 84–6; Petrie, *Royal Tombs I*, pp. 13–14 and plates 59, 66, and 67.
[55] Hoffman, *Egypt Before*, p. 276.
[56] Toby A.H. Wilkinson, *Early Dynastic Egypt*, New York: Routledge, 1999, p. 237.
[57] Emery, *Great Tombs II*, pp. 37–42; Emery, *Archaic Egypt*, pp. 86–87; and Green, "Human Sacrifice", p. 224.
[58] Emery, *Archaic Egypt*, pp. 90–1; and Green, "Human Sacrifice", p. 224.
[59] See Reisner, *The Development of the Egyptian Tomb Down to the Accession of Cheops*, p. 128; Petrie, *Royal Tombs I*, p. 14 and plates 59, 60, 66, and 67; Emery, *Archaic Egypt*, pp. 101–3; and Green, "Human Sacrifice", p. 228. For a report on Per-ibsen's tomb, which contained no subsidiary burials, see Werner Kaiser and Peter Grossmann, "Umm el-Qaab. Nachuntersuchungen im frühzeitlichen Königsfriedhof. 1. Vorbericht", *MDAIK* 35, 1979, 161–2. For a further discussion of this

felt were probably examples of sacrificial servant burials, noting that the state of the tomb made it impossible to locate other specific burials.⁶⁰ As with Abydos Tomb 10, the weight of the pattern in other rulers' tombs forces historians to conclude that Tomb 5 was at least possibly the site of sacrificial servant burials.

Khasekhemwy Khasekhemwy is the final king for whom we find evidence of sacrificial servant burial.⁶¹ Thus, our task is to now summarize the findings and draw conclusions. Of the fifteen tombs containing subsidiary graves as part of the original structure, six include nearly irrefutable evidence that retainers were buried with the tomb owner. Two others contain almost certain evidence that retainers were buried simultaneously with the tomb owners, and two more hold very likely evidence of such burials. In three cases, the architecture yields inconclusive indications, and the state of preservation of two others makes an estimation impossible. This gives us eight solid examples of sacrificial servant burial, and seven which may or may not be. While the array of numbers representing sacrificial servant burial is somewhat confusing (Kemp's numbers will be used in the charts in chapter 9), the cumulative weight of the evidence definitely indicates that sacrificial servant burial was a real and consistent part of royal burial practice. The recent work by O'Connor greatly strengthens this conclusion: since decisive evidence for sacrificial servant burial stems from the first two and nearly last two tombs with subsidiary burials, it very strongly suggests—indeed, almost mandates—that the subsidiary graves between the two temporal terminals would also have been part of this practice. This conclusion is further augmented by scholarly reasoning about the Egyptian ideological basis for conducting such a practice. The longevity of the practice—about two hundred years—argues against the concomitant burials being the result of catastrophe or warfare.⁶² Alternative explanations have become less and less sustainable to the point that they begin to appear ephemeral. It is tempting to conclude that many Egyptologists will conceive of any possible scenario other than admitting that their beloved civilized Egyptians would do something so barbaric.

Davies, an anthropologist who has written much about human sacrifice, surmises that since the ancient Egyptians felt that their king was partially in the divine sphere, they "would have been aghast at the idea that their king, so glorious in life, should be abandoned in death, that he who had been their vital force in this world should be left to fend for himself in the next."⁶³ He also argues that prestige, both in this life and in the next, was partially determined by the size of the king's entourage.⁶⁴ Green asks if it is "conceivable that [the king's] immediate domestic attendants should be expected to follow him at 'their' discretion, when they succumb to natural death."⁶⁵ Clearly, the continued existence of these servants in the afterlife was crucial. The preservation of their names and functions, as brought about by the stelae, ensured that these people would actually exist in the afterlife and would continue to meet the needs of the kings or nobles whom they served. Were they not intended to be present in this desired afterlife, there would be little reason to include the names in the stelae. Wengrow has noted "a direct relationship between ritual killing and the establishment of the tomb is suggested by the contents of a subsidiary grave in which residues of green, red, black and yellow paint, traces of which were also noted on the mastaba façade."⁶⁶

To more accurately assess these burials, we should also look at the preceding time period to determine whether there is continuity of practice. In Nagada—a culture that would become part of the dominant culture during the Early Dynastic Period—a number of pertinent graves dug several generations before the Early Dynastic Period were discovered. The people interred were consistently of the wealthy class and were accompanied by other people who were apparently buried simultaneously with the main occupation of the grave.⁶⁷ When Reisner re-examined these graves, comparing them to other sites that were possible examples of sacrificial servant burial, he reluctantly concluded that the Nagada graves were indeed of the sacrificial type.⁶⁸ Additionally, examples of sacrificial burial from the period immediately preceding the First Dynasty come from el-Adaima and Hierakonpolis.⁶⁹ Evidence presented in the first part of this chapter further denotes that ritual slaying was part of the culture from the era of the tombs under discussion. Trigger provides a context for the practice by comparing Egypt in its earliest stages of dynastic civilizations to

---

tomb, see David O'Connor, "Boat Graves and Pyramid Origins. New Discoveries at Abydos, Egypt", *Expedition* 33, 1991, 7–8.

⁶⁰ Hoffmann, *Egypt Before*, p. 276; Reisner, *The Development of the Egyptian Tomb Down to the Accession of Cheops*, p. 128.

⁶¹ Other actions may be considered as such, but they are of a very different nature. See chapter 5, the section on sacrifices associated with burials.

⁶² See Jean-Pierre Albert, Éric Crubézy, Béatrix Midant-Reynes, "L'Archéologie du sacrifice humain. Problèmes et hypothèses", *Archèo-Nil* 10, 2000, 15–16, where they discuss these as possible alternative hypotheses for simultaneous burials.

⁶³ Nigel Davies, *Human Sacrifice in History and Today*, New York: Morrow, 1981, 16.

⁶⁴ Davies, *Human Sacrifice in History and Today*, p. 21. See also Albert, "L'Archéologie du sacrifice humain. Problèmes et hypothèses", p. 1 4.

⁶⁵ Green, "Human Sacrifice", p. 230.

⁶⁶ Wengrow, *The Archaeology of Early Egypt*, 243.

⁶⁷ See Reisner, *The Early Dynastic Cemeteries of Naga-ed-Dêr*, Leipzig: University of California Press, 1965, graves 7016, 7024, 7027, 7036, 7037, 7045, 7055, 7057, 7058, for some examples. See also Petrie, *Naqada and Ballas*, Warminster, UK: Aris & Phillips, 1974; and Green, "Human Sacrifice", pp. 214–18.

⁶⁸ George Andrew Reisner and Joint Egyptian Expedition of Harvard University and the Boston Museum of Fine Arts, *Excavations at Kerma*, Cambridge, MA: Harvard University Press; Dows Dunham, Sue D'Auria, George A. Reisner, Museum of Fine Arts Boston Dept. of Egyptian and Ancient Near Eastern Art, *Excavations at Kerma Subsidiary Nubian Graves Excavated by the late George A. Reisner in 1915–1916, not included in his Excavations at Kerma, I–III and IV–V, published by him in the Harvard African studies, V and VI, 1923*, Boston: Museum of Fine Arts, 1982; Reisner, *Development of the Egyptian Tomb*; and Green, "Human Sacrifice", pp. 216–18.

⁶⁹ Crubézy and Midant-Reynes, "Les sacrifice humains", pp. 21–40; Bertrand Ludes and Éric Crubézy, "Le sacrifice humain en context funéraire: problèmes posés à l'anthropobiologie et à la médicine légale. L'exemple prédynastique", *Archèo-Nil* 10, 2000, 43–53; and Renee Friedman, "More Mummies: The 1998 Season at HK43", and "Trauma at HK43", *Nekhen News* 10, 1998, 4–7.

other cultures in a similar phase that also exhibited sacrificial burials as part of royal funerals.[70]

Some have argued that the subsidiary burials, even those with contiguous ceilings, were burials of important courtiers who had died before the king and then had their graves included in the king's superstructures when the ruler died and was buried. However, the low status of almost all the occupants of the subsidiary graves, the lack of evidence for other ceiling structures, the cultural continuity from earlier practices, and the anthropological arguments presented in this chapter sabotage such a suggestion. These improbable suggestions seem to be motivated by a frantic desire to escape from what Emily Teeter describes when she says that subsidiary burials are "embarrassing for Egyptologists, who like to stress how relatively humane the ancient Egyptians were."[71] The amount and consistency of the evidence, coupled with a compelling ideological argument, leads to the conclusion that the rulers of the Early Dynastic Period did indeed carry out a systematic program of sacrificing retainers for the tombs of royalty. Those tombs of which the structure did not allow a firm conclusion become much more likely candidates for sacrificial servant burial when assessed in this light. In the end, it becomes less important to determine which tombs were actually party to this rite and which may not have been; instead, it is important to realize that this was a common practice. Sacrificing retainers ensured that the social order proscribed by Ma'at for this world continued in the afterlife.

Archaic Period Evidence of Sanctioned Killing

Violence	Weak Evidence	Plausible Evidence	Strong Evidence	Very Strong Evidence
Beheading of enemies by Narmer			X	
Ritual Slaying at festival by Aha				X
Ritual Slaying at festival by Djer				X
Ongoing process of Ritual Slaying of prisoners		X		
Sacrificial servant burial at Saqqara Tomb 3357 (Aha)			X	
Sacrificial servant burial at Abydos Royal Mortuary Enclosure (Aha)				X
Sacrificial servant burial at Abydos Tomb O (Djer)				X
Sacrificial servant burial at Saqqara Tomb 3503 (Merneith)			X	
Sacrificial servant burial at Abydos Tomb Y (Merneith)			X	
Sacrificial servant burial at Saqqara Tomb 3504 (Djet)				X
Sacrificial servant burial at Abydos Tomb Z (Djet)				X
Sacrificial servant burial at Giza Tomb V (Djet)			X	
Sacrificial servant burial at Saqqara Tomb 3506 (Den)				X
Sacrificial servant burial at Abydos Tomb T				X
Sacrificial servant burial at Giza Tomb (Den?)			X	
Sacrificial servant burial at Abydos Tomb X (Anedjib)	X*			
Sacrificial servant burial at Saqqara Tomb 3111 (Anedjib)			X	
Sacrificial servant burial at Abydos Tomb U (Semerkhet)				X
Sacrificial servant burial at Abydos Tomb Q (Ka'a)				X
Sacrificial servant burial at Saqqara Tomb 3505 (Ka'a)			X	
Sacrificial servant burial at Saqqara Tomb 3500				X
Sacrificial servant burial at Abydos Tomb V (Khasekhemwy)		X*		

* State of preservation was such that an accurate assessment is unrealistic

---

[70] Bruce G. Trigger, *Early Civilizations: Ancient Egypt in Context*, Cairo: The American University in Cairo Press, 1993, pp. 95–8.

[71] Wilford, "With Escorts to the Afterlife, Pharaohs Proved Their Power", p. 16.

Chapter 3

SLAYING UNDER THE AEGIS OF THE GOD-KING: THE OLD KINGDOM

All people, all officials, all subjects, all men, all eunuchs, all women, all rulers . . . all messengers, who will rebel, who will conspire, who will talk of rebelling, who will fight, who will talk of fighting, every rebel who speaks of his rebellion . . . will be destroyed for all time.

—*Rebellion Formula, Execration Texts*

Uncertain of his fate, the bound prisoner was dragged before the stately nobleman. He knew he was kneeling before a person of prestige, for Mereruka was the vizier of Egypt, second in power only to the king. The captive knew that few people in the world would ever have as much control over others as did Mereruka. Hopeful for just a moment that he would be brought into the great vizier's household for service, the captive began to despair when tethered to a stake; for perched atop this stake were the severed heads of two other Nubians. The executioner brought his great blade forward, and soon Mereruka had another trophy adorning his ceremonial post.

Out of the formidable foundation laid by the kings of the Early Dynastic Period would rise rulers who, like the pyramids they built, would reach heights of power seldom equaled in the history of the world. While Early Dynastic Egypt was an astounding accomplishment, it pales in comparison to the grand culture and ideology of Old Kingdom Egypt. (It is this advancement which causes Egyptologists to designate a new time period, applying the label of *Old Kingdom*.) Art, architecture, foreign dominance, and royal prestige would all approach apexes hitherto not reached by any in the world. In many ways, when we think of Egyptian culture and heritage, images of the Old Kingdom come to mind.

It would be tempting to believe that, because sacrificial servant burials ceased at the dawn of the Third Dynasty, the rulers of the Old Kingdom were more benevolent and benign than their predecessors. We cannot make this assumption. A change in funerary practice does not necessarily indicate a change in the cultural character, ruling philosophy, or rituals that were associated with non-funerary spheres. As Tyldesley points out, "It would be wrong to imagine Old Kingdom Egypt as a gentle land of tolerance and non-violence."[1] We shall see that outside of the funerary realm, though some of our evidence comes from that sphere, there is substantial evidence for sanctioned killing in the Old Kingdom.

Compared to later periods, there is a dearth of textual evidence from the Old Kingdom. Royal inscriptions are noticeably absent from this time period. Our most abundant textual sources are private tomb inscriptions and some caches of administrative papyri. Both of these are genres in which we would expect to find little evidence for our study. Therefore, as with so many other aspects of the period, our evidence for this topic is scanty. Nevertheless, many clues are available to us in our quest to reconstruct the phenomenon of sanctioned killing.

In this quest, we should not be surprised to find that the most popular methods of killing eradicated Isfet from both this world and the next. If sanctioned killing was used by the king and society for the building up of *Ma'at* and the destruction of Isfet, then the types of killing that would most fully extirpate any chaotic element would be expected. In this study, I have not searched for evidence to confirm a preconceived hypothesis. Instead, I have examined every available evidence of slaying I could find, and I have let that evidence speak for itself. Yet it is unsurprising to see that the Egyptians most often employed methods of slaying that created destruction of unwanted elements in multiple spheres. Thus, in the Old

---

[1] Joyce A. Tyldesley, *Judgement of the Pharaoh: Crime and Punishment in Ancient Egypt*, London: Weidenfeld & Nicolson, 2000, p. 69. See also Alberto Ravinel Whitney Green, "The Role of Human Sacrifice in the Ancient Near East", Ph.D. Dissertation, University of Michigan, 1973, 290–1.

Kingdom the killing which we know about takes the forms of decapitation and burning, both accompanied by ritualistic elements. All of these methods affect multiple spheres of existence.

Execution

In our attempts to uncover the past, we must take upon ourselves many roles. We cannot be archaeologists only, because uncovering the bodies of those who died in the Old Kingdom is not enough. For this study we need to know how (and, if possible, why) they died. So, we also have to don the persona of forensic detectives, applying the techniques and technologies of modern crime investigation units. Thus, as if we were the stars in a strange episode of *CSI: Egypt*, we must thoroughly examine the bodies. Often the corpses are the only available evidence to determine the cause of death. While many tombs and graves from this time period have been discovered, forensic work has been done on only a minute percentage of the bodies recovered. We are, therefore, at the mercy of happenstance regarding both discovery and forensic examination. Fortunately, some forensic work has been done pertaining to the topic at hand. Often such forensic work is our only hope for solving the mysteries of the past.

In 1993 and 1994, six mummies from the Fourth or Fifth Dynasties were examined for DNA evidence. Two had died when elderly, two at middle age, and two while children. DNA testing demonstrated that they represented three related generations, probably grandparents, parents, and children: "X-rays also showed that all six had been executed, as evidenced by their broken necks."[2] This conclusion of execution is hard to escape, since other circumstances that could neatly break the necks of a multi-generational family at the same time are hard to imagine. We know nothing about the reason for this execution, yet it confirms the practice of execution in the Old Kingdom.

The possibility that this discovery is an example of decapitation is strengthened by pictorial evidence and indirect textual witnesses. Jean Capart has demonstrated the consistent use of a telling determinative (an Egyptian hieroglyph that categorized the word to which it was attached) in the Old Kingdom. It shows a man with his arms bound behind him and his neck tied to a stake; significantly, he has no head:[3] Forms of this determinative in which the captive has his head were also used, so the missing head must be intentional and instructional. Having studied this and other forms of punishment, Bedell concludes that "decapitation was a common form of execution in the Old Kingdom."[4]

Besides the consistent use of the determinative outlined above, there is other textual evidence of decapitation in the Old Kingdom. In the Pyramid Texts, the king desires to pass by baboons who threaten to "cut off" (*sni*) heads.[5] To prevent this, he ties his head to his neck. Great care must be taken before considering anything from the Pyramid Texts as representative of actual events in mortal life.[6] However, it is likely that funerary texts, especially those as early as the Pyramid Texts, had some basis in mortal life. While the practices described in funerary literature may not have occurred in the mortal realm, events portrayed therein likely reflect everyday reality. If, in the Pyramid Texts, the king worries about his head being separated from his body, then it suggests that severing heads as a punishment was a known concept.

Another determinative may also relate to the punishment of decapitation. The determinative which is T18 — in Gardiner's sign list is described as a crook with a knife (probably more than one) lashed to it.[7] Capart is sure it represents a decapitation device.[8] Sethe, in commenting on Pyramid Text 230, which speaks of an instrument of torture and uses this sign as a determinative, agrees with this interpretation.[9] Later the Amduat uses this glyph as a weapon in a vignette.[10] On the other hand, Gardiner, while noting these interpretations, feels that the sign represented "the equipment of an early chieftain's attendant."[11]

Two tomb depictions also demonstrate the trend of decapitation. One comes from the well-preserved tomb of Mereruka, a nobleman of the Sixth Dynasty whose mastaba rests just north of Teti's pyramid. Mereruka's tomb contains a myriad of scenes, one of which shows possible decapitations in progress. A nude prisoner is shown crouching before a stake to which he is bound. On top of the stake are two human heads (see fig. 3.1). Possibly these heads belonged to prisoners already

---

[2] Judy Greenfield, "Secrets of the Ancient World Revealed Through DNA: A lecture presented to the ESS by Dr. Scott Woodward, Professor of Microbiology, Brigham Young University, 20 April 2001", *The Ostracon, Bulletin for the Egyptian Study Society* 12, 2001, no. 1, 22.

[3] Jean Capart, "Note sur la décapitation en Égypte", *ZÄS* 36, 1898, 125–6. This sign is represented as A216b or its variant A219c in Rainer Hannig, *Grosses Handwörterbuch Ägyptisch-Deutsch: (2800-950 v. Chr.): die Sprache der Pharaonen*, Kulturgeschichte der antiken Welt, Mainz: P. von Zabern, 1995, p. 1121.

[4] Ellen D. Bedell, "Criminal Law in the Egyptian Ramesside Period", Ph.D. Dissertation, Brandeis University, 1973, 157.

[5] Pyr. 286b. *Wb* 3, 457, who list the definition of this verb as "the heads cut off," and "also: the necks." Hannig, *Grosses Handwörterbuch Ägyptisch-Deutsch: (2800-950 v. Chr.): die Sprache der Pharaonen*, p. 713, says "cut off (head, neck)." Raymond O. Faulkner, *CD*, p. 230, defines it as "cut off heads . . . sever necks."

[6] See Mpay Kemboly, *Violence and Protection in Early Egyptian Funerary Texts*, Oxford University Master's Thesis, 2000, 3–9.

[7] Alan Gardiner, *Egyptian Grammar, Being an Introduction to the Study of Hieroglyphs*, 3rd ed. rev., Oxford: Oxford University Press, 1982, p. 513.

[8] Capart, "Note sur la décapitation en Égypte", p. 125. See also Richard H. Wilkinson, *Reading Egyptian Art: A Hieroglyphic Guide to Ancient Egyptian Painting and Sculpture*, London: Thames and Hudson, 1992, p. 187.

[9] Kurt Sethe, *Übersetzung und Kommentar zu den altägyptischen Pyramidentexten*, Glückstadt: J.J. Augustin, 1935, commentary on Pyr. 230c.

[10] Amduat VIII, center register; Zandee, p. 226.

[11] Gardiner, *Egyptian Grammar*, p. 513.

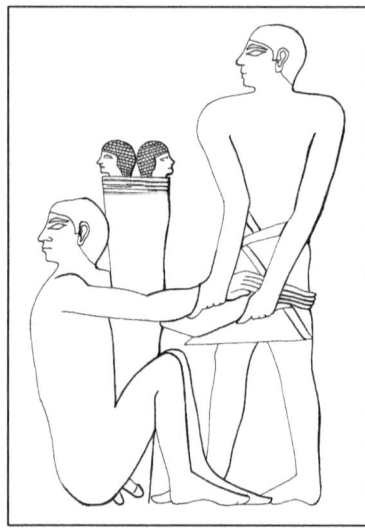

Figure 3.1 – Scene from the Tomb of Mereruka

executed.[12] A similar scene was painted in the tomb of Khentika. A close examination of the heads on the stake in Mereruka's tomb depiction reveals some traces which suggest that they are the heads of foreigners. This has led some to suggest that these were sculpted heads, intended to identify Egyptian criminals with the characteristics generally associated with vile foreigners.[13] However, even sculpted heads imply decapitation.

We must be careful when connecting tomb scenes to daily life. However, it is difficult to imagine why this representation was included if it did not reflect something from the lives of Mereruka and Khentika. Even if the scene was meant to ensure something was to happen in the afterlife, it probably resulted from something each nobleman experienced while living. It is very likely that the paintings commemorated Mereruka's and Khentika's overseership of executions. Since Mereruka served as vizier and since later evidence indicates that the vizier's responsibilities may have included overseeing executions, this seems plausible. In light of evidence to be presented below, we cannot rule out the possibility that the scenes represent a ritual associated with the burial rites of Mereruka and of Khentika. We must also remember that large mastabas, such as this one, included enough art work that they contained mimetic qualities.[14] In other words, in such depictions we have our best chance of finding an event too unsavory to be shown in official sources. Regardless of the purpose of the deaths, whether it be for burial ritual or to commemorate the tomb owners' overseeing executions, it seems quite possible that Mereruka and Khentika recorded actual beheadings.

The broken necks of six individuals described earlier in the chapter appear indisputable evidence of capital punishment. Decapitation is a form of execution which may have been regularly inflicted. Taken together, the bound headless determinative, the Pyramid Text reference, the weapon determinative, and the scenes in Mereruka's and Khentika's tomb, present extremely compelling evidence that this was actually the case. How often and for what reason we do not know.

There is also a theological rationale for decapitation as a method of execution. Missing a head made an afterlife impossible. Thus, decapitation effected complete destruction in both the mortal and the post-mortal life. Such would be the fate desired for any individual who was perceived as a representative of Isfet.

The autobiography of Weni, a fifth-dynasty official, informs us that he oversaw an investigation into an intrigue in the harem. If this case was anything like the harem conspiracy under Ramesses III discussed in chapter 7, then executions would have been involved. However, Weni was extremely discreet, and left no information as to the nature of that which he investigated, nor of the action taken.

Execration Texts

The Execration Texts, written on papyrus, pottery, or fashioned figures, are lists of individuals, groups, and areas which were perceived as hostile—or potentially so—to Egypt (see fig. 3.2). The ritual destruction of these items rendered such forces impotent.[15] This prophylactic magic was used by varying strata of society.[16] Several such figures from the Old Kingdom were found at Balat and Elephantine.[17] These finds were not large, and they probably did not represent state action. What certainly were old-kingdom state execration texts were found at Giza. Four related deposits have been uncovered there, consisting of figurines packed into pottery jars. The texts bear the names of Nubians, Egyptians, chiefs, military commanders, Nubian countries, and abstract threats like evil thoughts and plans.[18] A smaller but similar find was also made in Saqqara. This find also included Asiatic names.[19] The Giza and Saqqara deposits also contained an

---

[12] See Prentice Duell and University of Chicago Oriental Institute Sakkarah Expedition, *The Mastaba of Mereruka*, Chicago: The University of Chicago Press, 1938; Capart, "Note sur la décapitation en Égypte", p. 126; Bedell, "Criminal Law in the Egyptian Ramesside Period", p. 157.

[13] Nathalie Beaux, "Ennemis Étrangers et Malfaiteurs Égyptiens. Signification du Châtiment au pilori", BIFAO 91, 1991, 33–53. See also Hans Fischer-Elfert, *Abseits von Ma'at. Fallstudien zu Aussenseitern im Alten Ägypte*, Würzberg: Ergon Verlag, 2005, 22-26.

[14] See Antonio Loprieno, *Topos und Mimesis. Zum Ausländer in der ägyptischen Literatur*, Ägyptologische Abhandlungen, 1998, vol. 48, p. 14.

[15] See Kerry Muhlestein, Execration" in UCLA Encyclopedia of Egyptology, http://www.uee.ucla.edu (May, 2008).

[16] See also G. Belova, "The Egyptians' Ideas of Hostile Encirclement", in *Proceedings of the Seventh International Congress of Egyptologists*, C.J. Eyre (ed.), Orientalia Lovaniensia Analecta, Leuven: Uitgeverij Peeters, 1998, 145; and Harco Willems, "Crime, Cult and Capital Punishment (Mo'alla Inscription 8)", JEA 76, 1990, 46–7.

[17] See Jürgen Osing, "Ächtungstexte aus dem Alten Reich (II)", MDAIK 32, 1976, 133–86.

[18] Abu Bakr, Abdel Moneim, and Jürgen Osing, "Ächtungstexte aus dem Alten Reich", MDAIK 29, 1973, 97–133; Osing, "Ächtungstexte aus dem Alten Reich (II)", pp. 133–85; Hermann Junker, *Giza VIII*, Vienna: Akademie der Wissenschaften, 1947, pp. 30–38; and Stephan J. Seidlmayer, *Gräberfelder aus dem Übergang vom Altern zum Mittleren Reich. Studien zur archäologie der Ersten Zwischenzeit*, Heidelberg: Heidelberger Orientverlag, 1990, pp. 488–9.

[19] Edda Bresciani, "Foreigners", in *The Egyptians*, ed. Sergio Donadoni, Chicago: University of Chicago Press, 1997, p. 222.

Figure 3.2 – An Execration Figure

early version of the Rebellion Formula, which is more classically articulated in the Middle Kingdom:

> All people, all officials, all subjects, all men, all eunuchs, all women, all rulers, all from the region of Horus and Wawat, and Upper and Lower Egypt, all soldiers, all messengers, who will rebel (*sbi.ti=sni*), who will conspire (*w3.ti=sni*), who will talk of rebelling (*ddw sbi=sn*), who will fight (*ꜥh3.ti=sni*), who will talk of fighting (*dd.w ꜥh3=sn*), every rebel who speaks of his rebellion (*sbi=f*) [will be destroyed for all time].[20]

Such a ritual would have been a potent defense against Isfet. Assmann has identified similar rituals in Pyramid Text 23.[21] He also links a ritual of smashing red pots to execration rituals, considering them to be essentially equivalent.[22] He writes that in these rituals real and sacramental meanings overlapped.[23] This is a point to which we will return after examining the Mirgissa and Avaris finds.

Giza remained a site for execration rituals through the Thirtieth Dynasty, witnessing over two thousand years of the practice.[24] However, larger and better preserved finds come from elsewhere. Some of the most important finds originate from the Middle Kingdom,[25] which we must now examine in order to better understand our Old Kingdom examples. The most important of these, especially for our study, was at Mirgissa.[26] Mirgissa was a large fort along the bank of the Nile in Kush (Nubia), built during the Middle Kingdom to protect Egypt's interests in the area. Here over 175 execration texts were found, along with models of birds and ships. Most significant to our study is the body of an actual human who was forced to participate in the execration rites. A human skull, without a mandible, was found buried upside down in a pottery cup.[27] Surrounding this find were many small traces of beeswax dyed with red ochre, probably the remnants of melted figurines;[28] about twenty centimeters from the skull was buried a flint knife.[29] Ritner has convincingly demonstrated that this flint knife was the traditional blade for ritual slaughter.[30] The rest of the body was found nearby, apparently thrown away instead of buried.[31] Examination suggests that the body was Nubian.[32] This corpse was undeniably the human counterpart to the clay figures of the execration ritual.[33] Ritner calls it "indisputable evidence for the practice of human sacrifice."[34]

A human execration victim at Mirgissa significantly changes the lens through which all other execration finds are viewed. It is difficult to know how much can be extrapolated from this find. Mirgissa is the most complete deposit associated with execration rituals we have discovered, possessing all elements found elsewhere. Similar, though not as complete (including lacking human remains), deposits have been found at other Nubian forts—Uronarti and Shalfak.[35] Finds in Egypt are less regular in patterns and elements,[36] though most of

---

[20] Georges Posener, *Cinq figurines d'envoûtement*, Cairo: Institut français d'archéologie oriental du Caire, 1987, pp. 30-43, texts 63957 and 63959.

[21] Jan Assmann, "Spruch 23 der Pyramidentexte und die Ächtung der Feinde Pharos", in *Hommages à Jean Leclant*, Catherine Berger, Gisèle Clerc, and Nicolas-Christophe Grimal (eds.), Cairo: Institut français d'archéologie orientale, 1994.

[22] Assmann, "Spruch 23 der Pyramidentexte und die Ächtung der Feinde Pharos", p. 53. See also Robert Reitner, *The Mechanics of Ancient Egyptian Magical Practice*, Studies in Ancient Oriental Civilization, no. 54, Chicago: The Oriental Institute of The University of Chicago, 1993, pp. 144–53.

[23] Assmann, "Spruch 23 der Pyramidentexte und die Ächtung der Feinde Pharos", p. 51. See also Renate Müller-Wollermann, *Vergehen und Strafen. Zur Sanktionierung abweichenden Verhaltens im alten Ägypten*, Leiden: E.J. Brill, 2004, p. 45.

[24] Alfred Grimm, "Ein Käfig für einen Gefangenen in einem Ritual zur Vernichtung von Feinden", *JEA* 73, 1987, 205. A picture of the ship can be seen in H. Chevrier, "Rapport sur les travaux de Karnak (1952–1953)", *ASAE* 53, 1955, no. 1, pl. 7.

[25] See Georges Posener and Baudouin van de Walle, *Princes et pays d'Asie et de Nubie. Textes hiératiques sur des figurines d'envoûtement du moyen empire suivis de Remarques paléographiques sur lest textes similaires de Berlin, par B. van de Walle*, Brussels: Fondation égyptologique rein Élisabeth, 1940; and Kurt Sethe (ed.), *Die Ächtung feindlicher Fürsten, Völker und Dinge auf altägyptischen Tongefässcherben des mittleren Reiches, nach den Originalen im Berliner Museum*, Berlin Deutsche Akademie der Wissenschaften Berlin: Akademie der Wissenschaften u. Gruyter, 1926.

[26] See Seidlemayer, *Gräberfelder aus dem Übergang vom Altern zum Mittleren Reich. Studien zur archäologie der Ersten Zwischenzeit*, 488, who writes that "the most important find relating to execration rituals of the Middle Kingdom comes from outside the Egyptian fortress at Mirgissa in Lower Nubia." See also Andre Vila, "Un Dépôt de Textes D'Envoutement au Moyen Empire", *Journal des Savants* 41, 1963; and Yvan Koenig, "Les textes d'envoûtement de Mirgissa", *RdE*, 1990, 101–28.

[27] Andre Vila, "Un rituel d' envoûtement au Moyen Empire Égyptien", in *L'Homme, kier et aujourd'hui. Recueil d' études en hommage a' Andrè Leroi-Gourhan*, Marc Sauter (ed.), Paris: Éditions Cujas, 1973, pp. 145-7 and fig. 6; Koenig, "Les textes d'envoûtement de Mirgissa", p. 309 and fig. 4; and Ritner, *The Mechanics of Ancient Egyptian*, p. 163.

[28] Vila, *Un rituel*, p. 631, fig. 15; and Ritner, *The Mechanics of Ancient Egyptian*, p. 163.

[29] Vila, *Un rituel*, p. 638.

[30] Ritner, *The Mechanics*, pp. 163–7, especially n. 758.

[31] Vila, *Un rituel*, pp. 628–31; and Ritner, *The Mechanics*, p. 163.

[32] Vila, *Un rituel*, pp. 637–8.

[33] Vila, *Un rituel*, pp. 628–31.

[34] Ritner, *The Mechanics*, pp. 162–3.

[35] Vila, *Un rituel*, pp. 638–9.

[36] Ritner, *The Mechanics*, p.154.

these finds are in more archaeologically cluttered and difficult sites. Mirgissa and her sister forts are the perfect place to find the most complete rites, for there is less archaeological noise and happenstance through which to filter.

The study is complicated by an eighteenth-dynasty find at Avaris. Recent excavations have uncovered one certain execration pit, and another nearly certain execration pit, from an Egyptian strata. These pits, associated with Ahmose, were most likely used by him after the capture of Avaris as strong magic to prevent further incursions by foreigners. In the first pit, Locus 1055, three male skulls attest to human inclusion in the execration rites.[37] Moreover, accompanying these skulls were the fingers from the right hands of three males (probably the same males).[38] As Willems has pointed out in personal correspondence, this is reminiscent of the manner of sacrificing animals, wherein the foreleg was severed and presented, along with the head, as part of the sacrifice. The similarities make a sacrificial context almost inescapable. Besides this example, the excavator, Fuscaldo, is convinced that Locus 1016 was also an execration pit,[39] because two male skeletons were found there lying face down. Fuscaldo believes that the skulls are similar to the skull deposited at Mirgissa. She also avers that whereas at Mirgissa the next nearest execration pit contained broken figurines, at Avaris the figurines were not substitutes, but instead they represented real humans that were sacrificed, as evidenced by the two full human skeletons found at the tomb.[40] This additional finding of human execration victims broadens the generalizability of the Mirgissa deposit.

Concerning Concerning execration rites, as noted above, Assmann believes they can share sacramental and actual physical manifestations.[41] Nordh writes "execration rituals may have walked hand in hand with the execution of the punishments stated in the legal statutes. They seem to have complemented one another when it comes to certain kinds of crime."[42] To assess these statements, we must also examine Egyptian actions concerning rites in general. The Egyptians focused on a system of redundancy in order to ensure the efficacy of their rites. For instance, mummification ensured a place for the *ka*. However, in case there was a problem with the mummified body, a statue, or many statues, was also often provided (resources permitting), along with spells, drawings, anthropomorphoid coffins, and spare heads. Likewise, while actual offerings were provided for the dead, the redundancy system included drawings of offerings, funerary spells, and inscriptions for passers-by to read—all aimed at ensuring the provision of offerings. It is therefore not outside the Egyptian religious character to use spells, pots, clay figures, and humans in rites designed to protect Ma'at, and thus the country. On the contrary, while we cannot say that other redundant ritual actions demand the same type of redundancy of the execration rite, we can say that it is probable.

It would certainly be overly ambitious to opine that execration rites always featured human sacrifice; however, it is very fair to postulate that many did so. The lack of other human remains makes it difficult to say more, though the accident of preservation allows the possibility that this may have been a regular feature, at least in the Middle and New Kingdoms, from whence our two known examples come. Perhaps little can be said for the Old Kingdom. The execration deposits in our crowded Giza and Saqqara finds likely did not have a human element to the rites. Still, it is plausible, and the evidence will be categorized thus.

Other Forms of Ritual Slaying

The excavations at the Great Pyramid of Giza uncovered a spectacularly preserved boat. Even in the Old Kingdom, ritual boat processions were an age-old expression of kingship and royal power over the forces of Chaos, and thus boats had been buried with many kings before Khufu, the builder of the Great Pyramid. Not far from this boat pit in Giza, a very curious object was found: a framed box which had been carefully buried (see fig. 3.3). In 1985, Lehner and Lacovara puzzled together a purpose for this object. Based on many bits of evidence, they concluded that it was a frame used for transporting ka statues of the kind just mentioned above.[43] Two years later, a much more convincing argument was proffered.

In 1987, Grimm noticed a relief from a block at Karnak which shed light on the question of the boat in Giza. Pictured is a large ship sailing along the Nile, purportedly in a festival of triumph over enemies; hoisted on its bow is a prisoner suspended in a cage which matched exactly the enigmatic object found at Giza (see fig. 3.4).[44] The cage at Giza, Grimm noted, contained just enough room for a prisoner to stand without being able to move—the frame was designed such that the bars were built in the appropriate places for binding a prisoner at the feet and upper body with an aperture left for the head.[45] Grimm

---

[37] Perla Fuscaldo, "Tell al-Dab'a: Two Execration Pits and a Foundation Deposit", in *Egyptology at the Dawn of the Twenty-first Century. Proceedings of the Eighth International Congress of Egyptologists, Cairo, 2000*, Zahi Hawass (ed.), Cairo: The American University in Cairo Press, 2003, vol. 1, p. 186.

[38] Manfred Bietak, Josef Dorner, and Peter Janosi, "Ausgrabungen in dem Palastbezirk von Avaris Vorbericht tell El-Dab'a/'Ezbet Helmi 1993-2000," in Ägypten & Levante 11 (2001): 62-64.

[39] Fuscaldo, "Tell al-Dab'a: Two Execration Pits and a Foundation Deposit", p. 186. Bietak, *et al.*, "Ausgrabungen in dem Palastbezirk von Avaris," 67-74, are not as sure as Fuscaldo that the finds are part of an execration ritual.

[40] Fuscaldo, "Tell al-Dab'a: Two Execration Pits and a Foundation Deposit", pp. 188–7.

[41] Assmann, "Spruch 23 der Pyramidentexte und die Ächtung der Feinde Pharos", p. 51.

[42] Katarina Nordh, *Aspects of Ancient Egyptian Curses and Blessings: Conceptual Background and Transmission*, Stockholm: Gotab, 1996.

[43] M. Lehner and P. Lacovara, "An Enigmatic Wooden Object", *JEA*, 1985, 71.

[44] Grimm, "Ein Käfig für einen Gefangenen in einem Ritual zur Vernichtung von Feinden", pp. 203–4.

[45] Grimm, "Ein Käfig für einen Gefangenen in einem Ritual zur Vernichtung von Feinden", p. 204.

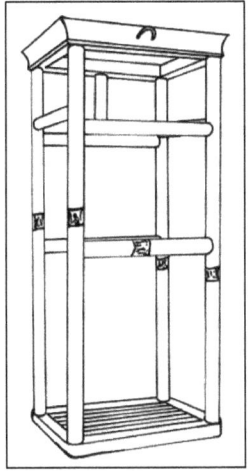

Figure 3.3 – Cage found buried near Khufu's boats at Giza

Figure 3.4 – Relief of Tutankhamun boat with suspended prisoner

also noted that none of the pictures used in the previous study had actually shown such a frame being used to drag ka statues.[46]

Grimm's interpretation can best be understood in light of other events, some of which will be discussed more fully in chapter 6 but must be mentioned now in order to properly evaluate Grimm's claim. The cage at Giza likely represents the continuation of a practice evidenced in pre-dynastic times. A rock drawing of a royal procession in Gebel Sheikh Suleiman from the late Pre-dynastic Period, roughly contemporary with Narmer,[47] depicts an Egyptian warship possibly cruising over enemies who are being cast in front of its keel. Besides the enemies who are (perhaps) flung into the water, one is shown bound to the front of the ship, seemingly hanging over the water.[48] It is impossible to tell whether or not those who were being thrown into the water were already dead; though the possibility that they could escape the river if not dead makes their deceased state more likely. The bound prisoner appears to almost certainly be alive. This is somewhat reminiscent of scenes from Hierakonpolis Tomb 100 and of the Painted Linen from Gebelein in Turin, in which smiting a prisoner is also associated with a royal barque.[49] A royal barque is also depicted above the decapitated prisoners on the Narmer Palette. Taken together, we see a steady stream of evidence that transporting and slaying prisoners in association with the royal barque was part of royal processions from the era of Hierakonpolis Tomb 100 (c. 3500 BCE) through at least the Giza era (c. 2500 BCE).

Moreover, events from later than the Giza find are also important. It is reported that Thutmosis I slew a Nubian and hung him upside down on his barque as he returned home from crushing a rebellion. Likewise, Amenhotep II, after a victorious battle, tied seven enemy princes upside down to the prow of his ship and paraded up the Nile; then he ritually slew them. One of the corpses was then taken by ship to be displayed in Napata while the other six became showpieces in Thebes. The Tutankhamun cage so closely parallels the actions of Amenhotep II that he may have employed the same item in his transport of prisoners bound for slaughter. Moreover, from the Eighteenth through the Twenty-first Dynasties come several known depictions of royal boats on which smiting-scene-decorated kiosks are pictured.[50]

There is a significant difference between a dead and a live, bound prisoner sported on the bow of a ship; yet clearly, they are closely associated. This issue will be more fully addressed below, but the propinquity among Thutmosis I binding a slain leader to his ship; the picture of Tutankhamun's cage; the upside-down future victims of Amenhotep II; and the kiosk smiting scenes of Akhenaten, Nefertiti, and Ramesses III must be noted. Undoubtedly these indicate a trend affiliating royal boats and dead or alive prisoners. Tutankhamun's cage ties this

---

[46] Grimm, "Ein Käfig für einen Gefangenen in einem Ritual zur Vernichtung von Feinden", p. 203.

[47] See Whitney Davis, *Masking the Blow: The Scene of Representation in Late Prehistoric Egyptian Art*, Berkeley: University of California, 1992, p. 126.

[48] Bruce Williams, Thomas J. Logan, and William Murnane, "The Metropolitan Museum Knife Handle and Aspects of Pharaonic Imagery before Narmer", *JNES* 46, 1987, 253, 263–4, 282–4. Because Emery first identified this scene as from the time of Djer, and most especially because he refers to it as the Wadi Halfa inscription whereas later scholarship has dubbed it the Gebel Sheikh Suleiman inscription, confusion has often led to identifying these as two separate depictions. It is, in fact, the same picture known by two different names.

[49] H. Case and J.C. Payne, "Tomb 100: The Decorated Tomb in Hierakonpolis", *JEA* 48, 1962, pl. 1; see also Williams, Logan, and Murnane, , "The Metropolitan Museum Knife Handle and Aspects of Pharaonic Imagery before Narmer", pp. 251–6, wherein they discuss the royal barque procession; and Kerry Muhlstein, "Death by Water: The Role of Water in Ancient Egypt's Treatment of Enemies and Juridical Process", in *L'Acqua Nell'antico Egitto: Vita, Rigenerazione, Incantesimo, Medicamento*, Alessia Amenta, Michela Luiselli, and Maria Novella Sordi, (eds.), Rome: L'Erma di Bretschneider, 2005, pp. 177–8.

[50] Emma Swan Hall, *The Pharaoh Smites His Enemies: a Comparative Study*, Münchner ägyptologische Studien, no. 44, München: Deutscher Kunstverlag, 1986, pp. 25–26, 36, figs. 39, 40, 66, and 82.

practice to the Giza cage and evokes the Gebel Sheikh Suleiman depiction, suggesting that the tradition was very old,[51] likely stemming from a time when the barque was the most important instrument of rule.[52]

The existence of such a cage in connection with the fourth-dynasty complex is strong evidence that such a practice was part of that time period. Indeed, it is hard to imagine that it would be included in the funerary complex of Khufu if it were not an important and consistently needed ritual object. We can therefore postulate that in the Fourth Dynasty, and probably on a continual basis from at least the time of the Gebel Sheikh Suleiman predynastic depiction more than half a millenia earlier, enemies were regularly carried on ships as part of a ritual that almost certainly included their slaughter. The later new-kingdom examples also indicate that this remained a feature of Egyptian culture.[53] Because of the charged power of ritual and water's super-destructive nature (water could deprive a body of burial and thus continued existence), the combination of the two was a potent force in destroying Chaos.

Another possible piece of evidence for sanctioned killing comes from one of the most famous and controversial sections of the Pyramid Texts: the Cannibal Hymn. The traditional analysis of this hymn is an interesting story behind the story. In the early days of Egyptology, when Egyptologists were apt to see primitive practices among the ancient Egyptians, this hymn was quickly interpreted as evidence of cannibalism, even before thorough examinations were performed. As the pendulum of the discipline's culture swung toward only seeing elements of high culture—probably because Egypt was viewed as the ancestor of high Western culture—the evidence for such a savage scene was dismissed. As I noted in the first chapter, it is difficult for scholars to maintain objectivity in matters that broach their political or religious views or that touch on topics with emotional charge. Because of the connection felt with ancient Egyptian culture, the topics of ritual slaying and cannibalism evoke emotional, political, and religious reactions, and thus it is a topic which seems to shield itself from objectivity; scholars on both sides of the issue have something at stake. In some instances, scholars analyzed the evidence with great proficiency, but just as they zeroed in on the target, they seemed to lose their nerve, veering off course. As pendulums generally do, the scholarship regarding this area is swinging back again, hopefully with a smaller arc. Today, younger Egyptologists are seeing evidence heretofore ignored.

As we attempt to come to a reasonable understanding of the hymn, the section which gives the notorious text its name is precisely the passage that concerns us:

It is N who judges with Amun whose name is hidden

On the day of slaughtering the eldest

N is owner of offerings, knotter of ropes

N is a maker of offerings for himself

N is an eater of men, living on gods

An owner of those who bring tribute, a dispatcher of messengers[54]

It is the grasper of top knots who is as a kettle, lassoing them for N

He who is sacred of brow[55] is he who protects them for him, thwarting them for him

It is he who is over the reddening[56] who binds them for him

It is Khonsu, cutter of the lords, he slices their throats for N

He removes for him that which is in their bellies

He is the messenger that he sent to restrain[57]

It is *Shesmu*[58] who slaughters them for him

Cooking for him the things inside them in his cauldron of the evening meal

N is he who eats their magic, a swallower of their *akhs* [souls]

Their great ones are his morning meal

Their middle-sized ones for his evening meal

Their little ones his night meal

Their old men and old women are for his incense burning[59]

It is the great ones of the upper sky who get the fire for him

For the cauldrons containing them, with the forelegs of their eldest ones[60]

---

[51] See Toby A.H. Wilkinson, *Early Dynastic Egypt*, New York: Routledge, 1999, pp. 32–3, for a discussion on the royal boat ritual procession.

[52] Jan Assmann, *The Mind of Egypt: History and Meaning in the Time of the Pharaohs*, trans. Andrew Jenkins, New York: Metropolitan, 2002, p. 46.

[53] See Muhlestein, "Death by Water", pp. 174–5.

[54] Hartwig Altenmüller, "Bemerkungen zum Kannibalenspruch", in *Fragen an die altägyptische Literatur: Studien zum Gedenken an Eberhard Otto*, Eberhard Otto, *et al.* (ed.), Wiesbaden: Reichert, 1977, p. 20, translates "a master of messengers, who gives orders." Miriam Lichtheim, *Ancient Egyptian Literature: A Book of Readings. Volume I: The Old and Middle Kingdoms*, Berkeley: University of California Press, 1973, p. 37, translates "Master of messengers who sends instructions."

[55] Altenmüller, "Bemerkungen zum Kannibalenspruch", p. 21, translates "The Serpent with raised head"; Similarly, Lichtheim, *Ancient Egyptian Literature*, p. 37, translates "It is Serpent Raised-head who guards"; and Raymond O Faulkner, *The Ancient Egyptian Pyramid Texts*, Oxford: Oxford University Press, 1969, p. 81, writes "It is the Serpent with raised head", but I have left my translation more literal.

[56] Lichtheim, *Ancient Egyptian Literature*, p. 37 and note 5, translates "he-upon-the willow". However, the determinative denoting red ink in the Teti version dictates that *trw* be translated with its red connotations.

[57] Altenmüller, "Bemerkungen zum Kannibalenspruch", p. 21, translates "Der Olpressengott is es, der sie zerstückelt für WT." Lichtheim also renders this as "to punish." Faulkner, *Pyramid Texts*, p. 81, translates "restrain," as I do. The word $ḥsf$ can have either meaning. See Faulkner, *Concise Dictionary*, p. 197; Hannig, *Grosses Handwörterbuch Ägyptisch-Deutsch*, p. 620; and *Wb* 3, 320. Since the stanzas above contain an alternating interplay between restraining and killing, I have maintained the interplay in this stanza by choosing the "restrain" meaning of the word.

[58] *Shesmu* is a god often associated with butchery and human sacrifice.

[59] Lichtheim, *Ancient Egyptian Literature*, p. 37, translates this as "the oldest males and females are for his fuel"—less literal but a better idiomatic rendering.

This text is undoubtedly a ritual text transferred to the walls of pyramids. Altenmüller notes that in the pyramid of Unas and in the spell's coffin-text descendants are other ritual-text supporters.[61] He also identifies a different textual context for the other occurrence of this spell in Teti's pyramid,[62] where it is set in the midst of transformation spells. However, Assmann has determined that transformation spells also stem from ritual.[63] Elsewhere Assmann has noted that the Pyramid Texts do not replace rituals, but instead "the cult is simply performed in two distinct media: ritual recitation and inscriptional record."[64] Hence, while the Cannibal Hymn may have been set in different contexts over time, it seems that it maintained its ritual identity. This makes it nearly indisputable that its original context was that of some ritual. Funerary literature is most applicable to this study when it involves ritual, since it would thus reflect actions carried out in the mortal sphere. The questions we must ask are what form the ritual took, and in which time period was that form preserved and used?

It is apparent that whatever its physical manifestation, this ritual induced the absorption of magical powers.[65] The transformation spells surrounding the ritual in Teti's pyramid also concern our topic.[66] Absorbing powers for transformation lends itself to the idea of ritual slaughter. Altenmüller writes that slaughtering in a particular way releases the magical powers which are to be eaten, and that in order to accomplish this, magical spells were recited during slaughtering rituals.[67] In light of this, we must conclude, as Altenmüller did, that this text was either an actual ritual, or the echo of a ritual, that was recited at the end of an offering or possibly a slaughtering.[68] Eyre believes that there was a corresponding ritual in at least the late Fifth Dynasty.[69]

But what was offered or slaughtered? Could it really be humans, as the text suggests? We have no reason to conclude that it was not, other than a preconception that Egyptians of the Old Kingdom just did not do this sort of thing. If we divest ourselves of this belief, there is nothing to indicate that the ritual text misportrayed the ritual itself.

Debate: Cannibalism or Not

As with Faulkner before him,[70] Spiegel concludes that the hymn did represent human sacrifice.[71] Altenmüller disagrees, not with the suggestion that human sacrifice occurred, but with Spiegel's idea that the sacrifice was to the king. Altenmüller feels that it would have been a sacrifice to the Sun God rather than to the king.[72] However, Altenmüller assumes that no human sacrifices were performed during the Old Kingdom and that such events must have taken place in archaic times.[73] He argues instead that cattle were sacrificed. As evidence he points out scenes in which cattle were brought for sacrifice—sometimes big cattle for morning meals and small cattle for evening meals—sometimes big for morning, medium for midday, and small for evening meals.[74] From this he concludes that the Cannibal Hymn lines referring to eating big ones in the morning, middle-sized ones at midday, and small ones in the evening could not refer to humans, since this practice was applied to cattle. While this parallel to the hymn is clear, there are two problems with his reasoning. First, he has based it on an assumption that the old-kingdom national character can be pigeonholed into a human-sacrifice-eschewing society. There is little evidence one way or the other on this issue, but the evidence we have cited thus far indicates that Altenmüller's assessment is the less supported position. Furthermore, the cattle parallel does not preclude its human counterpart, as the human victims very well may have been the precedent for the cattle. The idea of offering different-sized or different-aged victims at different times of the day is by no means exclusive to one species at a time. Sacrificial cattle is non sequitur; it is an illogical leap to postulate that if cattle were offered in a particular manner, then humans could not be. Instead, it is more likely that all species being offered would fit a certain regimen.

In a manner similar to Altenmüller, Eyre disputes that ritual slaying of humans was part of the ritual associated with the Cannibal Hymn. He continually cites the spell referring to eating gods,[75] overlooking the fact that the text explicitly calls the king "an eater of men, living on

---

[60] See Pyr 399b–406b, the Unas version.
[61] Altenmüller, "Bemerkungen zum Kannibalenspruch", p. 28.
[62] Altenmüller, "Bemerkungen zum Kannibalenspruch", p. 28.
[63] Jan Assmann, "Egyptian Mortuary Liturgy", in *Studies in Egyptology*, Sarah Israelit-Groll (ed.), Jerusalem: Magnes, 1990.
[64] Assmann, *Mind of Egypt*, p. 89.
[65] This opinion is independently arrived at by Altenmüller, "Bemerkungen zum Kannibalenspruch", p. 31. For more in general about cannibalism and its ability to add to immortality see Monique Halm-Tisserant, *Cannibalisme et Immortalité*, Paris: Les Belles Lettres, 1993, pp. 49–88.
[66] Altenmüller, "Bemerkungen zum Kannibalenspruch", p. 30. See also Christopher Eyre, *The Cannibal Hymn: A Cultural and Literary Study*, Bolton: University of Liverpool, 2002, p. 55, who writes of the offering of meat to statues as constituting a transformation spell. John L. Foster, "Some Observations on Pyramid Texts 273–274, the So-Called 'Cannibal Hymn'", *JSSEA* 9, 1979, pp. 58–9, believes that the text is concerned with the transformation of "resurrection, transfiguration, and assumption into heaven. Brutal and primitive as parts may be, they cannot negate the strains of transcendence that are actually there in the poem's religious conceptions. Our problem then is as follows: Can we moderns recover any of the imagination and feeling, any of the religious tones of hope and triumph, from this hymn without having the poetry destroyed by our revulsion at the eating of human (or divine) flesh?" Foster does not address whether the text had something to do with actual human slaughter, but this statement seems to intimate that he felt it was possible.
[67] Altenmüller, "Bemerkungen zum Kannibalenspruch", p. 31.
[68] Altenmüller, "Bemerkungen zum Kannibalenspruch", p. 35.
[69] Eyre, *The Cannibal Hymn*, p. 49, 55. He poses the question of whether the Cannibal Hymn is a commentary on the ritual or a replacement of the ritual. It is plain that he connects it with the former, though he does not explicitly answer this question.
[70] Raymond O. Faulkner, "The 'Cannibal Hymn' From the Pyramid Texts", *JEA* 10, 1924, 102–3.
[71] Joachim Spiegel, "Das Auferstehungsritual der Unas-Pyramide", *Archäologischer Anzeiger* 23, 1971, 434.
[72] Altenmüller, "Bemerkungen zum Kannibalenspruch", p. 36.
[73] Altenmüller, "Bemerkungen zum Kannibalenspruch", p. 38.
[74] Altenmüller, "Bemerkungen zum Kannibalenspruch", p. 37.
[75] See Eyre, *The Cannibal Hymn*, pp. 131–3.

gods." Furthermore, he roundly denounces the existence of cannibalism as a regular feature of any ancient society except during times of famine.[76] While Eyre believes that the ritual slaughter of cattle was part of the rite of the Cannibal Hymn, he believes that the cannibalism aspect was a metaphor and does not discuss whether the killing of people could be an actualized part of the metaphor as well as the killing of cattle.[77] Eyre spends a great deal of ink reiterating his belief that everything associated with humans in the text is symbolic.[78] His reason for this seems to stem from his idea that no human societies regularly engaged in cannibalism and from a belief hidden in one of his footnotes, wherein he argues against the hypothesis that ritual slaying of humans was part of the rite, with the justification that "it is difficult to see anything other than a priori assumptions to support such an argument."[79] While Eyre's work is an exceptional piece of scholarship, this particular point of reasoning seems to be turned on its head. Interpreting a text which describes the ritual slaying of humans as an example of ritual slaying is not based on a priori assumptions. Instead, since the text explicitly refers to the slaughter of people, without evidence to refute this, the rejection of ritual slaying must be based on a priori assumptions.

Such assumptions like those made by Eyre and Altenmüller are to be expected, for it is inevitable that scholars operate in light of their own experience; as outlined in chapter 1, the topic of violence seems to lend itself particularly well to post-modern interpretations. Additionally, in some known cases animals eventually did serve as substitutes for humans.[80] For example, one of the Cannibal Hymn's coffin-text descendants only refers to the slaughter of cattle.[81] However, another states that both human evildoers and cattle were to be slaughtered.[82] If, as the spell was being rewritten to its coffin-text form, humans were still included in the spell, it is arguable that the practice had not fallen out of use hundreds of years before.

As mentioned above, Baud and Etienne have suggested that the Cannibal Hymn may be the ritual text associated with the sacrifices pictured on the labels of Djer and Aha. These kings were buried with a varied population of retainers; this variety may echo the differing groups the hymn dictates will be eaten at differing times. Additionally, there are prisoners bound (lassoed) whose organs may be in the process of being removed and eaten, explaining the presence of a basin in the early-dynastic labels.[83]

There is theological argument for the case as well, especially if evildoers were victims in the ritual. Cooking, which was interrelated with burning,[84] completely annihilated the essence of a person, denying them existence in this life and in the next.[85] And so, "the topos of 'cooking', for example, which is so central to the Cannibal Spell, could at the same time signify both a destructive act—the annihilation of enemies—and a creative one—the transformation of the cooked animals/enemies into a powerful substance that could be absorbed by the receiver of the cooked offerings."[86] It is quite possible that criminals were the victims of this rite, since a Coffin Text descendant of the spell indicates such.[87] The idea of tying the destruction of criminals with a re-creation is preserved even up to the creation of the Shabaka Stone, which, in the midst of creation theology notes that while life is given to those who do good (ꜥnḫ n ḥr(i) ḥtp), death is given to those who do criminal acts (mwt n ḥr(i) ḫbntw).[88] We should expect that evildoers, those associated with Isfet, would be ritually destroyed in a manner that would eliminate them completely. This conclusion is strengthened by the presence of Shesmu as the one who butchers the victims in the Cannibal Hymn. Shesmu is often associated with protection provided by his role as a butcher who destroys enemies.[89]

As with so many occurrences examined in this book, we cannot be certain if the Cannibal Hymn represents a ritual that actually involved ritual slaying. However, its ritual context and theological implications indicate that it probably did. Assuming the existence of such a rite as is described in the hymn, we are still unsure of when it was enacted, but it is likely that the rite existed for some time before its immortalization in the pyramids and that it continued to exist at least to its middle-kingdom expression in the Coffin Texts, where it specifies what types of people were to be slaughtered. Of this Eyre correctly writes that while the recopying of the Cannibal Hymn essentially in its original form probably represented a textual transmission, that the transmission from the Pyramid Texts to the Coffin Texts "seems more likely to involve a continuous development in

---

[76] See Eyre, *The Cannibal Hymn*, pp. 156–7.
[77] See Eyre, *The Cannibal Hymn*, p. 159.
[78] See Eyre, *The Cannibal Hymn*, p. 166–72.
[79] See Eyre, *The Cannibal Hymn*, p. 162n45.
[80] J. Gwyn Griffiths, "Human Sacrifices in Egypt: The Classical Evidence", *ASAE* 48, 1948, 419–20.
[81] See CT VI, 179a, and Altenmüller, "Bemerkungen zum Kannibalenspruch", p. 31.
[82] See CT VI, 181h, and Altenmüller, "Bemerkungen zum Kannibalenspruch", p. 31.
[83] Michel Baud and Marc Etienne, "Le vanneau et le couteau. Un rituel monarchique sacrificiel dans l'Ègype de la Ire dynastie", in *Archèo-Nil* 10, 2000, 63.

[84] For more on this, see Eyre, *The Cannibal Hymn*, pp. 107–10, 173–4.
[85] Katja Goebs, "Symbolic Functions of Royal Crowns in Early Egyptian Funerary Literature", PhD Dissertation, Oxford, 1998, 196; Anthony Leahy, "Death by Fire in Ancient Egypt", *Journal of the Economic and Social History of the Orient* 27, no. 2, 1984, 201; Wolfgang Boochs, "Religöse Strafen", in *Religion und Philosophie im Alten Ägypten*, Ursula Verhoeven and Erhart Graefe (ed.), Leuven: Uitgeverij Peeters, 1991, p. 62; J. Zandee, *Death as an Enemy According to Ancient Egyptian Conceptions*, Leiden: E.J. Brill, 1960, pp. 13–14, 133–9; Tyldesley, *Judgment of the Pharaoh*, p. 67; Erik Hornung, *Altägyptische Höllenvorstellungen. Mit 7 Lichtdrucktafeln und 6 Abbildungen im Text, Abhandlungen der Sächsischen Akademie der Wissenschaften zu Leipzig, Philologisch-historische Klasse Bd. 59, Heft 3*, Berlin: Akademie-Verlag, 1968, p. 28.
[86] Goebs, "Symbolic Functions of Royal Crowns", p. 196; see also E.A. Wallis Budge, *Osiris and the Egyptian Resurrection*, New York: Dover, 1911, p. 175.
[87] See CT VI, 181h.
[88] Shabaka Stone, line 57.
[89] M. Ciccarello, "Shesmu the Letopolite" in *Studies in Honor of George R. Hughes*, Studies in Ancient Oriental Civilisation 39, Chicago: Oriental Institute, 1976, pp. 49-51.

performative use."⁹⁰ Like ritual boat processions, the Cannibal Hymn combines ritual potency with the hyper-destructive power of burning to ensure the annihilation of Isfet.

Despite all their efforts to preserve Order, the power and momentum of the Old Kingdom could not consistently control Chaos. Eventually Egypt outlived the majesty of her great monarchs, and for a time, Isfet gained the upper hand.

Old Kingdom Evidence of Sanctioned Killing

Violence	Weak Evidence	Plausible Evidence	Strong Evidence	Very Strong Evidence
Execution of six family members				X
Ongoing undetermined cases of decapitation				X
Specific example of decapitation from tomb of Mereruka and Khentika			X	
Ongoing Ritual Slaying as part of boat processions		X		
Ongoing human sacrifice as execration ritual		X		
Ongoing human sacrifice as part of ritual reflected in Cannibal Hymn			X	

---

⁹⁰ Eyre, *The Cannibal Hymn*, pp. 23–4.

Chapter 4

SANCTIONED KILLING IN THE TIME BETWEEN: THE FIRST INTERMEDIATE PERIOD
(Dynasties 7 through 11)

Drive him away! Kill his children! Erase his name! Destroy his neighbors! Expel his memory and the memory of those who supported and loved him.
—The Teaching for Merikare

The smell of incense rose thickly, intermingling with the strong and unmistakable scent of blood. The proud and haughty nomarch Ankhtifi was no stranger to battle, but the ceremonial flint knife he now grasped was a weapon to which he was not well accustomed. Still, he knew how to sever the leg from a mighty bull, and Hemen demanded this sacrifice. As he engaged in his grisly work, a thought struck him. As he held the butchered limb aloft, the desire crystallized in his mind. If any ever dared to desecrate the grand tomb he was building, they would take the place of the bull in the sacrifices to Hemen.

As spectacular and lasting as the displays of Old Kingdom power were, even this grand era would inevitably end. Stability and continuity were long lasting for the great Egyptian rulers and their political structure, but eventually power sifted through the monarchs' fingers into the hands of local leaders, and inexorable fragmentation occurred. The united lands of Egypt broke into smaller areas; local leaders vied for control. Like a sacrificial animal, Egypt was quartered among those seeking to become the new great king. Egyptologists call this era the First Intermediate Period.

Much of our evidence from the First Intermediate Period comes from a substantial proliferation in biographical statements. The tomb and memorial inscriptions that contained these statements also frequently contained another element which increased in volume along with the biography: the tomb curse.[1] Extrapolating information gained from curses is complicated by many factors. We must, therefore, devote some time to the matter.

Egyptian Inscriptional Curses

It is not surprising that during an era of decreased centralized control, with its incumbent lack of policing and of protecting cultural norms, that concern would arise for the protection of tombs. Threat Formulae—or curses—began to occur with regularity from the Fifth Dynasty onward.[2] Even before this period, curses were employed sporadically in tombs, invoking divine judgment.[3] As this genre proliferated in the First Intermediate Period, it also became more reliant on a divine tribunal.[4] This was probably due to the lack of a properly organized government that could enforce earthly tribunals.[5] The curses usually employed conditional statements, warning the reader of what would happen if the reader either desecrated the tomb or failed to comply with its inscriptional requests.

Because of their perceived ability to affect both this world and the next, curses were a perfect way to uphold *Ma'at*.[6] The tomb desecrator was seen as an expression of

---

[1] For excellent studies on curses, see Scott Morschauser, *Threat-Formulae in Ancient Egypt*, Baltimore: Halgo, 1991; and Katarina Nordh, *Aspects of Ancient Egyptian Curses and Blessings: Conceptual Background and Transmission*, Stockholm: Gotab, 1996.

[2] See Morschauser, *Threat-Formulae*, p. 145.

[3] Hans Goedicke, "Ankhtyfy's Threat", in *Individu, Société et spiritualité dans l'Égypte Pharaonique et Copte*, Christian Cannuyer and Jean-Marie Kruchten (ed.), Brussels: Editions & Imprimerie Illustra, 1993, p. 111.

[4] Morschauser, *Threat-Formulae*, p. 163.

[5] For a discussion of the relation between the First Intermediate Period's social conditions and burial customs, see Stephan J. Seidlmayer, *Gräberfelder aus dem Übergang vom Altern zum Mittleren Reich. Studien zur archäologie der Ersten Zwischenzeit*, Heidelberg: Heidelberger Orientverlag, 1990, pp. 431–41. See also Jan Assmann, *The Mind of Egypt: History and Meaning in the Time of the Pharaohs*, trans. Andrew Jenkins, New York: Metropolitan Books, 2002, p. 99.

[6] A large part of the thesis for Nordh's monograph is based on this concept. See Nordh, *Aspects of Ancient Egyptian Curses*, pp. 35–49.

Isfet—a rebel (*sbi*).⁷ This dangerous element had to be dealt with, and one manner of dealing with a rebel was to enact the threat formula, which was designed to restore Ma'at.⁸

What we must ascertain for the purposes of this study is the degree of abstraction present in the curses. Were they completely symbolic, or did they contain elements that represented, and perhaps dictated, real life?

Real or Imagined? Excursus on Threat Validity

Assmann has argued vociferously that curses only refer to acts outside of this world: "In Egypt also, cursing is not an act of legislation. It seems to me mistaken to assume that what these texts depict as the consequences of an act of profanation or violation corresponded to legal penalties. The execution of legal punishments belongs to the state and its juridical institutions. The execution of curse, however, belongs to deities and demons in the hereafter and—this is typically Egyptian—to that world's juridical institutions."⁹ Elsewhere he writes, "Curses and laws are parallel in that both establish a link between crime and punishment, the defining difference being that curses are to be enforced by superhuman powers and laws by legal institutions."¹⁰ Similarly, Morschauser writes that supernatural forces are expected to enact the threats contained in threat formulae, even those that are specified as being carried out by the king.¹¹

Specific examples of threats that could only be acted out by the supernatural are abundant. Threats such as those condemning someone to the knife of Amun-Re, the fire of Sekhmet, the tribunal of the Ennead, or similar fates, illustrate this point. Clearly these, and a myriad of similar curses, cannot be enforced by any human agent.

There is some evidence, however, that curses may have contained a literal element as well. It is apparent that many threats mirror legal actions. Morschauser writes, "The threats used in such texts, however, certainly had some roots in the sphere of law; more precisely they are imitative of legal models and concepts."¹² Sotas has compared threats from the Old Kingdom with royal decree punitive clauses.¹³ Nordh notes that the threat formulae used in execration rituals, discussed above, often coincided with a legal enactment of their texts.¹⁴ Goedicke and Morschauser have outlined threat formula terminology that indicates the pronouncement of capital punishment.¹⁵ More specifically, Willems has pointed out that the loss of burial and identity prescribed in threats is a well-known juridical punishment.¹⁶ By the time a person arrived at a tribunal in the next life, it would be too late to deny him a burial, indicating that the denial of burial was at least intended to be enacted by the living. Willems also demonstrates that curses of death by fire perfectly mirror texts which are certainly juridical.¹⁷ He argues very strongly that tomb curses could be literally acted out.¹⁸

Despite his objections to a living enactment of threats as outlined above, Morschauser indicates that the punishment for tomb robbing and desecrating—the topic of most curses—was indeed enforced by legal authorities to the extent possible.¹⁹ He also outlines several threats dealing with the disruption of a functioning mortuary cult. The threats specifically call for adjudication from living officials.²⁰ Other curses address property damage to the tomb, asking for similar measures that we know were taken at times.²¹ Lorton points out a document which stipulates that the disruption of a mortuary cult would result in the person being "accused in the name of the king."²² Another text proclaims that the tomb inhabitant was "protected by the king as a tomb owner."²³

As noted above, it may seem that no provision for enforcing threats existed. However, if tomb curses paralleled legal procedures, and if there were officials who enforced these legal procedures regarding tombs, would these officials not, in effect, be called upon to enforce the applicable sections of tomb threats? Though Morschauser felt that there was no provision for their enforcement, he paradoxically writes, "All free persons within the social matrix theoretically were responsible for the protection of the deceased's tomb and mortuary property."²⁴ This is to be expected if the aim of curses was to uphold Ma'at, an occupation that concerned everyone, especially those officials responsible for such matters.

As Assmann has stated, the custom of reversing offerings and tomb visits "required that an organization stand guard

---

⁷ David Lorton, "Legal and Social Institutions of Pharaonic Egypt", in *Civilizations of the Ancient Near East*, Jack M. Sasson (ed.), New York: Scribner's Sons, 1995, p. 348.
⁸ Nordh, *Aspects of Ancient Egyptian Curses*, pp. 87, 95.
⁹ Jan Assmann, "Inscriptional Violence and the Art of Cursing: A Study of Performative Writing", *Stanford Literature Review* 9, no. 1, 1992, 59–60.
¹⁰ Jan Assmann, "When Justice Fails: Jurisdiction and Imprecation in Ancient Egypt and the Near East", *JEA* 78, 1992, 162.
¹¹ Morschauser, *Threat-Formulae*, p. 20; Renate Müller-Wollermann, *Vergehen und Strafen. Zur Sanktionierung abweichenden Verhaltens im alten Ägypten*, Leiden: E.J. Brill, 2004, p. 206, also holds this view.
¹² Morschauser, *Threat-Formulae*, p. 20–21, 146.
¹³ Henri Sottas, *La préservation de la propriété funéraire dans l'ancienne Égypte, avec le recueil des formules d'imprécation*, Paris: H. Champion, 1913, pp. 36–40.

¹⁴ Nordh, *Aspects of Ancient Egyptian Curses*, p. 95.
¹⁵ Morschauser, *Threat-Formulae*, p. 155; and Hans Goedicke, "Juridical Expressions of the Old Kingdom", *JNES* 15, 1956, 58–9.
¹⁶ Harco Willems, "Crime, Cult and Capital Punishment, Mo'alla Inscription 8", *JEA* 76, 1990, 42.
¹⁷ Willems, "Crime, Cult and Capital Punishment, Mo'alla Inscription 8", p. 42. See also chapter 5, the section on burning.
¹⁸ Willems, "Crime, Cult and Capital Punishment, Mo'alla Inscription 8".
¹⁹ Morschauser, *Threat-Formulae*, p. 146.
²⁰ Morschauser, *Threat-Formulae*, p. 148.
²¹ Morschauser, *Threat-Formulae*, pp. 149–51. See also T. Eric Peet, *The Great Tomb-Robberies of the Twentieth Egyptian Dynasty*, Oxford: Clarendon Press, 1930.
²² See David Lorton, "The Treatment of Criminals in Ancient Egypt", *Journal of the Economic and Social History of the Orient* 20, no. 1, 1977, 7.
²³ *Urk.* I, p. 223.
²⁴ Morschauser, *Threat-Formulae*, p. 161.

over the tombs to prevent their being damaged, defiled, plundered, or broken up for building material."[25] Furthermore, Willems notes that "many biographies from the Old Kingdom inform us that tombs and equipment were gifts from the king himself. In view of this state commitment to the Afterlife of the nobility, it is logical that the central government was also responsible for the protection of the burial grounds and funerary chapels."[26] This supposition is supported by two cases from a later time period in which we know of court intervention. In one case, a man suspected of stealing from a tomb was forced to swear that if he stole again he would have his ears and nose cut off and then he would be impaled.[27] In the other case, a man who had tried to take illegal possession of an unused tomb was told never to enter the tomb again, upon penalty of beatings and open wounds.[28] Lorton correctly points out that these were criminal cases, but they may have been considered such because the state was involved.[29] However, the state's involvement demonstrates that the government had a role in maintaining the sanctity of tombs. This supposition is strengthened by the standard tomb offering formula: ḥtp-di-nsw, "an offering which the king gives." This standard formula indicates that the state claimed some control over the establishment and maintenance of tombs. The degree of actual involvement may be less than is indicated by the inscriptions, but the salient point is that the state is inscriptionally depicted as being in control of tombs, offerings, and inscriptions. We know that in the Nineteenth Dynasty men were executed for robbing nonroyal tombs.[30]

While some curses could only be enacted by supernatural agents, some threatened consequences that could only be acted out by the mortal living, such as the curse forbidding burial as noted above. Another example is the threat that a rebel will have no tomb and his body will be thrown into the river.[31]

Informatively, we can see a similar idea in wisdom literature stemming from this time period. There is some debate about the creation of the *Instructions for Merikare*. While the manuscript is later, arguments can be made for authorship in the First Intermediate Period,[32] Middle Kingdom,[33] or early Eighteenth Dynasty. Regardless, it seems to have its contextual roots in the First Intermediate period.[34] While it is likely pseudepigraphic, it is still a piece that reflects the *topos* of this time. This text explicitly states that god will smite the rebel, but it is also clear that the king will enact this.[35]

The problem with scholars' divergent views, as outlined above, is that they are operating under a false dichotomy. It is entirely possible that the ancient Egyptians intended both the otherworldly enactment of which Assmann speaks and the worldly discharge for which Willems argues. This would occur in the redundancy system presented in our examination of the Execration Texts.[36] While some aspects of tomb curses were clearly intended only for the divine/supernatural realm, others could apply equally to both spheres. Assmann argues that curses were a back-up used in case measures taken in this world did not work.[37] This same argument, intended to demonstrate that only supernatural intervention was being called for, in fact actually supports our point. Would not the Egyptians desire that both the officials of this life and those of the next life carry out those aspects of the curse which pertained to their respective spheres? The redundancy of invoking supernatural possibilities for these events is exactly the back-up Assmann outlines, but only if the expected actors in this realm failed. Why provision for those times "when justice failed," if justice were never expected to succeed? Instead, it exemplifies the same overlapping of spheres which Assmann describes as existing in the realm of execration-type rites.[38]

We must rid ourselves of this false dichotomy and see in the curses a call for action in both spheres.[39] Mirroring legal terminology, threat formulae relied on ancient Egypt's most common form of law—case law.[40] They were deliberately ambiguous, calling for an actual realization of their threats in this world, but the curses hedged the bet by also calling on the next world to act. They further increased their chances of restoring Ma'at by asking for punishments from another sphere that could only be conceivably enacted in that sphere.

Understanding the bispheric nature of threat formulae allows us a greater understanding of potential punishments. Attempting to ascertain which individual threats

---

[25] Assmann, *Mind of Egypt*, p. 88.
[26] Willems, "Crime, Cult and Capital Punishment, Mo'alla Inscription 8", p. 41.
[27] Lorton, "The Treatment of Criminals", 40.
[28] Lorton, "The Treatment of Criminals", 40.
[29] Lorton, "The Treatment of Criminals", p. 41.
[30] See chapter 7, the section on The Great Tomb Robberies.
[31] Joyce A. Tyldesley, *Judgement of the Pharaoh: Crime and Punishment in Ancient Egypt*, London: Weidenfeld & Nicolson, 2000, p. 71; William Kelly Simpson, *The Literature of Ancient Egypt: An Anthology of Stories, Instructions, and Poetry*, New Haven: Yale University Press, 1973, pp. 198–200.
[32] See Miriam Lichtheim, "Didactic Literature," in *Ancient Egyptian Literature: History and Forms*, ed. Antonio Loprieno (New York: E.J. Brill, 1996), 247.
[33] See Richard Parkinson, *The Tale of Sinuhe and Other Ancient Egyptian Poems* (Oxford: Oxford University Press, 1997), 212.
[34] See discussion below in this chapter.
[35] Miriam Lichtheim, *Ancient Egyptian Literature; a Book of Readings. Volume I: The Old and Middle Kingdoms*, Berkeley: University of California Press, 1973, p. 100.
[36] See chapter 3, the section on Execration Texts.
[37] Assmann, "When Justice Fails."
[38] See chapter 3, the section on Execration Texts, and Jan Assmann, "Spruch 23 der Pyramidentexte und die Ächtung der Feinde Pharos", in *Hommages à Jean Leclant*, Catherine Berger, Gisèle Clerc, and Nicolas-Christophe Grimal (ed.), Cairo: Institut français d'archéologie orientale, 1994, p. 51.
[39] See Kerry Muhlestein, "Empty Threats? How Egyptians' Self-Ontology Should Affect the Way We Read Many Texts," in JSSEA 34, 2007, 115-130.
[40] See Ellen D. Bedell, "Criminal Law in the Egyptian Ramesside Period", PhD dissertation, Brandeis University, 1973, 2, 12; Monica Marie Bontty, "Conflict Management in Ancient Egypt", Los Angeles: UCLA, 1997, p. 27; Girgis Mattha, *The Demotic Legal Code of Hermopolis West*, Bibliothèque de Étude, Cairo: Institut français d'archéologie orientale, 1975; and C.J. Eyre, "Crime and Adultery in Ancient Egypt", *JEA* 70, 1984, p. 92.

were actually enacted is fruitless. A knowledge of this is far beyond our ability to deduce. However, the curses found on tomb walls give us an idea of potential punishments. Furthermore, due to their mimicking quality, wherein they intentionally mirror their juridical counterparts, they provide a window into the types of penalties in Egyptian jurisprudence. By studying the curses of the First Intermediate Period we are, in effect, studying Egyptian case law. Because the chaotic events were not often recorded on a durable medium like stone, we would not expect to find many examples of actual cases. But because the threat formulae included potential punishments in an effort to preserve Ma'at, they constitute a unique genre in which chaotic elements are portrayed. Hence, curses form an invaluable source for learning of sanctioned punishment in ancient Egypt.

Figure 4.1 – Hekaib Sanctuary on Elephantine Island

The Threats of the First Intermediate Period

A number of inscriptions include curses pertinent to this study. One comes from the sanctuary of Hekaib (see fig. 4.1), located in southern Egypt on Elephantine Island. This is Stela 9, belonging to Sarenput I[41]:

> As for any governor, any wa'b-priest, any ka-priest, any scribe or any nobleman, who will take it [the offering] from my statue, his arm will be cut off like a bull and his neck will be severed like a bird (*mnt ts=f mi 3pd*)[42]; his position will not exist; the position of his son will not exist; his house in Kush will not exist; his tomb in the necropolis will not exist. His god will not accept his white bread. His flesh is for the fire, and his children for the flame. His body will smell the earth. I will be against him as a crocodile in the water, as a snake on the earth, and as an enemy in the necropolis.[43]

Here we see many forms of punishment, two of which concern us. First, the offender's neck will be severed, as a sacrificial bird's would be. This severing continues the form of punishment that we witnessed in the Old Kingdom.[44] Again, we need not concentrate on whether anyone was actually beheaded for violating this particular tomb. Instead we can conclude, based on the mimicking nature of the threat, that beheading was a form of punishment practiced when this inscription was made, in the late First Intermediate Period. It is also notable that sacrificial terminology was employed; clearly the author of this inscription felt that there were ritual/sacrificial elements to the punishments.

A second type of punishment is listed. The guilty party and his children are also destined for the fire. Fire will be discussed further in chapter 5,[45] but let us briefly mention in this chapter that fire effected total destruction, wiping out the possibility for an afterlife in a manner similar to cooking, as mentioned in chapter 3.[46] This could explain why offenders might be burned after being beheaded. In this stela, though, his children apparently would also suffer this horrific punishment. We cannot know if this was enacted, but we can see that burning was a form of punishment during the First Intermediate Period.[47] Speaking of the offender's body, Stela 9 records that the offender will smell the earth as a final indication that he will indeed die, inhaling dirt instead of the breath of life.

Another stela probably from the First Intermediate Period contains similar phraseology.[48] Anyone who harmed the stela would be judged and "his neck cut off like a bird" (*iw shitw ts=f mi 3pd*). Again a human decapitation is compared to a sacrificial animal's. Willems suggests that such terminology indicates a ritual element in the punishment.[49] If the intent was to destroy Isfet and restore Ma'at, this may very well be so. We will discuss the idea of ritualization further.

Two tombs in Assiut are also relevant. Tomb III's doorjamb inscription threatens one who fails to protect the tomb or its contents that "his god will not accept his white bread, he will not be buried in the West, and his flesh will burn together with the criminals, being made

---

[41] See Labib Habachi, Gerhard Haeny, and Friedrich Junge, *The Sanctuary of Heqaib (Elephantine)*, Mainz am Rhein, Germany: P. von Zabern, 1985, pp. 36–7.
[42] It should be noted here that a sacrificial bird's neck was usually wrung, not severed. However, metaphors often have imperfect applications.
[43] Other translations in Assmann, "Art of Cursing", p. 58; and Willems, "Crime, Cult and Capital Punishment, Mo'alla Inscription 8", p. 34.
[44] See chapter 3, the section on Execution.
[45] See chapter 5, the section on Burning.
[46] See chapter 3, the section on Other Forms of Ritual Sacrifice.
[47] Erik Hornung, *Altägyptische Höllenvorstellungen. Mit 7 Lichtdrucktafeln und 6 Abbildungen im Text*, Abhandlungen der Sächsischen Akademie der Wissenschaften zu Leipzig, Philologisch-historische Klasse Bd. 59, Heft 3, Berlin: Akademie-Verlag, 1968, p. 22, writes that in the First Intermediate Period, burning is attested as a punishment. He apparently infers this from the same information we are culling here, though he does not make this explicit.
[48] Ludwig Borchardt, Dia Abou-Ghazi, and Alexandre Moret, *Denkmäler des alten Reiches (ausser den Statuen) im Museum von Kairo, nr. 1295–1808*, al-Misri Mat'haf (ed.), Catalogue général des antiquités égyptiennes du Musée du Caire; v. 97, etc., Berlin: Reichsdruckerei, 1937, p. 111.
[49] Willems, "Crime, Cult and Capital Punishment, Mo'alla Inscription 8", p. 36.

one who does not exist."⁵⁰ Similarly, the entrance of Tomb IV curses "any rebel (sbi) and any who are ill-disposed (h3k-ib), who will do wrong despite having heard these things, [that] his name will not exist, he will not be buried in the necropolis, he will be cooked together with the criminals whom god has cursed."⁵¹

Within these two inscriptions are references to burning or cooking. Both assume that their readers know that criminals, including tomb desecrators, were burned. They likewise strengthen the assertion that burning and cooking wipe out people's existence completely, making them "ones who do not exist." The phraseology of these curses demands the conclusion that the burning of criminals was a feature of ancient Egypt at this time. Edel refers to the possibility of fire as a "hell threat" (Höllendrohungen).⁵² However, nothing in the inscriptions indicates that these threats are not literal, and Edel's comments are most likely a product of the false dichotomy that has been debunked above. Even if these inscriptions did intend only afterlife consequences, as we have noted several times, the curses were mirrors of the legal system, and thus they at least indicate what was happening there. This parallels the idea of burning or cooking criminals as presented in the coffin-text descendant of the Cannibal Hymn, as noted in chapter 3.⁵³

Another Assiut text contains a further element of sanctioned killing. Anyone who failed to recite the desired spell was bound to "fall to the anger of his city-god, and to the slaughter of the king (tḫs n nswt). He will not be remembered among the spirits and his name will never again be pronounced on earth, he will not be buried in the West, no offerings will be made for him, he will be burned together with the criminals, because Thoth has condemned him."⁵⁴ Here, besides the now-customary burning-of-criminals reference, we also learn of "the slaughter of the king," something that will be referred to with increasing frequency in ensuing eras. This phrase may be a euphemism for ritual slaying.

As mentioned above, Assmann argues that these curses could not possibly imply an earthly enforcement, because curses could not legislate.⁵⁵ Here he is missing a subtle, yet important, point. The curses are not legislating; they are appealing to case law. And it is just this element that concerns us. To sum up the telling case law appeals—in the form of curses—cited above, we have learned of decapitation (perhaps ritual in form), burning or cooking, and the ambiguous "slaughter of the king." The tomb curses constitute very strong evidence that these events were an ongoing part of the legal process.

A Royal Decree (Coptos Decree R)

In a very similar vein, we can learn something from a royal decree of the Eighth Dynasty.⁵⁶ Demedjibtawi's Coptos Decree is specifically legal in nature. In protecting the funerary cult of a favored nobleman, King Demedjibtawi declared of any who desecrated the site, "My Majesty cannot allow that their property or the property of their fathers will remain theirs, neither that they join the spirits in the necropolis, nor that they be among the living (ꜥnḫw)."⁵⁷ Unfortunately, the key phrase here, "nor that they be among the living," can be translated and interpreted in different ways. Willems rendered it with a literal translation, and I have done the same, ꜥnḫw literally means "those who are living,"⁵⁸ and is used thus in hundreds of descriptions to indicate people who are alive on this earth.⁵⁹ John Wilson translates, "Or that they be among the living [upon earth]."⁶⁰ Of this, Wilson writes, "Just how would a pharaoh carry out this provision of the decree? In mundane terms, their property would be confiscated, they would be executed, and they would be denied a normal burial in a necropolis."⁶¹ Others have translated it as a cessation from living as well.⁶² It is almost certain that Demedjibtawi intended for those who subverted the cult of this tomb to be killed. We cannot determine whether any ever were.

Translating to Fit the Mold

However, Goedicke feels that ꜥnḫw must mean *free citizen* and that the phrase stipulated a loss of free status, not life. His argument for this translation is that without such an interpretation of the word, the decree would have reference to capital punishment, and so he feels an alternative translation must be sound.⁶³ Thus, the plain Egyptian phrase is given a new interpretation so that the conception of a nonviolent Egyptian culture can be maintained. This is a particularly unconvincing and

---

⁵⁰ Elmar Edel, *Die Inschriften der Grabfronten der Siut-Gräber in Mittelägypten aus der Herakleopolitenzeit: eine Wiederherstellung nach den Zeichnungen der Description de l'Egypte*, Abhandlungen der Rheinisch-Westfälischen Akademie der Wissenschaften Bd. 71, Oplanden: Westdeutscher Verlag, 1984, pp. 25–37 and fig. 5. For other translations, see Willems, "Crime, Cult and Capital Punishment, Mo'alla Inscription 8", p. 37; and Assmann, "Art of Cursing", p. 58.
⁵¹ Edel, *Die Inschriften der Grabfronten der Siut-Gräber in Mittelägypten aus der Herakleopolitenzeit*, pp. 120–7, fig. 15. See also Willems, "Crime, Cult and Capital Punishment, Mo'alla Inscription 8", p. 37; and Assmann, "Art of Cursing", p. 59.
⁵² Edel, *Die Inschriften der Grabfronten der Siut-Gräber in Mittelägypten aus der Herakleopolitenzeit*, p. 33.
⁵³ See chapter 3, the section on Other Forms of Ritual Slaying.
⁵⁴ Edel, *Die Inschriften der Grabfronten der Siut-Gräber in Mittelägypten aus der Herakleopolitenzeit*, pp. 190–5; Assmann, "Art of Cursing", p. 59.
⁵⁵ Assmann, "Art of Cursing", p. 59–60.

⁵⁶ See William C. Hayes, "Royal Decrees from the Temple of Min at Coptus", *JEA* 32, 1946, for the dating of this decree.
⁵⁷ As in Hans Goedicke, *Königliche Dokumente aus dem alten Reich*, Ägyptologische Abhandlungen Bd. 14, Wiesbaden: Harrassowitz, 1967, pp. 213–15.
⁵⁸ Willems, "Crime, Cult and Capital Punishment, Mo'alla Inscription 8", p. 39.
⁵⁹ For example, tomb inscriptions often address a number of entities, including all the ꜥnḫw, which is generally translated as the living and understood as referring to those who are alive.
⁶⁰ John A. Wilson, "The Oath in Ancient Egypt" *JNES* 7, 1948, p. 149.
⁶¹ Wilson, "The Oath in Ancient Egypt", p. 149.
⁶² Sottas, *La préservation de la propriété funéraire dans l'ancienne Égypte*, p. 40, writes "vivants," or "alive." So does Tyldesley, *Judgment of the Pharaoh*, p. 28.
⁶³ Goedicke, *Königliche Dokumente*, p. 218.

circular argument. Lorton renders the same translation,[64] presumably for the same reason, since Lorton denies the existence of capital punishment for anything but treason. Given the evidence presented thus far in this study, and in light of that which will follow, these arguments appear particularly weak. Assuredly there was a death penalty in ancient Egypt at this time, and it was carried out in a variety of ways for manifold reasons. Only a curious retrojection of modern European ideas about capital punishment could raise any questions regarding this matter. We have no evidence of any ancient civilization that did not employ capital punishment. If it satisfies Lorton's criteria for a death penalty somewhat, the contravention of this royal edict could quite possibly be construed as treason. However, we have already seen many appeals to the death penalty for tomb desecration. Additionally, as Willems has noted, this inscription is evidence of the idea that the protection of tombs, at least the great number that were established under the auspices of the king, fell under government authority.[65]

The Tomb of Ankhtifi

One of the most complex and striking examples of a tomb curse that may relate to our topic is Ankhtifi in Mo'alla, known as Mo'alla Inscription 8.[66] Ankhtifi was a particularly proud and independent local ruler who had steadily expanded his realm. The pertinent passage reads[67]: "As for any ruler who will rule in Mo'alla who will act wrongfully and badly against this coffin or against any monument of this tomb, his arm shall be cut off for Hemen[68] at his mighty[69] procession."[70] The inscription continues with several parallel passages, indicating that the arm is to be cut off during different phases of the processions for Hemen. Willems has argued convincingly that this part of the inscription threatened the ritual sacrifice of future rulers who desecrated Ankhtifi's mortuary complex.[71] He marshals evidence of the tomb inscriptions that demand capital punishment,[72] and he shows how the particular tomb fits in with cultic and mythical practices.[73] He suggests that the guilty party would be a Seth-like rebel, an identity that demands ritual activity and that ties into the scenes of hippopotamus hunting presented just to the south of where this text was found; the two are separated only by scenes of ritual slaughter.[74] Willems believes the text demands that the offender replace the bull that was regularly sacrificed in the cult of the local god.[75] Willems further notes, "Nothing in these texts suggests that they should *not* be taken literally."[76] His thesis has since been buttressed by striking archaeological confirmation. The aforementioned severed fingers accompanying the execration finds at Avaris seem to be remains of just the type of sacrifice Ankhtifi was asking for. Just as Willems posited, clearly the severing of limbs as part of sacrifice, which was such a consistent part of animal sacrifice, could also be enacted on humans.

Debate: Was Willems Right?

Despite the cogency of Willems's arguments, and the seeming large acceptance of them, the idea has met substantial published resistance, most notably from Assmann and Goedicke. Assmann has twice argued that such an interpretation is not possible because tomb curses were not intended to be enforced in this life.[77] Though he does not state so explicitly, Assmann must mean that they could *never* have the intention of being enforced in this life or else his argument holds little sway. While his arguments are eloquently written, this line of thinking has been addressed and refuted above. Moreover, Assmann seems to have later changed his opinion somewhat, most recently writing that this inscription "is not, then, a curse in the normal sense but the announcement of laws; malediction and jurisdiction intermingle in a curious way."[78] Goedicke also disagrees with Willems and partially bases his dissent on the same arguments as Assmann.[79] However, he also treats several other issues. While many of these do not impinge upon Willems's claim, several do.

Goedicke claims that the reference to the severing of the arm ($hp\check{s}$) can refer to a bull or to a man's strength.[80] He bases this argument on a lassoing determinative for the

---

[64] Lorton, "Treatment of Criminals", p. 11.
[65] Willems, "Crime, Cult and Capital Punishment, Mo'alla Inscription 8", p. 41.
[66] See Jacques Vandier, *Mo'alla. La tombe d'Ankhtifi et la tombe de Sébekhotep*, Cairo: Institut français d'archéologie orientale, 1950; and Henry G. Fischer, "Notes on the Mo'alla Inscriptions and Some Contemporaneous Texts", *WZKM* 57, 1961, pp. 59–77.
[67] Mo'alla inscription no. 8, as in Vandier, *Mo'alla. La tombe d'Ankhtifi et la tombe de Sébekhotep*, p. 206.
[68] Disagreements over this translation will be discussed below.
[69] Willems, "Crime, Cult and Capital Punishment, Mo'alla Inscription 8", p. 29, translates "at his procession from (literally of) the district."
[70] Here I agree with the translation of Willems, "Crime, Cult and Capital Punishment, Mo'alla Inscription 8", pp. 28–29; and Nordh, *Aspects of Ancient Egyptian Curses*, p. 82; viewing this as a "going out" or a procession. See Willems's arguments for this reading on the pages just cited.
[71] Willems, "Crime, Cult and Capital Punishment, Mo'alla Inscription 8".
[72] Willems, "Crime, Cult and Capital Punishment, Mo'alla Inscription 8", pp. 33–43. He uses both inscriptions we have already discussed and many which we will discuss below, see chapter 5.
[73] Willems, "Crime, Cult and Capital Punishment, Mo'alla Inscription 8", pp. 43–51.

[74] Willems, "Crime, Cult and Capital Punishment, Mo'alla Inscription 8", pp. 4–46.
[75] Willems, "Crime, Cult and Capital Punishment, Mo'alla Inscription 8", pp. 46.
[76] Willems, "Crime, Cult and Capital Punishment, Mo'alla Inscription 8", pp. 47.
[77] Assman, "Art of Cursing"; and Assmann, "When Justice Fails". Eric Doret, "Ankhtifi and the Description of His Tomb at Mo'alla," in *For His Ka; Essay Offered in memory of Klaus Baer*, David P. Silverman, ed. (Chicago: Oriental Institute of the University of Chicago, 1994), 79 & 81, also felt that the inscription could only be cursing left for the divine to enact. However, he provides no evidence nor reasoning for this conclusion, he just states the conclusion as a matter of course.
[78] Assmann, *Mind of Egypt*, p. 99.
[79] Hans Goedicke, "Ankhtyfy's Threat", in *Individu, Société et spiritualité dans l'Égypte Pharaonique et Copte*, Christian Cannuyer and Jean-Marie Kruchten (ed.), Brussels: Editions & Imprimerie Illustra, 1993, 111–21.
[80] Hans Goedicke, "Ankhtyfy's Threat", p. 115.

verb form *sḫtw*, noting that a sacrificial bull had to be lassoed for slaughter but that a man would not be. He also asserts that *ḫpš* truly means foreleg and is used only for animals, except when it means a man's strength. Both of these points ignore the deliberate use of metaphor here. If Willems is right, the offender is replacing a sacrifice, and thus we would expect the sacrificial metaphor to be maintained by the employment of sacrificial terminology. We will see an example of this in the cases of Senusret I and Prince Osorkon, to be addressed below. Furthermore, the lassoing determinative may apply here, since criminals were often bound with a rope.

Another complaint Goedicke has against Willems's interpretation is that since the verb *ḫpš* is not accompanied by a knife determinative, it must not mean to sever but to maim.[81] He attempts to strengthen this argument by noting that severing an arm does not automatically kill a person, just as slaughter scenes do not begin with the severing of a foreleg. Again he ignores the metaphorical qualities of the passage. While he acknowledges that the terminology is appropriate for sacrificial rites regarding animals, he will not admit this for a possible human sacrifice, even if an animal metaphor is being employed.

In another point of disagreement, Goedicke searches for an agent for the passive verb *sḫtw*, writing, "Grammatically, the agent after a passive is introduced by the particle *in*, which is written here ⁓⁓⁓. As a result Hemen is not to be seen as the recipient of an act, but rather as the agent causing it."[82] While Goedicke's reading is possible, he does not admit that verbs in curses are usually not given a specific agent.[83] Therefore, it is Goedicke's rendering that would be unusual. Additionally, his reading would require the emendation of an *i* before the *n*, something which is possible but, since a less intrusive and more common reading is available, is hardly justified.

Goedicke believes that "it is in line with his [Ankhtifi's] role to hope and wish for divine interference, as he would have no authority to defend himself against later wrongdoings."[84] He supports this idea by noting that in none of the curses cited by Willems, outlined above, is the person able to enforce his curses himself.[85] This tired argument does not address several issues we have already noted. Goedicke does bring up one question which remains unanswered. Since the future rulers of the area are the potential offenders, who would possibly be able to enforce Ankhtifi's decree against these rulers?[86] This challenge does cast some small doubt on the picture painted by Willems.

Overall, Willems has presented a compelling case, and the disagreements have been less than convincing. We must admit that his reading is possible and maybe even likely, given the strong evidence he marshals. Even if we were sure of Willems's interpretation, it is impossible to generalize anything from the inscription. Ankhtifi ruled and built his tomb in a unique time in Egyptian history, using unique phraseology throughout, after ruling in a unique way. It is methodologically unsafe to generalize any practices from this area at this time.

The *Instructions for Merikare*

We find revealing information pertaining to this disquisition in the *Instructions for Merikare*. This piece of wisdom literature is purportedly the instructions of a reigning king to his successor, Merikare. The origin of this *speculum regum* is probably the Tenth Dynasty,[87] though it may be from the late Middle Kingdom.[88] While it is almost certainly pseudepigraphic, it still is a piece that reflects the *topos* of its time.[89] Yet concurrently its fictionality allows it to address elements that are not usually broached in *topos*-centered texts.[90] Therefore, while we will never be able to know if the precepts propounded therein were ever enacted, it does reveal the ideal for the time (and for the geographic area it represents—the Herekleopolitan kingdom). Additionally, as Lorton writes, "While this is not a juridical text, there is every reason to suppose that it reflects juridical realities."[91]

In this text, Merikare is admonished to "punish in accordance [with the crime]."[92] Many crimes discussed in the testament demand lesser punishments than that with which we are concerned. However, certain sections are revealing for our purposes. One such section states, "Do not strike down, it does not empower you. Punish with beatings, with captivity, and thus will the land be established. Except for the rebel (*sbỉ*) whose plans are discovered, for god knows those who plot treason, god smites his obstacles in blood."[93] Here it is expressed that god will smite the rebel, but it is clearly the god-like king who must enact this, lest he lose his throne. This is made clearer in the admonition "He who is silent toward the violent diminishes the offerings. God will attack the rebel

---

[81] Hans Goedicke, "Ankhtyfy's Threat", p. 116.
[82] Hans Goedicke, "Ankhtyfy's Threat", pp. 116–17.
[83] See all curses listed above.
[84] Goedicke, "Anktyfy's Threat", p. 117.
[85] Goedicke, "Anktyfy's Threat", pp. 120–1.
[86] Goedicke, "Anktyfy's Threat", p. 117.

[87] Miriam Lichtheim, "Didactic Literature", in *Ancient Egyptian Literature: History and Forms*, Antonio Loprieno (ed.), New York: E.J. Brill, 1996, p. 247.
[88] Richard Parkinson, *The Tale of Sinuhe and Other Ancient Egyptian Poems*, Oxford: Oxford University Press, 1997, p. 212.
[89] Lichtheim, *Egyptian Literature*, p. 97.
[90] Parkinson, *Tale of Sinuhe*, pp. 15–16.
[91] Lorton, "Treatment of Criminals", p. 51.
[92] P. Leningrad 1116A and P. Moscow 4658, as in Joachim Friedrich Quack, *Studien zur Lehre für Merikare*, Wiesbaden: O. Harrassowitz, 1992. Also used is Aksel Volten, *Zwei altägyptische politische Schriften. Die Lehre für König Merikare (Pap. Carlsberg VI) und die Lehre des Königs Amenemhet*, Copenhagen: Einar Munksgaard, 1945. Reconstruction from Lichtheim, *Egyptian Literature*, p. 99.
[93] P. Leningrad 1116A, lines 47–50. Lorton, "Treatment of Criminals", p. 13, feels that only intentions are spoken of, and thus the king cannot punish but only god can. He musters no evidence that the king cannot punish for intent, applying this Western ideal in the face of examples of the king punishing for intent in later periods. See chapter 7, the section on the Harem Conspiracy.

(*sbi*) for the sake of the temple."[94] Again the reference is to god attacking the rebel, but implicitly Merikare is warned that this attack must come from him because of the danger in being silent toward violence. In an earlier and more broken section of the text, in the midst of speaking of those who incite rebellion, we read, "Repulse him, kill [him] (*sm3* [*sw*])[95], blot out his name."[96] In these passages, we see, even with a lack of evidence of its actuation, that treasonous acts demanded capital punishment.

Servant Burials

Nebhepetre Mentuhotep built his magnificent tomb/temple in the cliff face of Deir el-Bahri.[97] Near this temple a mass grave was discovered.[98] Sixty soldiers' bodies had been interred together within this grave. It is possible that a small army was killed and interred upon the death and burial of the king so that he would have his army with him in the afterlife.[99] However, due to wounds on many of those buried,[100] it is much more likely that these soldiers were killed in a battle serving Mentuhotep, perhaps in Nubia or against Herakleopolis, and had been placed in this early version of a war cemetery.[101] Also at this site, a burial termed "unknown man E" was found. Because of the horrific look on his face, some have supposed that he may have been buried alive. We have so little pertinent data for this burial that speculation is the only possibility. Such will not be entertained here.

A more likely case of sacrificial servant burial is that of a woman, who forensic evidence indicates was strangled, found in the tomb of a royal daughter.[102] We know nothing else of the servant's death, but the probability, given the evidence, is that she was a servant who accompanied her mistress to the afterlife. This strange, isolated case also demonstrates how much our knowledge of sanctioned killing depends on the happenstance of excavation and the aleatory nature of selecting finds for forensic examination. It seems probable that this case of sacrificial burial was not the only occurrence, but without more data we can say nothing of the regularity of the practice.

For Egyptologists, it is difficult to know exactly where to draw our artificial line to divide the First Intermediate Period from the Middle Kingdom. In part, this is because eras usually transition from one to another. After years of struggle, all the areas of Egypt were once again brought under the control of one ruling family. As Egypt became more unified and coalesced into her more traditional guise of a powerful solidarity headed by a stable monarchy and accompanied by the trappings of advanced culture, it is impossible to pick a point in time, draw a line, and say, "Before this time Egypt was not in a period of stability and advanced culture, and after this she was." This distinction was probably not as difficult for the ancient Egyptians. Nebhepetre Mentuhotep at least was sure that before him Chaos had held sway but that he had restored Order. There may be something to his claim.

First Intermediate Period Evidence of Sanctioned Killing

Violence	Weak Evidence	Plausible Evidence	Strong Evidence	Very Strong Evidence
Ongoing burning or cooking of criminals				X
Ongoing decapitation, perhaps in a ritualized setting				X
Ongoing "king's slaughter"				X
Death sentence for rebellion against the king				X
Sacrificial burial at tomb of Nebhepetre Mentuhotep	X			
Sacrificial burial princess's tomb			X	
Potential for ritual sacrifice of tomb desecrator at Mo'alla			X	

---

[94] P. Leningrad 1116A, line 110.
[95] Volten, *Zwei altägyptische politische Schriften*, pp. 8–9, restores "it." Parkinson, *Tale of Sinuhe*, p. 217, restores "his children."
[96] P. Leningrad 1116A, lines 23–24.
[97] Dieter Arnold and Herbert Eustis Winlock, *The Temple of Mentuhotep at Deir el Bahari*, New York: Metropolitan Museum of Art, 1979, vol. 21.
[98] Herbert Eustis Winlock and Metropolitan Museum of Art, Egyptian Expedition, *The Slain Soldiers of Neb-hep-et-Re Mentu-hotpe*, New York: Metropolitan Museum of Art, 1945.
[99] Nigel Davies, *Human Sacrifice in History and Today*, New York: William Morrow and Company, 1981, p. 37.
[100] See Winlock and Gae Callender, "The Middle Kingdom Renaissance," in *The Oxford History of Ancient Egypt*, Ian Shaw, Oxford: Oxford University Press (ed.), 2000, p. 151.
[101] See, Peter Clayton, *Chronicle of the Pharaohs*, London: Thames and Hudson, 1994, p. 74, for an example of this *communis opinio*.

[102] Karlheinz Pfeiffer, "Menschenopfer in den Hochkulturen der Welt", *Die Wage* 10, 1971, 215.

Chapter 5

DEATH BY DROWNING, BURNING, AND FLAYING: THE MIDDLE KINGDOM AND SECOND INTERMEDIATE PERIOD

She was put into the fire, and her remains were given to the river.

—*Papyrus Westcar*

The soldiers of Fortress Mirgissa looked on with intense concentration. Since they considered Mirgissa one of the key outposts protecting Egypt, any magical rite designed to ward off rebellious foreigners was of keen interest to them. Reciting potent words, the priest raised the clay figure shaped like a Nubian high into the air, and with a final magical cry the priest hurled it to the rocky ground, shattering the effigy of their enemies. The priest then signaled a few of the soldiers to bring in the last ceremonial object as he brought from underneath his sash a ritual flint knife. Ignoring the merciless southern sun beating upon his shaved head, the priest indicated approval as the guards threw a captured Nubian to the ground. He forcefully began reciting the same formula he had for the clay figure. In a place this important to the safety of the realm, no chances would be taken. Clay figurines were not enough—a human must also be part of the rite. The magic performed on clay was but a precursor to what the priest intended for his squirming human victim.

For the historian, the Middle Kingdom is a wonderful oasis. While archaeology, iconography, and ethnography provide valuable information in our efforts to (re)construct history, nothing is as helpful as texts. Under a stable, consistent monarchy, writing and literature took leaps forward during the Middle Kingdom, an era when culture reached a new apex. More architecture, official inscriptions, voluminous coffin texts, and great literary works are available from the Middle Kingdom than from all the preceding periods combined; the historian and philologist alike find themselves gleefully wading through the increased information. More evidence adds fun. It also allows us to clarify our picture. Gathering together this more evenly faceted collection of sources allows us to construct a better picture of sanctioned killing. Not surprisingly, we will find that as the centralized control dissipates, our sources decrease, and we know very little of the dynasties immediately following the strong middle-kingdom rulers of the Twelfth Dynasty. Within the Middle Kingdom and the Second Intermediate Period, we find tales of desecration, retribution, adultery, ritual slaughter, and curses. While uncovering these stories necessitates delving into details, as we turn back the pages of history for middle-kingdom Egypt we are in for high adventure.

Sacrifices Associated With Burials

Possible examples of ritual slaying associated with middle-kingdom burials can only be understood in light of the eighteenth-dynasty tomb of Mentuherkhepeshef, a Fan Bearer and Mayor. Thus, we must examine this tomb out of its chronological order. In the section of Mentuherkhepeshef's tomb concerning the preparations for burial is a depiction of two Nubians being strangled (see figure 5.1).[1] Two other prostrate Nubians appear to await the same fate. Davies describes the scene: "A cord is passed round the neck of two kneeling men, the ends of [the chords] are in each case in the hands of two men ('strong ones') who stand on opposite sides, and thus can in a moment throttle their prisoner. This person is described as 'a Nubian Anu,' that is, a native of the region south of the First Cataract. Precision seems meant to be added to this information by a fortified oval, such as serves to designate a captured place, which is here set on the victim's head and supported on each side by a tiny figure."[2]

---

[1] Norman de Garis Davies, *Five Theban Tombs (being those of Mentuherkhepeshef, User, Daga, Nehemawäy and Tati)*, Archaeological Survey of Egypt 21, London: Egypt Exploration Fund, 1913, pl. viii.
[2] Davies, *Five Theban Tombs*, p. 15.

Figure 5.1 – Strangling scene from Mentuherkhepeshef

The signs within the oval are two harpoon glyphs ( ). While the exact geographic location signified by these glyphs is unknown, the meaning of the scene is clear. These men represented their town or area, which had been subdued.[3] Their sacrifice most likely reconfirmed this defeat and, in turn, the defeat of all chaotic elements. This suggests an execration-like ritual for the tomb, which ensured that Mentuherkhepeshef would be protected from Disorder. Why were representatives of this particular town or area chosen for this sacrifice? We can only assume that they were Nubians who were available to Mentuherkhepeshef. Thus, these Nubians and their town were his *de facto* representation of Chaos. Alternatively, perhaps Mentuherkhepeshef participated in military action against this town, and the slaughter of these Nubians was somehow connected. Nothing in Mentuhekhepeshef's titles and roles indicates why this slaughter was depicted in his tomb.

As Davies and Griffiths have noted, it is possible that this depiction does not illustrate an actual sacrifice.[4] The main argument for such an interpretation is a general lack of evidence for human sacrifice in ancient Egypt, an argument that is becoming increasingly tenuous. Griffiths, in 1958, admitted the possibility of the sacrifice's actuality, but he writes that without contemporary evidence, the question should be left open.[5] The Mirgissa evidence already cited, coupled with additional examples in this chapter and the next, provides the contemporary evidence that Griffiths searched for. Without an indication to the contrary, we must assess this tomb depiction as very strong evidence for a real execration-like sacrifice. In so asserting, we are again wrestling with the high-society notion and its attendant circular arguments that the Egyptians did not engage in ritual slaying. The house of cards this argument is built on continues to fall.

Connected to the depiction in Mentuherkhepeshef's tomb is another common depiction that may indicate further ritual slaying. In this scene, a figure labeled *tekenu* is dragged toward a pit. We are unsure of tekenu's meaning. The tekenu, pictured in at least thirty-four tombs spanning a time period from the Middle Kingdom to the Twenty-sixth Dynasty,[6] is a very enigmatic figure. Often the details of the character are much less easy to decipher than the Nubians in Mentuherkhepeshef's tomb. In the tekenu scene, the tekenu is first a man approaching a sled, "as if to emphasize the voluntary nature of the performance."[7] He is then pictured crouching on the sled (see fig. 5.2). In the bottom register, the sled is in a burial pit. The pit contains glyphs that probably indicate "hacking" and "bones" (see fig. 5.3)[8]

Figure 5.2 – Relief from tomb of Mentuherkhepeshef, depicting the *tekenu* on a sled

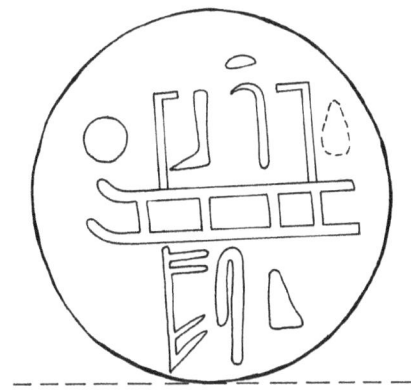

Figure 5.3 – Relief of *tekenu* sled and glyphs from the tomb of Mentuherkhepeshef

Taken alone, this scene certainly seems to signal that a tekenu was some kind of sacrificial burial. However, Griffiths, after examining evidence from other tekenu scenes, argues against this interpretation. His argument falters under the weight of the evidence.

Excursus on the Tekenu Rite

Griffiths outlines the different depictions of the tekenu, stating that while at times it is difficult to determine what the object labeled *tekenu* actually represents, it seems that it is consistently a human body covered in a skin.[9] He

---

[3] Davies, *Five Theban Tombs*, p. 15; John Gwyn Griffiths, "The Tekenu, the Nubians and the Butic Burial", *Kush* 6, 1958, 107–8.
[4] Davies, *Five Theban Tombs*, p. 15; Griffiths, "The Tekenu", p. 108.
[5] Griffiths, "The Tekenu", p. 110.
[6] Griffiths, "The Tekenu", p. 112.
[7] Davies, *Five Theban Tombs*, p. 14.
[8] Griffiths, "The Tekenu", p. 107.
[9] Griffiths, "The Tekenu", p. 113.

theorizes, as does Davies, that this may be the continuation of an ancient mode of burial, as opposed to human sacrifice; however, Griffiths and Davies do not indicate who or what would be buried in this proposed alternate form, which presumably accompanied the more modern burial of the tomb owner.[10]

Griffiths also observes that *sem priests* are sometimes depicted crouching and covered by skins in a manner somewhat similar to the tekenu. He supports this connection by drawing attention to the tekenu's and the sem priest's apparent connections to Horus. Willems and Reeder also suggest that the tekenu should be identified with the sem priest,[11] and by now the tekenu–sem-priest interpretation has become generally accepted. Some weight is added to this hypothesis by a depiction in the tomb of Rekhmire: The tekenu is shown on a couch that is identical to another couch on which a sem priest perches in another scene in the same tomb. This sem priest is wrapped, as is the tekenu, but in a very different shroud. While there is some merit to the sem-priest identification, the identification cannot explain the scenes indicating human slaughter. The sem-priest identification stems from a search for an alternate explanation, a search motivated by the assumption that the tekenu could not have been a ritual slaying. Again, this assumption is based on the tired and incorrect presumption that the Egyptians did not engage in human sacrifice. Once this bias is removed, most of the support for the tekenu–sem-priest theory falls by the wayside. A sem-priest depiction in a tomb does not a tekenu make.

Further arguing against a ritual-slaying interpretation, Griffiths remarks that where the tekenu and the Nubian-slaughter scenes are presented together, a different register depicts the sacrifice of bulls. Griffiths indicates that this "suggests rather that the tekenu consisted of the parts of a bull which were placed into a pit."[12] Taken by itself, this conclusion seems ephemeral. However, it is somewhat substantiated by another depiction from the tomb. In this depiction, a pit labeled *tekenu* also contains the signs for hair, ox foreleg, and heart (see fig. 5.4).[13] Still, the foreleg glyph in the tekenu pit and the bull slaughtering in another register are not compelling evidence that a bull was substituted in the tekenu ritual, especially when a human victim is so clearly destined for the pit. An explanation that more easily conforms to Occam's razor is that ox sacrifices were also included in

Figure 5.4 – Relief of *tekenu*, heart, hair, and foreleg glyphs from the tomb of Mentuherkhepeshef

the pit. Thus, the tekenu glyphs and the bull glyphs are both in the pit.

Griffiths also argues that, although the Nubians' slaying and the tekenu burial are painted next to each other in the same register, nothing indicates that the scenes are connected.[14] This argument twists the burden of proof. Are we not more justified in concluding, withouth contrary evidence, that since the Nubians' slaying and the tekenu burial are parts of a continuous scene, they must be connected?

Hornung believes that the tekenu may be all of the body parts which were extracted during mummification but were not put into the canopic jars.[15] This may be true, but we have no way of assessing this speculation. Barta thought that the froglike shape and skin of some tekenu depictions suggested that the rite was associated with Heket.[16]

The tekenu rite is maddening but tantalizing. It is important, ancient, and powerful. We are given tiny clues about the rite but clearly not enough clues to really know what was depicted. Thus, no conclusion can be sure. Still, the clues we have indicate a human and a sacrifice. Only grasping for contrary evidence casts doubt on this. Despite Griffiths' arguments that the tekenu was a bull sacrifice connected with sem priests and Horus, the weight of the evidence favors accepting the relief in Mentuherkhepeshef's tomb as it is depicted. Evidence to the contrary proves largely insubstantial. Thus, the involvement of ritual slaying in tekenu burials seems to be very possible.

Having examined this evidence, we may now return to the time period under study and observe that the middle-kingdom tomb of Sehetepibre, a steward of the king, in el-Lisht also contains tekenu depictions, though there are fewer portrayals than in Mentuherkhepeshef's tomb.

---

[10] Davies, *Five Theban Tombs*, p. 10; Griffiths, "The Tekenu", p. 114–15.
[11] Harko Willems, "The Coffin of Heqata (Cairo JdE 36418)", *Orientalia Lovaniensia Analecta* 70, 1996, 110–15; and Greg Reeder, "A Rite of Passage. The Enigmatic *Tekenu* in Ancient Egyptian Funerary Ritual," in *KMT* 5/3, 1994, 53-59. Reeder feels strongly that the tekenu is the sem priest, who fulfills a shamanistic function in the burial. His identification is based largely on the fact that both the tekenu and sem are depicted shrouded, though the shrouds look different.
[12] Willems, "The Coffin of Heqata (Cairo JdE 36418)", p. 115, italics in original.
[13] Willems, "The Coffin of Heqata (Cairo JdE 36418)", p. 107; Davies, *Five Theban Tombs*, pl. ix, bottom register. Griffiths writes that the hair, heart, and foreleg all belong to an ox, but there is nothing besides the accompanying foreleg glyph to indicate to whom the heart and hair belong.

[14] Griffiths, "The Tekenu", p. 120.
[15] Erik Hornung, *Idea Into Image: Essays on Ancient Egyptian Thought*, trans. Elizabeth Bredeck, Princeton: Princeton University Press, 1992, p. 169.
[16] Miroslav Barta, *JNES* 58/2, 1999, p. 1163.

Also, in Sehetepibre's tekenu depictions, the tightly wrapped tekenu renders it impossible to determine what form lies within. Nevertheless, as discussed above, the majority of tekenu scenes clearly depict a human who is being covered by some sort of animal skin, so we must assume that this tekenu is no different.

Similarly, Theban tomb 60, tomb of the middle-kingdom vizier Intefiqer, also depicts a tekenu ritual associated with the burial of Intefiqer. This tomb shows a kneeling tekenu covered in a skin as well, and the *tekenu* label undoubtedly refers to the same ritual as the one discussed above.[17] Moreover, we know that Intefiqer was a violent military leader. Thus, these two tombs quite possibly demonstrate what may have been a more widespread practice of ritual slaying as part of tomb preparation.[18]

Death by Fire and Other Unpleasant Methods

Eyre writes that "the single most important historical inscription of the Middle Kingdom is the damaged text of [Senusret] I from Tod."[19] Buchberger has called the dating of this inscription at the temple of Tôd into question.[20] This text is narrative in nature, marking the rudimentary beginnings of the genre of *Königsnovelle* (king's novel),[21] and must be approached with the critical cautions necessary for propagandistic literature.[22] Certainly the king casts himself in the typical role of discovering chaos and restoring it to order,[23] but this does not mean we should dismiss its historicity because it contains ideology. Such would introduce a false dichotomy. It is very likely that Senusret was indeed intending to cast himself in a mytho-ideological light, but it is unlikely he did so only in narrative. Instead we must assume he would have used real situations to enact real actions that would bring about an ideological statement in word and deed. "History as celebration"[24] doe not mean there was no history, and the act fits with the historical idea of Senusret inheriting the throne under political turmoil and taking violent steps in order to assert his rule firmly.[25] The textual account may stretch the truth; nevertheless, even if the events described therein are exaggerated and only partially represent actual events, they do suggest the types of punishment in the king's repertoire. Exaggeration in this text, if it occurs, is probably inflation of numbers, not fabrication of the king's actions. The inscription preserves one of the most dramatic examples of the virulent destruction of *Isfet*. Senusret I furiously razed opposition to *Ma'at*, adamantly insuring that Isfet would not gain the upper hand under his watch.

The inscription records that Senusret I found that the Temple of Tod was in a deplorable state. Weeds had overgrown it, its seals had been broken, portions of its wall had been broken down, and fire had been set to sections of its structure.[26] Senusret punished the desecrators: "[(As for) those who had cast] fire and flame on the temple, and those who had trespassed in this house, [My Majesty made a great(?) slaughter among them(?)] men and women, the valleys filled with the flayed (*srḥw*) and the hills with the impaled (*ptḥw*)."[27]

The word translated here as "impaled" is *ptḥw*, which generally means "to build," or perhaps *ptḥw* is a cognate of the Semitic word *ptḥ*, "to open."[28] Neither "built" nor "opened" make sense in the semantic context. However, as Redford has noted, the determinative used in this text is four upright stakes, bound together.[29] He correctly argues that the context, the determinative, and the Semitic cognate *ptḥ* or *paḫātu* (the arrangement of signs could easily be read *pḫtw*) all point to an interpretation of *ptḥw* (or *pḫtw*) as "to impale" or "to transfix."[30] Additionally, it seems that some had met the very unpleasant fate of being flayed, whether they were flayed while dead or alive we do not know.

Another punishment may be elucidated directly after this description. The next word after *ptḥw* is *ḫrwy*, or "enemy." Following this word, the upper traces of the *m*

---

[17] Norman de Garis Davies, Alan Henderson Gardiner, and Nina M. Cummings Davies, *The Tomb of Antefoker, Vizier of Sesostris I, and of His Wife, Senet (no. 60)*, Theban Tomb Series 2, London: G. Allen & Unwin, 1920, pl. 6; Griffiths, "The Tekenu, the Nubians and the Butic Burial", p. 111.

[18] This possibility is discussed further below, see chapter 6, "Possible Examples of Ritual Slaying". Also on the subject of sacrifices associated with burial, it should be noted that the practice of sacrificial servant burials is attested within a middle-kingdom context. However, these finds, at Avaris, are associated with Levantine culture and thus do not really appertain to the subject of this study. See Manfred Bietak, "Servant Burials in the Middle Bronze Age Culture of the Eastern Nile Delta", in *Yigael Yadin Memorial Volume*, A. Ben-Tor, J.C. Greenfield, and A. Malamat (eds.), Jerusalem: Ben-Zvi, 1989.

[19] C.J. Eyre, "Crime and Adultery in Ancient Egypt", *JEA* 70, 1984, 431.

[20] Hannes Buchberger, "Sesostris I. und die Inschrift von et-Tôd? Eine philologische Anfrage," in Karola Zibelius-Chen and Hans-Werner Fischer-Elfert, eds. *Von Reichlich Ägyptischem Verstande, Festschrift für Waltraud Guglielmi zum 65 Geburtstag* (Wiesbaden: Philippika, 2006), 15–21.

[21] Eyre, "Crime and Adultery in Ancient Egypt", p. 431.

[22] As was pointed out by Wolfgang Helck, "Politische Spannungen zu Beginn des Mittleren Reiches," *Ägypten – Dauer und Wandel. Symposium anlaäßlich des 75 jährigen Vestehens des Deutschen Archäologischen Instituts Kairo am 10. Und 11. Okt. 1982*, 18 (1985): 49; and Wolfgang Helck, *Politische Gegensätze im alten Ägypten* (Hildesheim: Gerstenberg Verlag, 1986): 37.

[23] As suggested by Helck, "Politische Spannungen," 49. For just a few other examples, see Urk. 7:27; P. Leningrad 1116B, 69; as in Wolfgang Helck, *Die Prophezeihung des Nfr.tj* (Wiesbaden: O. Harrassowitz, 1970), 57; Urk. 4:2026; and Stela of Taharqa year 6, lines 3–5 (Kawa version) as in M.F. Laming Macadam, *The Temples of Kawa I* (London: Oxford University Press, 1949).

[24] Helck, "Polisische Spannungen," 49.

[25] Claude Obsomer, "Sinouhé l'Égyptien et les Raisons de son Exil," *Le Muséon* 112 (1999), 265–66.

[26] See lines X+28–30, as transcribed in Donald B. Redford, "The Tod Inscriptions of Senwosret I and Early 12th Dynasty Involvement in Nubia and the South", *JSSEA* 17, 1987, 42 and fig. 2.

[27] Reconstructions according to Redford, "The Tod Inscriptions of Senwosret I and Early 12th Dynasty Involvement in Nubia and the South", 42.

[28] *Wb* 1, 565; or Rainer Hannig, *Grosses Handwörterbuch Ägyptisch-Deutsch: (2800-950 v. Chr.): die Sprache der Pharaonen*, Kulturgeschichte der antiken Welt 64, Mainz: P. von Zabern, 1995, p. 298.

[29] Redford, "The Tod Inscriptions of Senwosret I", n. 68.

[30] Redford, "The Tod Inscriptions of Senwosret I", n. 68.

owl are visible, and then the text breaks. Significantly, the determinative for *ḫrwy* is a bound, headless man (𓀘). While the determinative may be headless to ensure that the artistic rendering of the word was bereft of power—though the binding could amply accomplish this purpose—it is more likely that decapitation was the enemies' fate, probably described in the broken section of the text.[31] Redford reconstructs the description of the punishment to conclude that the enemies' fate was burning to death. This is not an inevitable, but a possible conclusion, since the next legible portion of the inscription reads "him into the flame" (*sw r ḫt*).[32] Whether decapitation is reported in the previous passage or not, this fragment makes it clear that some perpetrators were punished by burning. What seems most likely is that the prisoners were struck with a knife and then burned, as was done with other types of sacrifices.

The next group of offenders to be described received the punishment of decapition—*dndn ḫrwy*.[33] The word *dndn* commonly means "to decapitate," especially when it is accompanied, as it is here, with a knife determinative (𓌪).[34] Significantly, the word *ḫrwy* is again determined by a bound and headless man, lending further weight to the idea that the illegible lines above this passage describe decapitation. Whether or not the first passage with a determination of a headless enemy described decapitation, the latter passage confirms that part of the punishment that Senusret I inflicted was decapitation.

While Senusret I's text is specific about applying these different killing methods, the text also hints that the killing took place in a ritual context. Senusret I informs us that "[the knife][35] was applied to the children of the enemy (*msw ḫrwy*, again the headless *ḫrwy* is pictured), Asiatics as sacrifices."[36] The word for sacrificial victim, *smȝyw*, is followed by a recumbent headless cow determinative. Being determined thus, *smȝyw* always means a sacrificial animal.[37] There can be no doubt that Senusret intentionally included a sacrificial element in the executions he had just enacted.[38] This sacrificial association is augmented by the fact that some temple sacrifices were burned during this middle-kingdom period.[39] The wording and setting of Senusret I's account are inextricably linked to ritual slaying.

The text becomes extremely broken at this point, but hints of more violent slayings are discernable. Line X+35 speaks of burning Asiatics. Line X+37 may associate Nubians, Asiatics, and "seizing." Line X+38 mentions certain Nubian Medjay turning back (*hȝy* with a reversed legs determinative 𓂾) and refers to their "not over-powering."[40]

Buchberger questions the dating of the inscription due to a number of grammatical and orthographic uses which he believes are anachronistic in the Middle Kingdom.[41] Thus he postulates either a New Kingdom date for the inscription, or a New Kingdom restoration of the original text. The latter would not really affect the date of the inscription. Moreover, many of those things he believes are not typical of the Middle Kingdom are, nevertheless, attested in that era, and he does not adequately account for the use of the name "Senusret" in the text,[42] which suggests a Middle Kingdom context. Additionally, Obsomer felt that the inscription fit with the political actions of Senusret I.[43] Buchberger's article should make us consider the post-composition history of the text, but does not really cast doubt on the original Middle Kingdom context.[44]

One wonders whether both Nubians and Asiatics were really the perpetrators of the crimes against the temple. Perhaps as foreigners, and thus representatives of Isfet, they were chosen as a scapegoat for the cultic crimes that had happened at Tod. It is also possible that the real perpetrators were punished but were textually described as foreigners. While the answers to these questions are elusive, it is clear that the king engaged in impalement, decapitation, and burning, and that all or one of these punishments were enacted in a ritual setting. Moreover, while some of the account may be exaggerated, it also seems inevitable that such practices were part of Senusret I's zeitgeist. Decapitating and burning rebellious enemies, as part of a sacrificial slaughter, was clearly part of the royal repertoire.

---

[31] Christophe Barbotin and J.J. Clère, "L'Inscription de Sèsostris Ier à Tôd", *Bulletin de l' Institut Français d'Archéologie Orientale* 91, 1991, 10, lines 116–21, translate, "I began to decapitate the rebel for him, the Majesty of Horus, [. . .] his [blood] of the body, in the wild heart of his youth, [his] slaughterhouse was (populated) with rebels' children, the cattle of the daily offering were (composed) of Asiatics (?) . . . which fulfilled the attacker's massacre." In this translation, they leave out much of the text that is surrounded by broken lines, but they preserve the essence of the event.

[32] X+30 as in Redford, "The Tod Inscriptions of Senwosret I", 43 and fig. 2.

[33] X+32.

[34] *Wb* 4, 983.

[35] Reconstruction by Redford.

[36] Line X+32.

[37] *Wb* 4, 123–4; Hannig, *Grosses Handwörterbuch Ägyptisch-Deutsch*, p. 703. See also Redford, "The Tod Inscriptions of Senwosret I", n. 81.

[38] Dennis D. Hughes, *Human Sacrifice in Ancient Greece*, New York: Routledge, 1991, p. 4, discusses the problem of the terminology of human sacrifice in the study of Greek religion and the semantic wrestle of scholars of that field; this wrestling parallels the terminology problem outlined in this study. Hughes concludes that cases in which humans are sacrificed in the place of animals and in which the slaying of humans is described using the language of animal sacrifice undoubtedly should be referred to as human sacrifice. While his point is well made, I will continue with the term of ritual slaying to avoid the pitfalls outlined in chapter 1, "The Terminology of Sacrifice".

[39] Byron E. Shafer, "Temples, Priests, and Rituals: an Overview", *Temples of Ancient Egypt*, Byron E. Shafer (ed.), Ithaca: Cornell University Press, 1997, p. 25. See also Christopher Eyre, *The Cannibal Hymn: A Cultural and Literary Study*, Bolton: Liverpool University Press, 2002, pp. 172–3.

[40] Redford, "The Tod Inscriptions of Senwosret I", 43 and fig. 2.

[41] Hannes Buchberger, "Sesostris I. und die Inschrift von et-Tôd? Eine philologische Anfrage," in Karola Zibelius-Chen and Hans-Werner Fischer-Elfert, eds. *Von Reichlich Ägyptischem Verstande, Festschrift für Waltraud Guglielmi zum 65 Geburtstag* (Wiesbaden: Philippika, 2006), 15–21.

[42] Line X+25.

[43] Obsomer, "Sinouhe", 265-66.

[44] See Kerry Muhlestein, "Royal Executions: Evidence Bearing on the Subject of Sanctioned Killing in the Middle Kingdom," in *The Journal of the Economic and Social History of the Orient*, 51/2 (2008), 191-192.

Willems notes that the late-period altar in the Temple of Tod contains many references to the Myth of the Destruction of Mankind and that traditionally the spot may have been a place for destroying those who had rebelled against deity.[45] This tradition may have sprung from the very act under study. In any case, Senusret I's action has almost been universally accepted as an example of the king employing burning as a death penalty.[46] An exception is Lorton, who believes that burning was not a form of execution used by the Egyptians, especially in the Middle Kingdom.[47] Lorton's position has been effectively refuted by Leahy,[48] and opinions contrary to Lorton's have been expressed by a host of scholars.[49]

Another royal inscription indicates that the king used burning as a form of execution. This inscription, Stela Cairo JE 35256, was probably carved during the Twelfth Dynasty but was usurped by Neferhotep I during the Thirteenth Dynasty.[50] The stela's original creation and later usurpation combine to provide pertinent information for both time periods, extending the stela's window of generalization. The stela was erected to protect the "sacred land" (*tȝ dsr*) around a cemetery in Abydos. On the stela, the king decreed that anyone, except a *wa'b* priest performing his duty, who trespassed or built in the sacred area would be burned (*ḥrtw bdtw=f*).[51] As mentioned above, Lorton has argued against burning as a form of punishment and hence translated "burning" as "branded."[52] Breasted also prefers "branded."[53] Leahy so effectively argues against this translation as to leave no question that it should be "burning."[54] Other scholars translate the passage to mean "burning."[55]

Both the Tod and Abydos royal inscriptions decree death for those who have profaned a sacred site. Most other examples, thus far presented, of burning as a punishment involve the desecration of a tomb. This commonality cannot be overlooked. It is likely that such a crime, which affected both mortal and immortal spheres, demanded a punishment that would annihilate such an Isfet-tinged element in all realms. Since burning completely destroyed the essence of a person, it was just such a punishment.

There are other references to burning from the Middle Kingdom. Papyrus Westcar indicates that, under the supervision of the king, the adulterous wife of a nobleman was burned for her crime (literally, "fire was put" (*rdi ḥt*) on her).[56] The possibility of an adulterer being punished by death is discussed later in the chapter. In the Tale of the Shipwrecked Sailor, the god-like snake, also associated with the king,[57] threatens the sailor with being turned to ashes as one who does not exist.[58] Both of these tales are fiction. Moreover, both stories involve magical elements. Nevertheless, the authors of these tales probably drew from reality to create punishments. In both cases, the king figure has the ability to bring about death by fire. This association likely reflects the authors' society.

A middle-kingdom graffito bears upon the subject. An Intefiqer, probably the vizier of Amenemhet I whose tomb we discussed earlier in the chapter, records that he led victorious campaigns in Nubia. During these campaigns he "put fire to their homes (*rdi=i ḥt m prw=sn*), as is done to a rebel against the king" (*mi irit sbi ḥr nswt*).[59] Whether Intefiqer really did all he claimed to have done, this passage provides strong evidence that rebels were burned. Intefiqer's metaphor would make no sense and would not have been employed without a real referent to existing, known situations. As did Senusret I, Intefiqer's contemporary, Intefiqer took no chance that Chaos would prosper while he was on guard. Here was a man who would not stand for chaotic rebellion—Isfet was eradicated.

---

[45] Harco Willems, "Crime, Cult and Capital Punishment (Mo'alla Inscription 8)", *JEA* 76, 1990, 43. See also Jean Yoyotte, "Héra d' Héliopolis et le Sacrifice Humain", *Annuaire École pratique des hautes études, Section–sciences religieuses* 89, 1980–1, 38; and *Urk.* 4, 17.

[46] Willems, "Crime", p. 41; A.G. McDowell, "Crime and Punishment", in *The Oxford Encyclopedia of Ancient Egypt*, Donald B. Redford (ed.), Oxford: Oxford University Press, 2001, p. 317; Joyce A. Tyldesley, *Judgement of the Pharaoh: Crime and Punishment in Ancient Egypt*, London: Weidenfeld & Nicolson, 2000, p. 66.

[47] David Lorton, "The Treatment of Criminals in Ancient Egypt", *Journal of the Economic and Social History of the Orient* 20, 1977, pp. 15–18. Renate Müller-Wollermann, *Vergehen und Strafen: Zur Sanktionierung abweichenden Verhaltens im alten Ägypten*, Leiden: E.J. Brill, 2004, p. 206, also believes that drowning, burning, and decapitation were punishments that only existed in the afterlife, a view which this study makes abundantly clear is untenable.

[48] Anthony Leahy, "Death by Fire in Ancient Egypt", *Journal of the Economic and Social History of the Orient* 27, 1984, 199. See entire article for full refutation.

[49] See Erik Hornung, *Altägyptische Höllenvorstellungen: Mit 7 Lichtdrucktafeln und 6 Abbildungen im Text*, Abhandlungen der Sächsischen Akademie der Wissenschaften zu Leipzig, Philologisch-historische Klasse 59, Heft 3, Berlin: Akademie-Verlag, 1968, p. 22; Tyldesley, *Judgment of the Pharaoh*, p. 66; McDowell, "Crime and Punishment", p. 317; Griffiths, "Menschenopfer", in *Lexicon der Ägyptologie*, Wolfgang Helck and Wolfhart Westendorf (eds.), Wiesbaden: Otto Harrassowitz, 1982, p. 1218; see also J. Zandee, *Death as an Enemy according to Ancient Egyptian Conceptions*, Leiden: E.J. Brill, 1960, pp. 14–15; Willems, "Crime", p. 41; and Harry Smith, "Ma'et and Isfet", *Bulletin of the Australian Centre for Egyptology* 5, 1994, 85, for a few examples.

[50] Anthony Leahy, "A Protective Measure at Abydos in the Thirteenth Dynasty", *JEA* 75, 1989, 46.

[51] Line 6, as in Leahy, "A Protective Measure", fig. 1.

[52] Lorton, "The Treatment of Criminals", p. 18.

[53] *ARE* 1, 338.

[54] Leahy, "Death by Fire", p. 199.

[55] For example, see McDowell, "Crime and Punishment", p. 317; Ellen D. Bedell, "Criminal Law in the Egyptian Ramesside Period", Ph.D. Dissertation, Brandeis University, 1973, 166; and Willems, "Crime", pp. 40, 54.

[56] P. Berlin 3033, col. 4, line 9. See Georges Posener, *Le Papyrus Vandier*, Paris: Institute Français d'Archéologie Orientale, 1985, p. 32, both the text and n. 3. Posener also compares this to the late Teachings of Ankhsheshonqy.

[57] See Kerry Muhlestein, "The Shipwrecked Sailor as Veiled Criticism of the King", *Lingua Aegyptia*, forthcoming.

[58] P. St. Petersburg 1115, lines 73–4.

[59] Zbyněk Žába, Fritz Hintze, and Miroslav Verner (eds.), *The Rock Inscriptions of Lower Nubia (Czechoslovak Concession)*, Ceskoslovenský Egyptologický Publications 1, Prague: Charles University, 1974, p. 99, inscription no. 73. Also translated in Richard B. Parkinson, *Voices from Ancient Egypt: An Anthology of Middle Kingdom Writings*, Norman, OK: University of Oklahoma, 1991, pp. 95–6; Redford, "The Tod Inscriptions of Senwosret I" 45, translates "Fire was set in their houses, just as is done to one that rebels against the king!"

Considered together, the two royal inscriptions from Tod and from Abydos, Intefiqer's graffito, and the two narrative fictions, Papyrus Westcar and the Tale of the Shipwrecked Sailor, provide very strong evidence for burning as a form of capital punishment. In all cases, royal power brought about the punishment. There is little room for doubt that such burnings were a feature of Egyptian society during this time period. Moreover, the phrasing of the snake's threat in the Tale of the Shipwrecked Sailor makes it clear that one consequence of being burned was the complete cessation of existence, a fate of particular horror to the ancient Egyptians.

Miscellaneous Punishments

There are several other tidbits of information regarding sanctioned killing from this time period. The fictitious tale recorded on Papyrus Westcar, mentioned earlier in the chapter, records that the partner-in-sin of the adulterous noblewoman was given, with the king's permission, to a crocodile.[60] This is probably fanciful since the crocodile is a magical part of the story and since his reception of the offender continues an ironic literary device. Nevertheless, some have interpreted the crocodile feeding as a real punishment, which is possible.[61]

More possible evidence for the seriousness of adultery is found in the Instructions of Ptahhotep, a document that may have originated in the late Old Kingdom but is more likely a middle-kingdom creation.[62] Goedicke writes that these instructions designate a death penalty for adultery.[63] The lines he cites for this assertion are more ambiguous than he indicates. The instruction informs the reader that being involved sexually with the women of another house is "a small moment, like a dream, and one reaches death by knowing them."[64] While this phrase could mean that such licentiousness was a capital crime, other interpretations of these lines are possible. Eyre believes that a consequence of adultery was indeed death but that "this death was, however, expected as the revenge of the deceived husband, not as the result of criminal proceedings."[65] However, as already mentioned, in Papyrus Westcar the revenge of the husband does not culminate in death until the king approves. The Herodotus account of Pheros burning women of infidelity is so fanciful that we cannot appeal to it for any further clarity.[66] In the face of such ambiguity, the most we may posit is the possibility that a death sentence was attached to adultery. The subject will be further discussed in chapter 6, as the topic arises again in the Eighteenth Dynasty.

A last insight is gained from an administrative document. This papyrus reads, "I found the royal servant (ḥm-nsw) Sobekemheb, for he had fled. See, I gave him to the Court of Hearings. . . . He is given to death in the Hall of Speaking."[67] It is important to note that fleeing conscripted workers were condemned to a life of forced labor, while runaway slaves—or at least royal runaways—were executed.[68] Since royal servants may have been condemned criminals, they may have been put to death because they were trying to escape from an already severe punishment. The forthrightness of the language in this text provides very strong evidence that runaway royal slaves, and possibly other runaway slaves, were indeed executed if caught.

Curses

As with the First Intermediate Period, the Middle Kingdom attests several inscriptional curses, creating a window into the world of juridical punishment. Also, these inscriptions afford us quick peeks into the lives of ordinary men who are often overlooked in the grand and sweeping stories of history. Inscriptional curses show us what the ancient Egyptians considered ordinary elements of their culture, however exotic the elements may seem to us. We will first examine the inscription of Knumhotep II at Beni Hasan.[69] This text clearly states that anyone who violates the tomb "will not exist." The text does not stipulate how this would be accomplished, just that the desecrator must no longer be. Such a threat implies that a punishment capable of destroying a person's essence, such as burning, would be employed.[70]

Relevant information is also found in a series of twelfth-dynasty inscriptions from lower Nubia. These graffiti do not accompany tombs, but the preservation of the names in the graffiti would have helped preserve the inscribers themselves. Inscription 57 threatens that anyone who destroyed the inscription would "die by the king's execution block" (mwt=f n nmt nswt).[71] Willems translates similarly,[72] but Zába translates "king's executioner"[73] (nmty nswt). Both translations are equally possible, and there is no effective difference between the

---

[60] P. Berlin 3033, col. 4, lines 5–8.
[61] See Bedell, "Criminal Law", p. 163; Griffiths, "Menschenopfer", p. 1218; and Wolfgang Boochs, "Religöse Strafen", in *Religion und Philosophie im Alten Ägypten*, Ursula Verhoeven and Erhart Graefe (ed.), Leuven: Peters, 1991, p. 62.
[62] Miriam Lichtheim, "Didactic Literature", in *Ancient Egyptian Literature: History and Forms*, Antonio Loprieno (eds.), Leiden: E.J. Brill, 1996, pp. 244, 247.
[63] Hans Goedicke, "Was Magic Used in the Harem Conspiracy Against Ramesses III?", *JEA* 49, 1963, 89.
[64] P. Prisse, col. 9, lines 7–11.
[65] C.J. Eyre, "Crime and Adultery", *JEA* 70, 1984, 97.
[66] Herodotus II, 111.
[67] P. UC32209, 1.4–6 and 2.4–5, as in *The UCL Lahun Papyri: Letters*, Mark Collier and Stephen Quirke (eds.), Oxford: Basingstoke, 2002. I take the t(w) as a passive, creating the above translation. Collier and Quirke translate the last line as "so you seem to be letting him die/languish? In the office of the reporter." Antonio Loprieno, "Slaves", in *The Egyptians*, Sergio Donadoni (ed.), Chicago, IL: University of Chicago, 1997, p. 200, translates, "He will thus be condemned to death in the Hall of the Speaker".
[68] Loprieno, "Slaves", p. 200.
[69] P. E. Newberry, *Beni Hasan*, London: K. Paul Trench Trübner, 1893, pl. xxv, lines 96–9.
[70] See also Willems, "Crime", p. 38.
[71] Zába, *The Rock Inscriptions of Lower Nubia*, p. 81, inscription no. 57.
[72] Willems, "Crime", p. 38.
[73] Zába, *The Rock Inscriptions of Cover Nubia*, pp. 81–4. The essential difference is whether nm.t is a noun of itself, or if an unrepresented yodh makes it a nisbe, ie. nm.ty.

two. While it is unlikely that someone damaging the graffito would ever garner enough attention to elicit capital punishment, it also appears certain that the king's executioner/execution block inflicted a real form of punishment.

Another graffito states that its damager would die by the hand of the executioner.[74] Again the conclusion is simple: execution under the auspices of the king was a part of middle-kingdom life. The barely legible traces of Inscription 56 have been restored by Zába to read, "As for him who will cut (this), death will be found for him."[75] A fourth text is less clear, reading that anyone who destroyed the inscription "will no more sail down stream."[76] While death is not explicitly threatened, it can be inferred from the other inscriptions that to "no more sail down stream" involves the cessation of the perpetrator's life. Taken together, all of these curses paint a convincing picture of capital punishment, especially at the hand of the king's executioner, in the Middle Kingdom.

Ritual Slaying

While some of the burning episodes discussed earlier in the chapter clearly have sacrificial connotations, as might the tekenu ritual, there is other evidence for ritual slaying in the Middle Kingdom. One example, the human execration at Mirgissa, was discussed in chapter 3. Here at Mirgissa, a human was clearly sacrificed as part of a religious ritual.[77] This case undoubtedly qualifies as a ritual slaying. Moreover, the archaeological remains of the full execration rite, of which slaying a human was only part, are consistent with those of a Ptolemaic ritual text describing a rite which was generally a human sacrifice in effigy: "Bind with the sinew of a red cow . . . spit on him four times . . . trample on him with the left foot . . . smite him with a spear . . . slaughter him with a knife . . . place him on the fire . . . spit on him in the fire many times."[78] The similarity between the two rites is illustrative; furthermore, as with Senusret I's, Tod's sacrifices used a knife, followed by burning.

Willems, in writing of later altars that appear to have been used for ritual slaying, states that "both altars date from the Late Period, but there is a possibility that another, from the Middle Kingdom, was also used for human sacrifices in case of necessity. I refer to the brick altar in the Hekaib sanctuary. This hypothesis cannot be proved, but it should nevertheless be noted that the installation is situated directly in front of the stela referring to human sacrifice."[79] With such inferential evidence, the practice should be acknowledged as having been possible, but more than this cannot be said.

An even more ambiguous reference comes from the Tale of the Shipwrecked Sailor, a narrative fiction we have discussed in this chapter. At the conclusion of this tale, the despairing count asks his attendant not to cheer him at the end of their failed mission, for "who gives water to a bird when the morrow dawns for its slaughter?"[80] The text is difficult to read, and this translation is not universally accepted. An entire article has been dedicated to the proper translation of these lines, concluding that only the general meaning of the lines, not an exact translation, can be completely agreed on.[81] Gulila writes that this meaning "is simply 'what good is there in giving water to a goose just before it is killed?'"[82] Widely varying interpretations have been attached to the count's rhetorical question. Otto even construes the saying as optimistic.[83] However, general consensus interprets a more negative connotation in the count's words than does Otto's interpretation.[84]

Of current interest is the reference to the slaughter of a goose, which probably was a sacrificial bird. Indubitably, the count is here comparing his fate to the bird's. It is too presumptuous to interpret the metaphor to mean that the count felt he would be sacrificed. Still, while this meaning is improbable, it should be acknowledged to be possible.

Funerary Literature

We now turn to the evidence garnered from funerary literature, using all the caution these texts demand. The Middle Kingdom witnessed the creation of a new genre of funerary literature: the Coffin Texts. These spells followed the Pyramid Texts and were primarily found on the coffins of the elite, though they were also found on stelae, papyri, tomb walls, canopic chests, and mummy masks.[85] The fresh creation of these spells, which certainly involved reuse and reworking of the Pyramid Texts and some pyramid-text ideas, maintained their reflection of contemporary society because the reworking allowed for the input of middle-kingdom practices. For

---

[74] Zába, *The Rock Inscriptions of Cover Nubia*, p. 52, inscription no. 24.
[75] Zába, *The Rock Inscriptions of Cover Nubia*, p. 79, inscription no. 56.
[76] Zába, *The Rock Inscriptions of Cover Nubia*, p. 85, inscription no. 58.
[77] See Andre Vila, "Un dépôt de Textes (Envoutement au Moyen Empire", *Journal des Savants* 41, 1963; and Robert Ritner, *The Mechanics of Ancient Egyptian Magical Practice*, Studies in Ancient Oriental Civilization 54, Chicago: University of Chicago, 1993, 161–5.
[78] P. Louvre 3129 B 44–8, in Siegfried Schott, *Urkunden mythologischen Inhalts*, Leipzig: J.C. Hinrichs, 1929, 5.
[79] Willems, "Crime", p. 43. For information on the altar and inscription, see Labib Habachi, Gerhard Haeny, and Friedrich Junge, *The Sanctuary of Heqaib*, Elephantine 4, Mainz-on-the-Rhine: P. von Zabern, 1985, p. 35.
[80] P. St. Petersburg 1115, lines 184–5.
[81] Mordechai Gilula, "Shipwrecked Sailor, Lines 184–5", *Studies in Honor of George R. Hughes*, Janet H. Johnson and Edward F. Wente (eds.), Chicago: Oriental Institute of Chicago, 1976.
[82] Gilula, "Shipwrecked Sailor, Lines 184–5", p. 82.
[83] E. Otto, "Die Geschichte des Sinuhe und des Schiffbrüchigen als 'lehrhafte Stücke'", *ZÄS* 93, 1966, 111.
[84] See Anthony Spalinger, "An Alarming Parallel to the End of the Shipwrecked Sailor", *GM* 73, 1984, 93; John Baines, "Interpreting the Story of the Shipwrecked Sailor", *JEA* 76, 1990, 61; Muhlestein, "Shipwrecked Sailor"; and Betsy M. Bryan, "The Hero of the 'Shipwrecked Sailor'", *Serapis, the American Journal of Egyptology* 5, 1979, 13, for some examples.
[85] Erik Hornung, *The Ancient Egyptian Books of the Afterlife*, David Lorton (trans.), Ithaca, NY: Cornell University, 1999, p. 7.

example, Eyre writes that the creative transmission from the Pyramid Texts to the Coffin Texts "seems more likely to involve a continuous development in performative use."[86] Thus, we can look to these texts to tell us something of middle-kingdom practice.

We have already noted that one of the descendants of the Cannibal Hymn indicates that evil-doers will be slaughtered.[87] This threat to evil-doers would not have been included in this coffin text if it reflected a practice that had died out hundreds of years earlier. The evidence for ritual slaughtering is somewhat strengthened by another text, in which the deceased asserts that he will not be made a slaughtering/offering (ꜥbt) by the doorkeepers of Osiris.[88] Neither of these references proves that people were slaughtered and offered anywhere outside the afterlife, but they indicate that ritual slaying may have occurred.

Another spell asks for the deceased to be saved from the Osiris's fishermen who chop off heads (ḥsḳ). The deceased then asserts that neither his head nor his neck will be chopped off.[89] Again, this may be something only to be feared in the afterlife. Yet we may presume that the punishments of the afterlife were patterned after the punishments of this life.[90] While these references may perpetuate archaic terminology, in light of the plenteous evidence for decapitation previously presented, the scant coffin-text references just cited are greatly bolstered as evidence for sanctioned killing.

If capital punishment by decapitation had been part of the Egyptian milieu for hundreds of years, as I have argued thus far, then these coffin-text references probably indicate its middle-kingdom continuation. This proposition will be further enhanced by later chapters, as the continued use of beheading in later periods is demonstrated. It is improbable that the Middle Kingdom represents an anomalous gap in the use of this technique. Some have construed a Papyrus Westcar statement, in which a magician demonstrates his magical restorative capabilities by declining to behead a human, to mean that beheading was proscribed by middle-kingdom culture. The magical nature of the magician's act disallows this kind of extrapolation from the story. It should also be remembered that the Tod inscription of Senusret I contains ample evidence of decapitation. Thus, we must conclude that decapitation was very likely employed in the Middle Kingdom.

Burning is likewise attested in the Coffin Texts. Coffin texts VII.1152; IV.270; II.276; II.379; IV.66; VII.1071; II.54; V.12; IV.329; V.319; and others refer to burning as a form of punishment.[91] The consistent afterlife use of burning as punishment and known mortal-life examples combine to indicate that burning was a prevalent form of punishment.

Drowning in the Second Intermediate Period

Our only pertinent text from the Second Intermediate Period is extremely ambiguous. This era is a complex phase of Egyptian history. As in the First Intermediate Period, there was fragmentation and dissolution of centralized power and control. But this time another element was thrown into the mix. As Egypt splintered, the group that garnered the most power and controlled Egypt for a long time consisted of foreigners: the Hyksos, or Semitic dynasts. While the Hyksos became Egyptianized in many ways, a significant portion of the Egyptian population would never accept the foreign rulers as anything but vile outsiders who wrongfully controlled the greatest people in the cosmos. From the Egyptians' viewpoint, foreigners were Isfet embodied, and foreign rulers were unbearable. Eventually, a Theban family led an army against the Hyksos and the Hyksos's Egyptian allies. The Thebans stylized themselves as the champions of Ma'at, determined to expel Chaos and to return the land and cosmos to their proper state. At least in the mind of the Theban family who came to rule Egypt, the Egyptians were led by the great warriors Seqenenre, Kamose, and Ahmose. These warriors were victorious in driving out Chaos and giving Order a desperately needed rebirth.

In the account of Kamose's expulsion of the Hyksos recorded on Carnarvon Tablet 1,[92] Kamose outlines his conquest of the rebel Tti, stating that he overpowered the rebel, butchered Tti's men, and "made his wife go down to the bank of the river (itꜣy r mryt)."[93] The meaning of this last phrase is not clear, though some light can be cast by a further investigation of the phrase "going to the bank of the river."

One argument that this phrase indicates a death penalty cites evidence from a later period: a juridical record from Deir el-Medina. In this record, the city judges recommend death for a woman who had stolen copper from Amun. As part of their argument for such a harsh penalty, they cite a precedent, in which the vizier orders another female thief to be taken "to the river bank (r mryt)." [94] The appeal to this precedent to justify a death penalty would make little sense if "going to the

---

[86] Eyre, *Cannibal Hymn*, pp. 23–4.

[87] See chapter 3, "Other Forms of Ritual Sacrifice"; CT VI, 181h; and Hartwig Altenmüller, "Bemerkungen zum Kannibalenspruch", in *Fragen an die altägyptische Literatur: Studien zum Gedenken an Eberhard Otto*, Eberhard Otto, et al. (ed.), Wiesbaden: Reichert, 1977, p. 31.

[88] See CT VI, 132d; and Zandee, *Death as an Enemy*, p. 147.

[89] CT III 295h–296e; and Zandee, *Death as an Enemy*, pp. 149–50.

[90] Bedell, "Criminal Law", pp. 157–8, uses this text to argue for the existence of decapitation.

[91] See Zandee, *Death as an Enemy*, pp. 133–5.

[92] See Alan H. Gardiner, "The Defeat of the Hyksos by Kamose: The Carnarvon Tablet No.1", *JEA* 3, 1916, pls. 12–13, for the publication of this tablet.

[93] Carnarvon Tablet I 112–14. See also Adina Haran, "Nationalism and the Sin of Conquest in the Texts of Kamose (K3-MS): Carnarvon Tablet No. 1, Stela No. I and Stela No. II", in *Jerusalem Studies in Egyptology*, Irene Shirun-Grumach (eds.), Wiesbaden: Harrassowitz Verlag, 1998, p. 266.

[94] Ostracon Nach 1, verso, lines 8–13, especially line 11, as in Jaroslav Cerný and Alan Henderson Gardiner, *Hieratic Ostraca*, Oxford: Oxford University Press, 1957, pl. 46; see also Bedell, "Criminal Law", 15.

riverbank" did not indicate that death would ensue. McDowell argues that "to take to the riverbank" instead indicated interrogation,[95] because interrogations were conducted at the riverbank during the Great Tomb Robberies, even though those robberies were punished by impalement.[96] She proposes that the riverbank served as an official "place of examination."[97] However, the Deir el-Medina appeal to precedent would have little effect if a death sentence is not implied by the phrase. Therefore, prudence forces the possibility that being taken to the riverbank sometimes meant that a person was to be drowned.

Drowning was a severe form of punishment because it prevented the proper burial and body preservation which would save the deceased from a second death.[98] For example, the corpse of a convicted criminal was ordered to be eliminated by throwing it into the Nile.[99] The Shabaka Stone indicates that Horus was anxious to have Isis and Nephthys rescue Osiris's already dead body from drowning (ḫwi=sn mḥi=f) in the Nile.[100] This must also be why, according to Herodotus, if ancient Egyptians found a body drowned in the Nile, the inhabitants of the nearest town were required to rescue the body and embalm it.[101] Drowning, like burning, was a punishment effective both in this life and in the next, particularly fitting for elements which represented Isfet in either life.

As for the case of Tti's wife, given the evidence, being taken to the riverbank (itȝy r mryt) probably did imply a death sentence. The wife of such a rebel would certainly be a dangerous and chaotic element. In addition, interrogating her makes very little sense. This deduction makes interrogation a very unlikely interpretation of the phrase. It is difficult to conceive that Kamose would not kill such a woman, so she must have been drowned at the riverbank.

Cases of sacrificial subsidiary burials found at Tel el-Daba from the Second Intermediate Period are almost certainly of Hyksos origin and are thus not included in this study. With the end of Hyksos domination, the Egyptians felt they were once again firmly under the rule of Ma'at. As the new dynasty would tell it, Order was firmly enthroned, and Egypt marched forward to its most powerful era yet.

---

[95] A.G. McDowell, *Jurisdiction in the Workmen's Community of Deir el-Medina*, Leiden: Nederlands Instituut Voor Het Nabije Oosten, 1990, pp. 157, 221.

[96] McDowell, *Jurisdiction in the Workmen's Community of Deir el-Medina*, pp. 218, 220. See also T. Eric Peet, *The Great Tomb-Robberies of the Twentieth Egyptian Dynasty*, Oxford: Clarendon, 1930.

[97] McDowell, p. 220.

[98] Kerry Muhlestein, "Death by Water: The Role of Water in Ancient Egypt's Treatment of Enemies and Juridical Process", in *L'Acqua Nell'antico Egitto: Vita, Rigenerazione, Incantesimo, Medicamento*, Alessia Amenta, Michela Luiselli, and Maria Novella Sordi (eds.), Rome: L'Erma di Bretschneider, 2005.

[99] See Hermann Kees, "Apotheosis by Drowning", in *Studies Presented to F.Ll. Griffith*, Oxford: Oxford University Press, 1932, p. 404; and Adolf Erman, "Ein Fall abgekürzter Justiz", in *Abhandlungen der Königlich preussischen Akademie der Wissenschaften zu Berlin, Philosophist Klasse*, Berlin: 1913, pp. 9–11.

[100] Shabaka Stone, lines 62–3.

[101] Herodotus, 2:90.

Middle Kingdom and Second Intermediate Period Evidence of Sanctioned Killing

Violence	Weak Evidence	Plausible Evidence	Strong Evidence	Very Strong Evidence
Slaying of tekenu at a burial			X	
General practice of slaying tekenu at burial		X		
Beheading/sacrificial slaughter of desecrators at Temple of Tod				X
Sacrificial burning of desecrators at Temple of Tod				X
Impalement of desecrators at Temple of Tod				X
Flaying of desecrators at Temple of Tod				X
Burning decreed for those who violate sacred land				X
Ongoing program of burning/cooking wrong doers				X
Ritual slaying as part of execration rite at Mirgissa				X
Ritual slaying on Hekaib altar		X		
Ongoing program of ritual slaying for failed execution of duty (as evidenced in the Shipwrecked Sailor)	X			
Capital punishment for adultery		X		
Capital punishment for runaway slaves				X
Kamose's drowning of the rebel Tti's wife			X	

Chapter 6

THE SLAYINGS OF THE GREAT PHARAOHS
(Dynasty 18)

It is the king who . . . binds the rebellious; who quiets the hostile; who is strong-armed toward robbers, applying violence to them who are violent, mighty-hearted against the mighty-hearted; who brings down the arm of him who is high; who shortens the hour of the cruel of heart; who causes the malcontent to perform the regulation of the laws, although his heart is unwilling, great in terror among criminals, lord of fear among the rebellious.

—The Stela of Intef

Almost at the end of their journey, the Kushite woman and her two children gazed in respectful awe at the remarkable stone features they were passing. Here just outside of Napata, the natural stone outcrop, truly resembling the sacred snake, protected the Kushites' southern capital. As the family rounded a bend in the road, the woman took her eyes from the scenery to see what lay before them as they approached the city. Quickly she grabbed her youngest, holding his face against her leg so that he could not see. There, in front of them, beside a sign warning the literate against a similar fate, was the impaled body of an enemy of Egypt. Such was the end of all those who dared rise in rebellion against the great warrior, King Amenhotep II.

When most of us think of ancient Egyptian architecture, the pyramids of the Old Kingdom come to mind. But when we think of Egypt's powerful pharaohs, the great rulers of the New Kingdom strike the most imposing figures: Thutmosis III, Amenhotep II, Seti I, and Ramesses the Great. These men's acts and self-created images rise out of the dust to invoke respect, even thousands of years later. If any Egyptian dynasty was the golden age of empire, it was the Eighteenth Dynasty. The warrior kings of this age carved out an empire which reached political, cultural, and military highs still admired. This dynasty produced enough compelling stories to entertain the avid reader for a lifetime.

The Eighteenth Dynasty witnessed the creation of new literary genres; additionally, more papyri, ostraca, and monumental inscriptions survive from this dynasty than from any of its predecessors. As a result, we have a tremendous amount of evidence for sanctioned killing from this single dynasty. Some of this evidence has already been discussed briefly in previous chapters, but it will now be placed in its proper historical context and its implications further explored. Furthermore, the evidence presented in this chapter will help us understand violence in the service of order far better than we have hitherto been able. Again we will see that Order was best served when Chaos was destroyed through ritual, burning, drowning, or decapitation. Other means of killing were employed, and often the means were not specified at all. But overall, these dynasts turned to forms of sanctioned killing with special theological meaning. The warrior kings who cultivated a reputation for battle prowess also passed on the greatest amount of evidence for prowess in sanctioned killing.

Possible Examples of Ritual Slaying

We begin by briefly revisiting some possible examples of ritual slaying associated with burial. It was during the Eighteenth Dynasty that Mentuherkhepeshef, a Fan Bearer and Mayor, was buried. The reader will recall that his tomb contained the depiction of two Nubians being strangled.[1] In the previous chapter, after assessing the evidence, we concluded that it was very likely that an

---

[1] Norman de Garis Davies, *Five Theban Tombs (Being Those of Mentuherkhepeshef, User, Daga, Nehemawȧy and Tati)*, Archaeological Survey of Egypt 21st Memoir, London: Egypt Exploration Fund, 1913, p. 15 and pl. 8. See also John Gwyn Griffiths, "The Tekenu, the Nubians and the Butic Burial", *Kush* 6, 1958.

actual execration-type ritual was depicted in this tomb. We can reasonably speculate that such a rite was not unique to the creation of this tomb, and that the rite happened elsewhere, especially since nothing in the titles of Mentuherkhepeshef set him apart for witnessing these slayings. Without further evidence, we can only conjecture, yet it is improbable that this one tomb, during the entire span of this dynasty, witnessed a burial rite that was practiced nowhere else.

It will further be remembered that Mentuherkhepeshef's tomb also contained an artistic representation of a rite involving a *tekenu* figure. We concluded that it was possible, perhaps even likely, that the tekenu depiction represented the ritual slaughter of a real person in association with burials. During Dynasty 18, the practice of depicting the tekenu rite in tombs truly flowered.

Eighteenth Dynasty Tekenu Tombs

Besides those already described in the tomb of Mentuherkhepeshef, depictions of a tekenu rite have been found in the Eighteenth Dynasty el-Kab tombs of Renni,[2] and Paheri (a mayor),[3] and in the Theben Tombs TT 24 (Nebamun, a Steward of the Royal Wife),[4] TT 81 (Ineni, Overseer of the Granary of Amun),[5] TT 15 (Tetiky, King's Son—not literally—and Mayor),[6] TT 42 (Amenmose, Captain of Troops and Eyes of the King in the Two Lands of Retjenu),[7] TT 260 (User, Scribe, Weigher of Amun, and Overseer of the Ploughed Lands of Amun),[8] TT 82 (Amenemhet, Scribe, Counter of the Grain of Amun, and Steward of the Vizier),[9] TT 100 (Rekhmire, Governor of the Town and Vizier),[10] TT 12 (Overseer of the Granary of the King's Wife and the King's Mother), TT 17 (Nebamun, Scribe and Physician of the King), TT 39 (Puimere, Second Prophet of Amun), TT 53 (Amenemhet, Agent of Amun), TT 55 (Ramose, Governor of the Town and Vizier), TT 78 (Horemeheb, King's Scribe and Scribe of Recruits), TT 92 (Sumnet, Royal Butler), TT 104 (Djehutinefer, Overseer of the Treasury and King's Scribe), TT 120 (Anen, Second Prophet of Amun), TT 122 (Amenhotep, Overseer of the Magazine of Amun), TT 125 (Duaneheh, First Herald and Overseer of the Estate of Amun), TT 127 (Senenmiah, King's Scribe, Overseer of All That Grows), TT 172 (Mentuywy, Royal Butler and Child of the Nursery), TT 224 (Ahmose called Hunay, Overseer of the Estate of the God's Wife), and TT 276 (Amenopet, Overseer of the Treasury of Gold and Silver, Judge, and Overseer of the Cabinet),[11] totaling 26 Eighteenth Dynasty tombs.

It is difficult to determine whether the sudden rise in tekenu depictions is due to an actual rise in the practice, to an accident of preservation, to a trend in tomb-scene depictions which allowed an already common event to be depicted, or to some other practice. There does not appear to be any pattern in the titles and roles of those whose tombs depicted this rite, other than that they were all powerful and influential men whose lives spanned from Ahmose's to Akhenaten's reigns. Nevertheless, not all powerful and influential men from this dynasty depicted this rite. Regardless of these complications, if the tekenu depiction does represent an actual sacrifice, which it seems to,[12] then we have evidence of a great number of ritual slayings in the Theban area during the Eighteenth Dynasty.

The existence of tekenu depictions in 26 tombs illuminates the possibility that the rite was performed elsewhere. The high number of representations suggests that perhaps dynastic practice represented the rite in the tomb of anyone who witnessed its enactment, but we cannot know. Possibly the ritual was more widespread than the attestations of its depiction. Extrapolation is further complicated by the near exclusivity of the practice in Theban tombs. The tekenu rite could be an example of a local custom. However, since a disproportionately large number of excavated tombs come from the Theban area, the apparent exclusivity may also be an accident of preservation or of excavation. It would be convenient to either generalize the existence of the rite elsewhere or to ascribe it to a peculiarity of the Theban necropolis, but we have insufficient data to do either of these.

We have also already mentioned another type of ritual slaying that was possibly connected to royal conquest during this era. Let us begin with the account of Ahmose, son of Abana. Among his many military adventures, this naval leader records that Thutmosis I crushed a Nubian rebellion and that on his return trip a Nubian was hung upside down[13] at the bow of the king's ship.[14] This Nubian may have been the first man that the king killed in battle, but in the light of similar cases, the possibility remains that the man either already had been a victim of, or was

---

[2] Joseph John Tylor, F. Lloyd Griffith, and Somers Clarke, *Wall Drawings and Monuments of El Kab. The Tomb of Renni*, London: B. Quaritch, 1900, pl. 8.

[3] Joseph John Tylor and F. Lloyd Griffith, *Wall Drawings and Monuments of El Kab. The Tomb of Paheri*, Boston: Egypt Exploration Fund, 1895, pl. 8.

[4] Urbain Bouriant, *Tombeau de Neb-Amon*, Cairo: Institut Français d'Archéologie Orientale, 1883, pp. 95–7.

[5] Tylor, Griffith, and Clarke, *Wall Drawings*, pp. 111–13.

[6] George Edward Stanhope Molyneux Herbert, Earl of Carnarvon *et al.*, *Five Years' Explorations at Thebes: A Record of Work Done 1907–1911*, London: H. Frowde, 1912, pl. 9.

[7] Nina M. Cummings Davies and Norman de Garis Davies, *The Tombs of Menkheperasonb, Amenmose, and Another*, London: Egypt Exploration Society, 1926, pl. 38.

[8] Tylor, Griffith, and Clarke, *Wall Drawings*, p. 113.

[9] Nina M. Cummings Davies and Alan Henderson Gardiner, *The Tomb of Amenemhet (no. 82)*, Society of Egypt Exploration (ed.), Theban Tombs Series 1, Oxford: Oxford University Press, 1973.

[10] Norman de Garis Davies, *The Tomb of Rekh-mi-Re at Thebes*, New York: Arno, 1973.

[11] Tylor, Griffith, and Clarke, *Wall Drawings*, p. 112.

[12] Besides the analysis in chapter 5, see Alberto Ravinel Whitney Green, "The Role of Human Sacrifice in the Ancient Near East", PhD dissertation, University of Michigan, 1973, 251–2, who, after analyzing the evidence, writes that the depictions "reveal that at the death of certain important individuals, human beings were offered as sacrifices along with animals in the burial ceremony."

[13] To understand the significance of being upside down, see Mikhail Chegodaev, "Lest One Be Turned Upside Down", *DE*, 1988, 40.

[14] *Urk.* 4, 1–11, especially lines 35–6.

destined for, ritual slaying. The evidence we will examine next will buttress this proposition.

If any king were proud of his ability as a warrior, Amenhotep II was. This was a man who ensured that he was known for his strength, ability, and ferocity in armed contests. Amenhotep II performed the most striking example of slaying connected with ritual water processions. Always one to ensure that his heroic deeds were well known, he erected two tablets, one at Amada and the other at Elephantine, which declared uniformly his acts. The only significant difference between the tablets is the scene depicted at the top. On the Amada stela, Amenhotep II offers wine to Amun-re and Harakhti. In the same place, the Elephantine stela shows the king receiving life and stability from Amun and Khnum. The text on the tablets is nearly identical. The crucial part of the text for our study comes after the description of a successful campaign in Upper Retjenu (Canaan). Upon his return, the king performed a ritual sacrifice: "His majesty returned with great joy to his father Amun. He slew the seven princes with his mace himself. They were from the area of Tachsi[15] and had been given upside-down to the prow of the King's ship by the name of 'Amenhotep-who-reestablishes-the-two-lands.'"[16]

The tenses of the verbs in this passage leave some ambiguity. The passage could be read with any of the verbs pluperfect, thus changing the chronological order of the events. However, the translation above does the least violence to the text and is most in harmony with our understanding of prisoners and water. The king had apparently hung the prisoners upside down on the prow of his ship as he sailed home, and then slew them with his own mace. Afterwards the bodies of six of the slain princes were hung before the wall of Thebes; the other body Amenhotep II hung in Napata, and undoubtedly he transported this victim to this far-off city on the prow of a ship. If this sequence of events is correct, then there can be little doubt that the slaying of these seven princes was a ritual act; the battle was long over, and the king had returned.[17] Even if the king slew the princes before the boat journey, he almost certainly killed them after the battle—it is unlikely the king met and slew seven princes in the battle. Furthermore, if these princes were slain after battle, it is improbable that they were slain in anything but a ritual setting.

Tutankhamun probably did a similar thing, as has been mentioned before. Grimm has pointed out that a relief from Karnak shows a large ship, on the front of which were hung dead prisoners and a cage containing a bound Asiatic prisoner.[18] Grimm postulates, with good evidence, that the ship is part of a festival of triumph over enemies, which Amenhotep II's and Thutmosis I's ships appear to have also been part of.[19] It will be remembered that the cage pictured in this relief matched exactly the real cage found near the boat pits in a Giza excavation, making it likely that this practice extended at least from the Fourth through the Eighteenth Dynasties[20]—and probably into the Pre-dynastic Period, if the depiction from Gebel Sheikh Suleiman is of a similar event. Furthermore, some reliefs depict royal boats with a kiosk sporting a smiting scene. We know of reliefs depicting such boat kiosks with Akhenaten, Nefertiti, Ramesses III, and Herihor smiting foreigners.[21] These depictions more strongly associate ritual slaying of prisoners with king's ships.

In the light of Amenhotep II's stelae and Tutankhamun's relief, it is quite possible that the event which Ahmose son of Abana records about Thutmosis I hanging a vanquished Nubian from the bow of his boat is an example of ritual slaying. The conclusion fits in perfectly with what was apparently a long standing tradition. Indeed, the knowledge that this ritual was performed by three kings of this dynasty naturally leads to speculation about whether hanging victims of ritual slaying on the prow of a boat was part of a festival that all eighteenth-dyanasty kings celebrated. The conclusion that all kings did celebrate their ritual is further justified by evidence from earlier periods. Deduction indicates that the rite was likely regular, but without further evidence, we can only categorize this conclusion as possible evidence of ritual slaying. Further analysis of the difference between dead prisoners and live prisoners being paraded on the royal barque will take place below.

Further light is cast on the issue of royal ritual slaying by the tomb inscription of Amenemheb. After serving successfully under Thutmosis III, Amenemheb preserved his account of the accession of Amenhotep II. Unfortunately, the text of the lines that interest us is somewhat broken, but we can make out that as part of his accession, Amenhotep did something in the "Red Land" and then "cut off the heads of their chiefs" ($dm.n=f\ tpw\ srw=sn$).[22] Breasted writes that "Amenemhab doubtless refers to the sacrifice of the seven kings of Tikhshi."[23] Piehl[24] and Green[25] hold the same view. This has become

---

[15] Rainer Hannig, *Grosses Handwörterbuch Ägyptisch-Deutsch: (2800-950 v. Chr.): die Sprache der Pharaonen*, Kulturgeschichte der antiken Welt, Bd. 64, Mainz: P. von Zabern, 1995, p. 1404, describes Tachsi as being between Kadesh and the Orontes.

[16] *Stela of Amenophis II, and Inscription of Meneptah*, Cairo, 1963, vol. 5, line 5 of pl. 4(facsimile), lines 16–17 of the insert of the stela of Amenhotep II (this publication is unbound, and the loose pages are unnumbered), *Urk.* 4, 1279; for another translation, see *ARE* 2, 313.

[17] Independently assessed but agreeing are Green, "The Role of Human Sacrifice in the Ancient Near East", pp. 245–8; and Nigel Davies, *Human Sacrifice in History and Today*, New York: William Morrow and Company, 1981, p. 36.

[18] Alfred Grimm, "Ein Käfig für einen Gefangenen in einem Ritual zur Vernichtung von Feinden", *JEA* 73, 1987, 203–4. A picture of the ship can be seen in H. Chevrier, "Rapport sur les travaux de Karnak (1952-1953)", *ASAE* 53, no. 1, 1955, pl. 7.

[19] Grimm, "Ein Käfig für einen Gefangenen", pp. 204, 206.

[20] Grimm, "Ein Käfig für einen Gefangenen", 204.

[21] Emma Swan Hall, *The Pharaoh Smites His Enemies: A Comparative Study*, Münchner ägyptologische Studien, Munich: Deutscher Kunstverlag, 1986, vol. 44, pp. 25–6, 36, figs. 39, 40, 66, 82.

[22] *Urk.* 4, 1408–13; see also Georg Ebers, "Das Grab und die Biographie des Feldhauptmanns Amen em heb", *Zeitschrift der Deutschen Morgenländischen Gesellschaft*, 1876, pl. 3; K. Piehl, "Varia II", *Zeitschrift für ägyptische Sprache*, 1885, p. 115.

[23] *ARE* 2, p. 319, n. b.

[24] Piehl, "Varia II", p. 115n3.

the generally accepted interpretation, though there is little reason for the interpretation's acceptance other than that the stelae and Amenemheb all record that Amenhotep II slew foreign leaders. Some doubt is cast on the theory by the fact that the Amada and Elephantine stelae record that Amenhotep used a mace, but Amenemheb reports that the heads were cut off. Most significantly, the slaying of seven princes mentioned in the Amada and Elephantine stelae were from the third year of Amenhotep II's reign. It is so improbable that Amenhotep II would have waited until the third year of his reign to perform his coronation rite that these two events are almost certainly separate.

The sacrifice of foreign leaders at Amenhotep II's accession is pregnant with the possibility of extrapolation. It is implausible that, in such a ritualized and stylized event as his coronation, Amenhotep II would have engaged in a rite that no one before or after him did. However, it is also doubtful that, if others had performed the same ritual, we would only know of Amenhotep's performance. This second implausibility is made more implausible by the fact that we learn of Amenhotep II's action from a fairly mimetic text, the long and very personal autobiographical inscription of Amenemheb. This mimetic source tips the balance in favor of such a rite being a regular part of accession rituals, but again we are in the realm of conjecture.

Under the heading of possible ritual slaying, we must place one more aforementioned event in its proper historical context: the human execration rites performed in eighteenth-dynasty Avaris, found in area H-3 of Tel el-Dab'a. As noted above, three human skulls were found in the midst of Egyptian pottery from what was presumably the execration version of the rite of "smashing the red pots."[26] Furthermore, two other men found in the adjacent pit appear to have been ritually slaughtered in execration rites. This find appears to be of the same order as the Mirgissa find and makes yet another example of ritual slaying almost inescapable.

Akhenaten slew a great number of people after a war. This may not have been an example of ritual slaying, the possibility of which will be discussed below. After a Kushite group rebelled, Akhenaten sent an army who crushed them. Upon subduing the Kushites, 145 were taken as living captives, and 225 more became "those who were impaled" (ntyw ḥr ḫt).[27] These men were obviously slain after victory was in the Egyptians' hands, and the men were under the control of Egypt's army. Furthermore, Akhenaten threatened a swaying vassal in the Levant that if he did not change his ways, he and his entire family would die by the king's ax.[28] While we cannot know if this type of threat was ever carried out against any vassal, the threat may attest to the notion that there was a known method of royal execution via ax. It also demonstrates the type of act deemed worthy of execution.

In summary, we have seen a great deal of evidence for various forms of ritual slaying in the Eighteenth Dynasty. Four Nubians were almost certainly killed in connection with the burial of Mentuherkhepeshef. Furthermore, killing humans was likely a part of the tekenu rite. The tekenu rite was depicted in at least 26 burials in Thebes and el-Kab alone during this dynasty. Additionally, Amenhotep II and Tutankhamun almost certainly ritually slew enemies and hung them from the prows of their ships, and Thutmosis I possibly did the same. These total to at least nine people killed in this ritual. Moreover, more were slain by Amenhotep II at his accession. Finally, a ritual slaying also appears certain at Avaris, as a human became part of an execration rite. If all of these events actually occurred, then we know of at least 40 ritual sacrifices in the Eighteenth Dynasty. If Akhenaten's slaying of prisoners of war was also performed in a ritual context, and if his numbers are reliable, then 225 more can be added to this tally. Furthermore, with three kings having slain prisoners for a water parade celebrating a victory over enemies, and four other rulers, two from this dynasty, depicting boats with smiting scenes on them, this was possibly a rite engaged in by all eighteenth-dynasty rulers. It is further possible that sacrifice upon accession was also more common than the single episode we know of, but we can only hypothesize.

The Death Penalty

The availability of a greater variety and number of texts from the Eighteenth Dynasty allows a greater knowledge of which crimes were worthy of death. Here we will examine the evidence and evaluate the possibilities that execution was carried out during this period. In chapter 9, after amassing a greater body of evidence, we will analyze what types of crimes were worthy of death, look for patterns, and attempt to understand why.

One of our probable cases of the death penalty has already been briefly mentioned. This is the case of the woman, Heria (ḥriɜ), who was found guilty of stealing a copper chisel. This incident took place in the Nineteenth Dynasty, but the case record alludes to another possible execution from the Eighteenth, and thus is considered here. Though Heria swore that she had not stolen the chisel, her house was searched, and there the missing object was found with some equipment stolen from the temple of Amun. After this examination, she was

---

[25] Green, "The Role of Human Sacrifice in the Ancient Near East", pp. 249–51.
[26] Perla Fuscaldo, "Tell al-Dab'a: Two Execration Pits and a Foundation Deposit", in *Egyptology at the Dawn of the Twenty-first Century: Proceedings of the Eighth International Congress of Egyptologists, Cairo, 2000*, Zahi Hawass (ed.), New York: American University in Cairo Press, 2003, vol. 1, p. 186.
[27] See the Buhen Stela as published in H. S. Smith, *The Fortress of Buhen: the Inscriptions*, London: Egypt Exploration Society, 1976, pp. 124–5 and pl. 29. See also Alan R. Schulman, "The Nubian War of Akhenaton", in *L'Égyptologie en 1979: Axes prioritaires de recherches*, Paris: Centre National de la Recherche Scientifique, 1982, vol. 2, 301–2. For a discussion on the term rendered here as *impalement*, see chapter 7, the section on royal inscriptions. The number of prisoners slain may have been exaggerated.
[28] *EA*, 162.

declared "worthy of death."²⁹ We do not know if Heria was executed, because the matter was referred to the vizier, and there the record ends. However, referral to the vizier appears to have been the normal procedure for possible death sentences. It is from the document recommending Heria's death, Ostracon Nash 1, that we learn of the circumstances. We have no document recording the vizier's actions in her case. Knowing exactly why this punishment was worthy of death is complicated by several factors, which will be discussed in chapter 9.³⁰

It is likewise from Ostracon Nash 1 that we learn of an eighteenth-dynasty possible case of capital punishment, which we have also in chapter 5. The reader will recall that as part of an argument for Heria's death penalty, the judges from Deir el-Medina brought to the vizier's attention a case law precedent for such acts. These judges state that earlier in their town a woman who had been caught stealing a copper object had been sent to the river bank. While it is inconclusive that being sent to the riverbank meant being drowned, the appeal to this case as an argument for giving Heria the death penalty seems to indicate that the phrase did imply death, at least in this situation.³¹

Another ambiguous case may involve a potential sentence of death. We read of a scribe who had conscripted a group of corvee laborers from the Temple of Thoth in Memphis to do work for the Temple of Hauron in Memphis. He was warned by a man called Djehutiemheb that such conscription was beyond his responsibility and that the scribe must immediately correct the situation. In a broken section, Djehutiemheb exhorts the scribe to return the men immediately. Following this exhortation, Djehutiemheb warns the scribe that "death is the way in which I am involved with you" (*mwt p3 nty tw=i im=f m-di=k*).³² This last phrase may mean that our errant scribe has committed something worthy of death, and that nothing can belay that sentence. Such an interpretation is strengthened when Djehutiemheb goes on to say "you wish to die (*mr.n=k mwt*) rather than live."³³ It is also possible that the stern words served as a warning that if the situation were not corrected immediately, then such a sentence would be carried out. Alternatively, perhaps this threat was merely a hyperbolic way of demonstrating the seriousness of the act.

A tantalizing bit of relevant information is presented in the Horemheb edict. Here the king warns against just such conscription, but the modifier describing how serious a crime this was (such as one "worthy of death") falls in a broken part of the text, and thus cannot be ascertained.³⁴ The poor preservation of both of these pertinent texts leaves us with little conclusive evidence. It is possible that unauthorized use of corvee labor—perhaps only of labor for temples—was a capital offense, but this is based on plausible, not strong, evidence.

The Horemheb edict does outline a crime which was "worthy of death." It explicitly states that any judge who opposed justice, possibly by accepting a bribe, was committing a "great crime worthy of death."³⁵ Of course, we have no idea whether or not this was ever enacted, but the knowledge that such venality was seen as a capital offense is important.

Another possibly royal instruction is that of Amenhotep III, found in the funerary temple of Amenhotep, son of Hapu. This inscription has been dated orthographically and grammatically to the Twenty-first Dynasty, but Varille, pointing out the historical accuracies on the hieratic inscription of this stela, argued that it was a rephrasing of an earlier text.³⁶ This stela contains instructions for guards of the Theban necropolis and decrees death for those who violated the tomb and chapel of Amenhotep, son of Hapu. Such violators would be "put on the burning flames of the king in the day of his wrath. His Uraeus will spit flame on their head, annihilating flesh, it will devour bodies. It will happen as with Apophis on the morning of the first day of the year."³⁷ As with all cases of inscriptional violence, this text may call for supernatural punishment as opposed to punishment that would be inflicted by governmental authorities. This interpretation is indicated by the reference to a spitting Uraeus and to Apophis. Antithetically, the reference to the furnace of the king is so similar to the Tod inscription we encountered earlier, and is so concrete, that the text may have an intended actualization in the here and now. As has been noted persistently, both applications may have been connoted

---

²⁹ See Ostracon Nash 1, Verso lines 2–3, as in Jaroslav Černý and Alan H. Gardiner, *Hieratic Ostraca*, Oxford: Oxford University Press, 1957, pl. 46. See also A.G. McDowell, *Jurisdiction in the Workmen's Community of Deir el-Medina*, Leiden: Nederlands Instituut Voor Het Nabije Oosten, 1990, p. 221; Ellen D. Bedell, "Criminal Law in the Egyptian Ramesside Period", PhD dissertation, Brandeis University, 1973, 14, 149; and Morris Bierbrier, *The Tomb-Builders of the Pharaohs*, London: British Museum, 1982, p. 106.

³⁰ See also Bedell, "Criminal Law in the Egyptian Ramesside Period", 149–52.

³¹ Bedell, "Criminal Law in the Egyptian Ramesside Period", pp. 15, 159–64, argues for this interpretation, while McDowell, *Jurisdiction*, p. 221, believes that it probably did not indicate capital punishment.

³² P. Turin A, 4, 9–10, as in Alan H. Gardiner, *Late Egyptian Miscellanies*, Brussels: Fondation Égyptologue Reine Élisabeth, 1937, p. 124. Ricardo A. Caminos, *Late Egyptian Miscellanies*, London: Oxford University Press, 1954, p. 456, translated, "What is the way of doing it [returning the laborers]? At once! The situation in which I am with you is death." T.G.H. James, *Pharaoh's People: Scenes From Life in Imperial Egypt*, London: Bodley Head, 1984, p. 87, translated, "How is the matter [returning the men] to be done? Immediately! Death is how I am involved with you."

³³ P. Turin A, 2, 5.

³⁴ Kurt Pfluger, "The Edict of King Haremhab", *JNES* 5, 1946, no. 4, 265.

³⁵ Benedict G. Davies, "Fascicle VI", in *Egyptian Historical Records of the Later Eighteenth Dynasty*, Barbara Cumming and Wolfgang Helck (eds.), Warminster, England: Aris and Phillips, 1982, p. 81; Pfluger, "Edict of King Haremhab", p. 265. Also Bedell, "Criminal Law in the Egyptian Ramesside Period", p. 152; and Hasan el-Saady, "Considerations on Bribery in Ancient Egypt", *SAK* 25, 1998, 297–8.

³⁶ A. Varille, *Inscriptions concernant l'architecte Amenhotep, fils de Hapou*, Cairo: L'Institut Francais D'archeologie Orientale, 1968, pp. 81–5.

³⁷ Text no. 27, line 8, as presented in Varille, *Inscriptions concernant l'architecte Amenhotep, fils de Hapou*, p. 71. See also C. Robichon and A. Varille, *Le temple du scribe royal Amenhotep, fils de Hapou*, Cairo: L'Institut Français D'archeologie Orientale, 1936, pp. 1–17.

and desired. Since the stela is intended to provide a protective force of men for the necropolis, and instructions for the performance of their duty, at least a partial earthly enactment is implied. It is preferable to see the Uraeus and Apophis images as a mythologization of an actual event instead of as a plea only to the supernatural realm. This issue will be treated at length below.

Moreover, the text outlines capital punishment for misappropriation of services designated for specific offerings, something attested from the first-intermediate-period decree of Demedjibtawy to the Ramesside era. Furthermore, it refers to the fire of the king, again something attested in the First Intermediate Period and something that will be consistently demonstrated throughout the duration of the time period treated in this study. Combining all of these factors creates the impression that Amenhotep III likely intended death by burning for those who interfered with the funerary cult of his trusted advisor.[38] It should also be noted that this text reaffirms the idea that burning brings about complete annihilation.

In Hatshepsut's Deir el-Bahri account of her coronation ceremony, wherein Thutmosis I purportedly enthroned her, Thutmosis I declares that "he who shall speak an evil thing in the path of her majesty shall die."[39] Such an edict, whether from Thutmosis I or Hatshepsut herself, was probably necessitated by Hatshepsut's particular need to suppress everything that would detract from her legitimacy. Nothing can be extrapolated from Thutmosis I's edict, but it is a clear description of a capital offense. It may never have been enforced.

Inscriptional Threats

From this period, we know of two inscriptions that contribute to our knowledge of death decrees in threat formulae. The first, on the Tefnakht stela, is somewhat like the decree of Amenhotep III listed above. It states that the offender will go to the fire that comes from the mouth of Sakhmet.[40] This sounds very much like a supernatural punishment, and it is probable that a supernatural punishment is intended. However, it is also possible that this inscription mythologizes a real punishment to be enacted in this lifetime.

The second threat is very specific about its earthly application. This inscription stipulates that the offender's "lifetime will not continue on earth."[41] Nothing could be more explicit about the end of a person's mortal life nor in its delineation of this punishment being enacted on Earth, a phrase that frequently designates those who live on this earth, not in another realm. The threat does not imply a second death.

Funerary Literature

Besides the textual windows afforded by tomb inscriptions, we can also gain a window into daily life events from the funerary literature of the Eighteenth Dynasty. This time period saw the rise of new funerary literature. Notable among these are the Book of the Dead ("the book of going forth by day") and the Amduat ("that which is in the netherworld"). As previously noted, funerary texts represent an idealized, not an actual, life, yet they still reveal the mindset and experiences of their creators.

We first turn to texts in the Book of the Dead. This new-kingdom collection of funerary spells was first written on mummy cloths and coffins and later appeared on papyri, which became the normal medium.[42] As with other funerary literature, its purpose was to give its owner all that was necessary to achieve the desired state in the afterlife. Some of the spells in the book contain references to decapitation. Spell 71 speaks of a *wedjet*-eye that chops off heads.[43] Part of spell 43 is designed to prevent a person's head from being chopped off.[44] The persistence in funerary literature, with its continual transformation of form and content, of the motif of decapitation points to a likelihood that this form of punishment was as longstanding as Egyptian civilization itself. Additionally, the Book of the Dead also contains many references to burning, such as demons and snakes that burn people,[45] gates that burn people, and gates that simultaneously cut and burn people.[46]

The Amduat is attested from the time of Hatshepsut or Tuthmosis III. From this time until Ramesses III, every royal tomb contained extensive portions of this book of the afterlife.[47] Its use changed and expanded after Ramesses III. The content of the Amduat essentially guided the deceased through the netherworld to the desired destination. Pictures played a more integral part in the book than in previous funerary literature. Within the Amduat text, we again find evidence for decapitation. A vignette within the Amduat shows a knife-wielding goddess standing near many headless victims. The caption for the picture is "chopping off your heads."[48]

Additionally, the *šms* glyph— which we have

---

[38] See also Harco Willems, "Crime, Cult and Capital Punishment (Mo'alla Inscription 8)", *JEA* 76, 1990, 40.
[39] *Urk.* 4, 257.
[40] As in W. Spiegelberg, "Die Tefnakhthos-stele des Museums von Athen", *Recueil des Travaux* 25, 1903, 190. Also Jan Assmann, "Inscriptional Violence and the Art of Cursing: A Study of Performative Writing", *Stanford Literature Review* 9, no. 1, 1992, 62.
[41] *Urk.* 4, 401, 2; see also Willems, "Crime, Cult and Capital Punishment", p. 42.
[42] See Erik Hornung, *The Ancient Egyptian Books of the Afterlife*, David Lorton (trans.), Ithaca: Cornell University Press, 1999, p. 13.
[43] *BD*, 71.
[44] *BD*, 43. See also J. Zandee, *Death as an Enemy According to Ancient Egyptian Conceptions*, Leiden: E.J. Brill, 1960, p. 154.
[45] *BD*, 17.
[46] *BD*, 146; Zandee, *Death as an Enemy*, p. 134; and Bedell, "Criminal Law in the Egyptian Ramesside Period", p. 166.
[47] Hornung, *The Ancient Egyptian Books*, pp. 27–30.
[48] Amduat XI. 76; Zandee, *Death as an Enemy*, p. 152.

already discussed as a possible device of decapitation, was pictured as a weapon.[49]

The Amduat also contains evidence of burning as a form of death. The references are too numerous to record here, but Zandee has gathered an impressive number of them, including references to being burned by the Uraeaus of the king—similar to the punishment mentioned in the stela of Amenhotep, son of Hapu—and several gates which burn enemies.[50] The bad things that could happen to a person in the afterlife become too numerous to list. Indeed, the Amduat constitutes a study unto itself. For our purposes, we can see that decapitation and burning remained concerns expressed in the funerary literature of the Eighteenth Dynasty, in all probability reflecting concerns which accompanied life on earth. The persistence of these two forms of punishment is revealed by their persistence and proliferation in funerary literature.

Even with the changes in the availability of textual evidence, we have seen that the forms of punishment employed in this period are consistent with those which preceded. The reasons for inflicting death we knew of from earlier dynasties also continued in this era, and we also have welcome additional information from the newfound genres. This new information probably did not represent a change in religious or juridical practice, though the possibility cannot be wholly excluded. It is more likely that the new information resulted from either new textual practices or from better preservation. Whatever the reason, it is abundantly clear that sanctioned killing was a part of the eighteenth-dynasty milieu.

Eighteenth Dynasty Evidence of Sanctioned Killing

Violence	Weak Evidence	Plausible Evidence	Strong Evidence	Very Strong Evidence
Four Nubians sacrificed in association with burial of Mentuherkhepeshef				X
Similar sacrifices performed with other burials			X	
26 tekenu sacrifices in association with burials			X*	
Similar sacrifices at other tombs		X		
Ritual sacrifice of enemy by Thutmosis I			X	
Ritual slaying of seven enemy princes by Amenhotep III				X
Sacrifice of enemy leaders at coronation of Amenhotep III				X
Ritual slaying of enemies by Tutankhamun				X
Ongoing ritual slaying of enemies by other kings			X	
Ongoing ritual slaying of enemies at coronation of other kings		X		
Human execration rite at Avaris—three skulls				X
Human execration rite at Avaris—two skeletons			X	
Impalement of 225** Nubian prisoners of war by Akhenaten				X
Death by drowning for an earlier copper thief at Deir el-Medina				X
Potential for death for diverting corvee labor				X
Potential burning for interference with mortuary cult of a favorite of the king			X	
Death decreed for rendering false rulings				X
Death decreed for those who speak against Hatshepsut				X
Burning decreed for tomb desecration		X		
Death decreed for tomb desecration				X
Ongoing practice of burning of criminals			X	
Ongoing practice of decapitation of criminals			X	

* Case borders between plausible and strong evidence
** Number may be exaggerated

---

[49] Amduat VIII, center register; Zandee, *Death as an Enemy*, p. 226.
[50] Zandee, *Death as an Enemy*, pp. 133–4; Bedell, "Criminal Law in the Egyptian Ramesside Period", p. 166.

Chapter 7

INSTANCES OF INTRIGUE: THE RAMESSIDE ERA

You may grant breath to him whom you like among them, and you may slay whom you desire.

—Medinet Habu

Ramesses III watched as the smoke from the sacred brazier wafted away in the wind, dispersing the last of the birds he had offered in gratitude for his successful Libyan war. Now that the ceremony was over, his Vizier dared approach him. "What does his majesty—life prosperity and health be yours—desire that we do with the captured Libyan chiefs?" Ramesses gripped his ritual blade all the tighter, turning to his Vizier with a look that matched the Uraeus on his brow, "Bring them forth, pinioned, as were our sacrificial birds."

After Dynasty 18 weakened, Egypt experienced a resurgence under a new line of kings. As Ramesses I brought a military family to the throne, Egypt rediscovered its military prowess and began pushing its borders back toward the expanse they had obtained during the heady days of the Eighteenth Dynasty's greatest kings. While Ramesses I's reign was short lived, his name lived on, after the successful rule of Seti I, in Ramesses II, otherwise known as Ramesses the Great. During his rule, Ramesses II not only recaptured most of Egypt's land, but he raised his personal, and thus Egypt's national, prestige to all-time heights. Through architecture, statuary, inscriptions, military campaigns, and longevity, Ramesses the Great ensured himself an eternal legacy. He commanded such respect that most of the rulers who succeeded him for the next dozen generations named themselves after him. Egyptologists refer to this period as the Ramesside Era.

Because of the discovery of many juridical texts, the Ramesside Era provides us with more specific information regarding sanctioned killing than does any other period. The Nauri Decree of Seti I, the documents concerning the Harem Conspiracy during the reign of Ramesses III, and the texts dealing with the Great Tomb Robberies all cast a great deal of light on our understanding of Egyptian ritual slaying. The latter two instances, the Harem Conspiracy and the Great Tomb Robberies, consist of so much intrigue, so many storyline twists and turns, and such an abundance of politics and legal wrangling that they are equal to any legal thrillers of our time. As with other periods, several other pieces of Ramesside-era evidence are also relevant.

Royal Inscriptions

Seti I was a stern, seasoned general. Building upon the brief reign of his father, Ramesses I, Seti forcefully returned Egypt to the path of glory. His building programs, military campaigns, and royal decrees reset the standard of Egyptian magnificence. One of Seti's royal inscriptions contains a possible stipulation for death. At Kanais, in southern Egypt, he built a small temple on the path leading to gold and stone quarries. Three inscriptions were commissioned for the sanctuary, the third of which concerns us.[1] Herein Seti I warns his successors that if they overthrow any of his plans, they will have to answer for it before a tribunal in Heliopolis. A break in the text makes a more certain identification of this tribunal impossible, though the end of the stanza refers to the Ennead, a group of nine founding gods. After the reference to the tribunal, Seti threatens the offenders with burning: "They [the tribunal] will be red like a hewn firebrand. They will burn the flesh of those who will not listen to me. They will punish he who ruins my plans. He will be delivered to the justice hall of the netherworld. [I

---

[1] S. Schott, *Kanais, der Tempel Sethos I. im Wâdi Mia*, Göttingen, Germany: Vandenhoeck & Ruprecht, 1961.

have said this to protect] you. He who is free of crime will be spared. But woe to him whose heart strays. The Ennead, they will judge him."[2]

While this is certainly a grim fate, the language begs the question as to whether this fate was meant to overtake the future king(s) while on the earth or in the afterlife. Several elements point toward the latter interpretation. First, who would have the authority to force a king to submit to the punishment? Second, the reference to Heliopolis and the Ennead suggests that the gods would be responsible for this punishment. Since the Ennead's representative on earth was the transgressor, it could not turn to him for a mortal realization of justice. Third, it is explicitly stated that the king will be delivered to a slaughterhouse in the *Du'at*, the netherworld. Taken together, it is hard to argue that this threat is applicable in the mortal realm.

However, the inscription continues by warning officials who suggest that future rulers remove workmen for the temple. These unfortunate souls were destined for fire that would consume them, since Seti I had created the place for the benefit of his dynasty and since god abhors those who interfere.[3] This threat may have been intended to stand as a law and the punishment to be carried out by future rulers. Such an interpretation is supported by Seti's reminder to future rulers that he has made the temple and decree for their good. This line could be encouragement to actually enforce the decree. However, the reference to god abhorring those who interfere casts a supernatural element into the scene. Possibly, a dual application—both in this realm and in the next—is intended. However, the previous appeals to otherworldly justice, combined with these stanzas, which also make appeals to deities for enforcement, make an interpretation of real-world application unlikely.

Seti I's Nauri Decree is a larger and more famous royal inscription. Upon building a cenotaph for Osiris at Abydos, Seti exempted a large estate from the taxes and other burdens that were to provide for the Abydos temple. In Nauri, between the second and third cataracts, a large inscription of the exemption decree was made. The statements thereon amount to royal laws. In an effort to prevent the mistreatment or misappropriation of the goods and personnel dedicated to the Osireion, Seti outlined a number of punishments for a number of possible crimes. Two particular portions of the inscription concern us. In the midst of a variety of misdeeds—most of which were punishable by exaggerated restitution, beatings, and wounds—one crime is designated as deserving of death:

> Concerning any keeper of cattle, any keeper of hounds, any herder belonging to the House who peculate any of the animals belonging to the House to another as with he who causes it to be offered in another venue, so that it is not offered to Osiris, his Lord in the House, punishment will be done to him by throwing him down and impaling him (*sḫr=f diw ḥr tp ḫt*), forfeiting his wife and children and all his property to the House, and requiring the head of animals from him to whom it was given as stolen goods from the House, at the rate of one hundred to one.[4]

After this dire decree, the inscription continues listing other sundry violations and their attached punishments, which all resemble the non-lethal punishments that had been delineated before. The only other anomaly is connected to the stipulation against officials who had interfered with or embezzled the proceeds. These people were to be punished by having the goods recovered, "but his majesty has avoided causing [those who had mishandled the proceeds to be thrown to the ground and] impaled (*ḥr tp ḫt*), desiring to let him be convicted in any council[5] of any city to which they go."[6] Why it was necessary to note that these people were spared impalement is not at all clear. Nor can we know what letting a city council convict the guilty means. Possibly, the city council was to enact the impalement, but since, as will be discussed below, capital punishment was usually the king's or the vizier's prerogative, this seems unlikely. Edgerton argues that the men were sent to a city council to prevent locals from taking capricious actions.[7] This may be, but only guesswork leads to this conclusion. Bedell believes that this passage demonstrates that the local authorities were fully authorized to dispense fatal judgments as outlined by the decree.[8] Again, nothing other than conjecture confirms this opinion. The purpose of Seti's caveat is yet to be determined.

The question remains, how was the crime for which impalement was to be meted out so different from other crimes? In contrast to the unauthorized conscription of corvée labor mentioned in chapter 6, anyone who took people away from serving Osiris was to be given blows and wounds.[9] Anyone stopping the estate's boats was to be given blows and wounds.[10] Anyone who moved the boundary of the land was to have his ears cut off and be relegated to hard labor.[11] Anyone who attacked the estate's hunters, who stole goods, or who assaulted the

---

[2] *KRI* 1, 69; reconstruction provided by Kitchen. Miriam Lichtheim, *Ancient Egyptian Literature, A Book of Readings: The New Kingdom*, Berkeley: University of California Press, 1975, p. 55, translates *ḥb.t* as "slaughterhouse."
[3] *KRI* 1, 70.
[4] My translation is indebted to that of F. Lloyd Griffith, "The Abydos Decree of Seti I at Nauri", *JEA* 13, nos. 1–4, 1927, pl. 42, lines 74–8. See also *KRI* 1:55–56.
[5] See I. Lourie, "A Note on Egyptian Law-Courts", *JEA* 27, nos. 1 & 2, 1931, 62–4; A.G. McDowell, *Jurisdiction in the Workmen's Community of Deir el-Medina*, Leiden: Nederlands Instituut Voor Het Nabije Oosten, 1990, pp. 143–78; and M.M. Bontty, "Conflict Management in Ancient Egypt", PhD dissertation, University of California at Los Angeles, 1997, 180–204, for discussions on the role of the *qnbt*.
[6] Reconstruction is Griffith's; Griffith, "Abydos Decree", pl. 43.
[7] W.F. Edgerton, "The Nauri Decree of Seti I: A Translation and Analysis of the Legal Portion", *JNES* 6, no. 4, 1947, 226, 230.
[8] E.D. Bedell, "Criminal Law in the Egyptian Ramesside Period", PhD dissertation, Brandeis University, 1973, 151.
[9] *KRI* 1, 52–3.
[10] *KRI* 1, p. 53.
[11] *KRI* 1, p. 54.

estate's herdsmen was to be given blows and wounds.[12] Other similar crimes required similar punishments, which always included exaggerated restitution if something had been stolen. Only the embezzling or misoffering of cattle by a keeper of cattle, a keeper of hounds, or a herdsman, demanded the death penalty. While we will further discuss which elements merit sanctioned killing below, here I submit that no plausible explanation for the severe consequences of this one act has been teased out of this conundrum. Such a lack of understanding makes any generalization from this decree impossible. Instead we may catalogue it as a singular incident, and no more.

Excursus on Reason for Harshness

Bedell argues that the betrayal of trust and sacrilege combined to bring about such dire consequences.[13] However, other acts combine the same elements but receive a lesser punishment. Lorton feels that the harsh punishment was because the property had been both stolen and alienated to a third party.[14] Similarly, McDowell notes that both selling embezzled sacrificial animals and sacrificing them to another god alienate the animals from their dedicated purpose, but does not venture this as a reason for the harshness of the penalty.[15] Again, other, less harshly treated acts, fit this description. Tyldesley writes that the death penalty was presumably for a breach of official duty.[16] As with all other ideas presented thus far, this reasoning fails because other breaches of official duty within the decree do not receive the same condemnation. Edgerton thinks that perhaps cattle held a special place in Osireion rites, accounting for the harshness of the penalty.[17] This is possible, but other crimes against cattle do not incur such a harsh treatment in the decree. It should also be noted that Edgerton feels that the term ḥr tp ḫt probably means impalement, but that the question is open.[18] Since his expression of that opinion, more evidence, which will be outlined below, has closed the question.

Seti I's grandson, Merneptah, also left behind inscriptions mentioning impalement. He commissioned an inscription on the walls of the temple of Amada, a site located between the first and second cataracts—the same temple in which Amenhotep II left one of his two inscriptions about his slaying of seven foreign princes. Merneptah's inscription in Amada effectively ends the debate about the meaning of the expression ḥr tp ḫt. The writing is badly damaged and worn, but photographs and squeeze sheets have made the key elements discernable. After outlining a victorious battle against the Libyans in which Merneptah slew great numbers, the text records in line 5 that "the remainder were put on the top of stakes, to the south of Memphis." The phrase "were put on top of stakes," dỉw ḥr tp ḫt, is followed by a determinative which shows a person stuck on top of a pointed stake face down, his legs hanging to one side, his arms to the other (see fig. 7.1).[19] This glyph clearly depicts an impalement scene, significantly to indicate, or *determine*, the meaning of the term ḥr tp ḫt. We learn from the inscription of the intentional killing of those who were apparently subdued enemies. Additionally, the impalement determinative and the phrase ḥr tp ḫt imbues the text with great value in our effort to understand this phrase. The question about whether or not impalement is meant can no longer be open.

Figure 7.1 – Determinative depicting impalement

This same inscription contains another critical phrase. Merneptah also dealt a harsh blow to Kushite rebels. As Hornung puts it, a large number of the Medjai prisoners of war were burned.[20] This seems to be the best interpretation for a phrase that literally reads "fire was thrown (ḫ3i ḫt) on the Medjai."[21] Other Medjai had their hands or ears cut off, or their eyes plucked out, and eventually a heap of them was made in the towns of Kush.[22] All of this was done *after* the prisoners were brought to Egypt—this punishment again had obviously been wrought against those who were already subdued. The text of Merneptah's inscription makes it clear that he

---

[12] *KRI* 1, pp. 54–5.

[13] Bedell, "Criminal Law in the Egyptian Ramesside Period", p. 151.

[14] David Lorton, "The Treatment of Criminals in Ancient Egypt", *Journal of the Economic and Social History of the Orient* 20, no. 1, 1977, 26–8.

[15] A.G. McDowell, "Crime and Punishment", in Donald B. Redford (ed.), *The Oxford Encyclopedia of Ancient Egypt*, London: Oxford University Press, 2001, p. 317.

[16] Joyce A. Tyldesley, *Judgment of the Pharaoh: Crime and Punishment in Ancient Egypt*, London: Weidenfeld & Nicolson, 2000, p. 29.

[17] Edgerton, "Nauri Decree of Seti I", p. 230.

[18] Edgerton, "Nauri Decree of Seti I", p. 224–5, n. 46.

[19] *Stela of Amenophis II and Inscription of Meneptah*, vol. 5, Cairo, 1963, line 5 of pl. 4 facsimile; pl. 5 reproduction of facsimile made by Breasted; pl. 8 photograph of stela. See also *KRI* 4, 1; see Henri Gauthier, *Le temple d'Amada*, Cairo: Institut Français d'Archéologie Orientale, 1913, p. 63, for a poor reproduction. He does not copy this figure, or several others, correctly. See also Ahmad Abdel-Hamid Youssef, "Merneptah's Fourth Year Text at Amada", *ASAE* 58, 1964, facsimile on pp. 274–5, photo on pl. 1.

[20] E. Hornung, *Altägyptische Höllenvorstellungen. Mit 7 Lichtdrucktafeln und 6 Abbildungen im Text*, Abhandlungen der Sächsischen Akademie der Wissenschaften zu Leipzig, Philologisch-historische Klasse Bd. 59, Heft 3, Berlin: Akademie-Verlag, 1968, p. 27.

[21] *KRI* 4, 1, line 7.

[22] *KRI* 4, 1, line 8. See also Youssef, "Merneptah's Fourth Year Text", p. 276.

slew prisoners of war on two occasions. Why one group was impaled and another was burned, we do not know. Such actions were likely taken to intimidate and to discourage future incursions and rebellions. Whether these executions were ritualistic or perfunctory killings bereft of religious trappings is not apparent. Thus it is difficult to know how to classify the events, but we can be sure that a great number of people were killed under the auspices of the king.

Similarly, Ramesses III records that in a Libyan war, after destroying the enemy, "their leaders were carried off and slain. They were cast down and were made as pinioned [ini(w) nȝ ḥȝwt smȝ(w) ḥdb(w) swt iriw m ḏnḥ]."[23] The text makes it plain that the battle was over and that the leaders were carried away before they were slain. Additionally, the reference to being pinioned echoes sacrificial terminology. In another incident, Ramesses III was visited by the father of a prisoner who came to plead for his son's life. In response the king "came down upon their heads like a mountain of granite" (ḥm=f ḥȝw ḥr tp=sn mi ḏw n mȝt),[24] a strong implication that Ramesses killed both men. These events will be revisited in chapter 10. All of the events discussed thus far show the king blazing out against Chaos.

Various Capital Offenses

Besides the capital offenses revealed by these inscriptions, we have other sources which impinge upon state-sponsored execution. The Instructions of Amenemope contains two stanzas of interest to us. While the known copies of this work are of a later date, the composition of the text is generally assigned to the Ramesside Era,[25] and thus the text is pertinent to our discussion of this time period. This text is difficult to translate and interpret, and thus the wording of key points has varied greatly in translation. The instruction is divided into stanzas, typically referred to as chapters. We will examine lines from chapters 11 and 20.

Chapter 11 of the Instructions of Amenemope contains a warning against coveting the goods of the poor. In arguing against this vice, the author reminds the reader that the poor are apparently examined with beatings, since sticks are used. After the examination, "he [the poor person] is seized and beaten to the executioner."[26] While the exact meaning of this phrase is opaque, clearly a poor person could be executed—presumably for a complete inability to pay debts—though this is inexplicit. It is difficult to conceive of such an example being included in these instructions were the practice not well known and ongoing. We can only conclude that for unknown reasons, perhaps inability to pay debt, the dependant poor were almost certainly executed frequently.

Chapter 20 of the instructions deals with the appropriate behavior of legal authorities. Quite a lengthy portion relates to the topic of sanctioned killing:

> Do not make for yourself documents falsely,
> They are a great treason worthy of death;[27]
> They [bring] the great oath of restraint;
> They [bring] a hearing by the herald.
> Do not falsify the oracles in the scrolls
> And in this way disturb the plans of god;
> Do not use the power of god for yourself,
> As if there were no Fate and Destiny.
> Give property to its owners,
> In this way you seek your own life;
> Do not raise your desires in their house,
> Or your bones are destined for the executioner.[28]

This stanza contains two possibilities of death, both related to one central concept. First, the creation of false documents while in a position of trust, assumedly for one's own good, can lead to an oath, presumably in a trial heard by a herald—doubtlessly a royal trial—who may pronounce a death sentence. Again, this punishment would only be included in the teachings if it were a standing and well-known practice.

The stanza continues by warning of the dangers of being false in a position of royal trust for one's own gain. Falsifying oracles should be avoided, because this disturbs god (nṯr). Serving a god or temple also allows a chance for abuse, which should be avoided. This reasoning is directly followed by the advice to hand over property to its owners as a way of seeking/maintaining one's own life. Since these lines follow four which concern a person in the service of a temple, the property spoken of would likely be temple property. Such reasoning also applies to the line about not raising one's

---

[23] KRI 5, 25, line 54. See also W.F. Edgerton and J.A. Wilson, *Historical records of Ramses III: The texts in Medinet Habu Volumes I and II*, Chicago: University of Chicago Press, 1936, plates 27–8.

[24] KRI 5, 70, lines 28–9.

[25] Lichtheim, *Ancient Egyptian Literature*, p. 147; and F. Lloyd Griffith, "The Teaching of Amenophis the Son of Kanakht. Papyrus B.M. 10474", *JEA* 12, 1926, 193.

[26] Papyrus British Museum No. 10474, XV, 274, as in Wallis Budge, *The Teaching of Amen-Em-Apt, Son of Kanekht*, London: Martin Hopkinson and Company, 1924, p. 208. Lichtheim, *Ancient Egyptian Literature*, p. 155, translates, "And he is led to the executioner." Griffith, "Teaching of Amenophis", p. 211, translates, "Where? is the executioner?" William Kelly Simpson, *The Literature of Ancient Egypt: An Anthology of Stories, Instructions, and Poetry*, New Haven, CT: Yale University Press, 1973, p. 253, translates, "Who is to have the execution?"

[27] Griffith, "Teaching of Amenophis", p. 218, translates, "Make not for thyself false documents; they are a gross treason worthy of death." Simpson, *Literature of Ancient Egypt*, p. 259, translates, "Do not make false [enrollment] lists, For they are a serious affair deserving death." Lichtheim's translation of "Do not make for yourself false documents, They are a deadly provocation", p. 158, carries the essential meaning, but Griffith's and Simpson's translations preserve more of a literal translation, and for our purposes probably convey the meaning better.

[28] P. BM 10474 XXI, 413—Budge, *Teaching of Amen-Em-At*, pp. 221–2. Lichtheim, *Ancient Egyptian Literature*, p. 158–9, translates this last phrase as "Don't raise your desire in their house, or your bones belong to the execution block." Griffith, "Teaching of Amenophis", p. 218, translates, "Let not thy heart build in their house, for thus thy bones are for the execution block." Simpson, *Literature of Ancient Egypt*, p. 260, as, "Let not your heart build in their house, for then your neck will be on the execution block."

desire in the gods' house, because this leads to execution—probably because such a desire leads one to inappropriate acts.

All of the lines after the mention of rendering false oracles possibly belong together, culminating in the execution block. This reading would reason that rendering a false oracle disturbs the plan of god. Such an act was equated with using the might of god for personal gain, which is akin to ignoring fate and destiny. Under this interpretation, these four lines form synthetic parallelism: falsifying oracles parallels using the might of god for personal gain, and disturbing the plan of god parallels ignoring fate and destiny. The parallelism is continued in the next lines, constituting an antithetical parallel. In contrast to falsifying oracles and using the might of god is handing over property to its (temple/god) owners; the appropriate way of seeking one's own life serves as a foil for disturbing the plan of god and ignoring destiny. The original pattern of the stanza returns with raising one's own desire/heart, which parallels falsifying oracles and using the might of god for personal gain and is antithetical to handing over property to its owner. Going to the executioner's block parallels disturbing the plan of god or ignoring destiny and contrasts seeking one's own life. Such parallelism is graphically represented thus:

Falsifying oracles	yields	disturbing plans of god
Using power for self	yields	ignoring fate and destiny
Giving property to owners	yields	seeking own life
Raising desires	yields	execution block

If this line of reasoning is correct, the punishment of the executioner's block is the result of all those things that parallel raising one's heart and are the antithesis of handing over property to the temple: rendering false oracles and using the might of god for personal gain. Thus, we can propose that rendering false oracles, and the rather nebulous act of using god's might for personal gain, could lead to execution. This reading is plausible, though we have only inductive reasoning to reach this conclusion. The crux of the matter seems to be the inappropriateness of trying to influence or speak for the gods.

The first part of chapter 20 is reasonably understandable. Making false documents while in a position of power is potentially a capital offense. The second part, as can easily be seen in the above analysis, requires much interpretation. Thus it is not entirely clear why building/raising one's heart would lead to the execution block, though the possible use of parallelism may answer this question. While we cannot be sure of the specifics, the connotations are that dishonest actions for personal gain performed while in an office of trust can bring about a death sentence. This agrees squarely with the Horemheb decree discussed above. Thus the *topos*-driven Instructions of Amenemope confirms that such punishments were accepted and practiced for some time. However, we must note that the Nauri Decree does not stipulate the death penalty across the entire spectrum of misuse of temple proceeds by an official. As discussed above, many of these offences proscribed other punishments. Such inconsistency makes it difficult to see a pattern or to extrapolate from the evidence we have.

While in most cases theft was a civil offense,[29] stealing royal property could bring about death. This is learned from Ostracon British Museum 5631. Herein it is recorded that two men found a jar containing several valuable objects which apparently belonged to the king. One wanted to open the jar and divide the contents between the two. The other replied that such would be a crime deserving execution, or being carved up (*ḫti*, written with a knife determinative:).[30] This story indicates that these men at least perceived that theft of royal property was a capital offense. We can only assume that such was the case. Furthermore, the Ramesside Era is the time period in which death was recommended for the Deir el-Medina woman, Heria, for stealing a copper chisel belonging to state workmen. One letter makes it appear that diverting corvée workers was a capital offense, but the same letter also intimates that the punishment would really be becoming a corvée worker instead; thus we cannot determine the true intent of the letter.[31]

Like the Instructions of Ptahhotep, the Instructions of Ani contain a warning against adultery. The reader is warned that to engage in adultery with a strange woman who is away from her husband is a "great crime of death."[32] Again, this may mean that capital punishment was attached to such adultery, but it may mean that a husband was free to pursue fatal revenge.[33] Eyre argues that "no doubt in practice adultery usually resulted in divorce or repudiation and not death."[34] This idea is buttressed by evidence from Deir el-Medina, where we know of people accused of (sometimes multiple) adultery, and have no record of their lives being sought after,[35] though we must be careful of such arguments of silence. As with the Ptahhotep lines, here I conclude the possibility of a death sentence being attached to adultery, but cannot make a stronger determination.

---

[29] McDowell, *Jurisdiction*, p. 233; and Jaroslav Cerný, "Restitution of, and Penalty Attaching to, Stolen Property in Ramesside Times", *JEA* 23, no. 2, 1937, 186–9.

[30] Jaroslav Cerný and Alan Henderson Gardiner, *Hieratic Ostraca*, Oxford: Griffith Institute, 1957, pl. 88, lines 3–9; Adolf Erman, "Ein ehrilicher Beamter", *ZÄS* 42, 1905, 104; and Bedell, "Criminal Law in the Egyptian Ramesside Period", p. 148.

[31] P. Anastasi IV.

[32] P. Boulaq 4, 16, as in Joachim Friedrich Quack, *Die Lehren des Ani. Ein neuägyptischer Weisheitstext in seinem kulturellen Umfeld*, Fribourg: Universitätsverlag Freiburg Schweiz und Vandenhoeck & Ruprecht Göttingen, 1994, pp. 94, 288.

[33] See C.J. Eyre, "Crime and Adultery in Ancient Egypt", *JEA* 70, 1984, 95.

[34] Eyre, "Crime and Adultery in Ancient Egypt", 98.

[35] For example, see the stories of Pa-nb and Mry-Sumt. These cases may be anomalous, since both were known for being adept at manipulation of the system and bribery. See Jac J. Janssen, "Two Personalities," in *Gleanings from Deir el-Medina*, ed R.J. Demarée and Jac. J. Janssen (Leiden: Nederlands Instituut voor het Nabije Oosten te Leiden, 1982), 114, 119-20.

Possible Examples of Ritual Slaying

From the Ramesside Era, a few possible examples of ritual slaying are attested. The first type is by now familiar to the reader. Evidence of *tekenu* rites exists in the Ramesside tombs TT 41,[36] TT A.26,[37] TT 49, TT 284, and TT C.4.[38] As with most of the tekenu depictions in the preceding dynasty, all of these tombs are in the Theban area. Thus it is likewise difficult to determine whether this likely example of sacrifice associated with burial is a local custom or whether an accident of preservation and excavation has given us a small sample of a much more widespread practice.

An intriguing and mildly controversial possibility of ritual slaying during this time period comes from the Amman area of Jordan. There a structure was found which some have contended was a small temple.[39] The structure was in use for about one hundred years, its final occupation ending with the thirteenth century BCE.[40] The excavators discovered fragments of Mycenaean, Cypriot, and Midianite ware, along with hundreds of fragments of Egyptian stone ware.[41] It has been postulated that a substantial part of the presence in this structure was Egyptian.[42]

Most intriguing among the material recovered are thousands of bone fragments contained within were almost exclusively—between 92 per cent and 95 per cent—human.[43] These bones were scattered throughout every room of the building and are present in every strata. Concentrations were unusually high in some "small roughly circular groups associated with ash and hardened clay patches."[44] Another high concentration was found in the area of an incinerator.[45] Even with such a great number of bone fragments, not a great number of bodies are represented. It has also been determined that these bodies were burned. Hennessey argues that these finds, coupled with a number of weapons, demonstrate that the bodies were slaughtered and shortly afterwards burned; he further argues that the location of the site in an area which has traditionally been associated with human sacrifice leads to the conclusion that this temple was used for occasional human sacrifice.[46] The apparent Egyptian presence leads some to the deduction that Egyptians participated in these rites.

The conclusions are not as clear as Hennessey has made them. Mumford argues that the evidence could also support the hypothesis that the site was a fort that was conquered, and its soldiers had been destroyed and burned.[47] The great distance between the site and any area controlled by Egypt during the Ramesside Era makes it unlikely that Egypt played a major role in the use of the building, whatever its function was. Additionally, whether human sacrifice was carried out there is altogether unclear. Burning a building to destroy it is common. Other destructive measures could have scattered the bones. The large number of weapons housed within the structure could point toward a violent rite, but it is more likely that they were used for warfare and defense. Thus, while Egyptians could possibly have used the Amman structure for ritual slaying, the evidence is weak, and it seems unlikely.

Two ostraca from Deir el-Medina contain tantalizing questions put to an oracle. We cannot be certain of the dates of these texts. One poses the question "should I burn him?" (*n3 wbd sw*).[48] Similarly, another asks "should he not be burned?" (*tm wbd.t=f*).[49] Certainly these are oracles relating to the possibility of death by burning, but, as discussed above, the inclusion of the verb *wbd* indicates that it may have ritual connotations. At the very least we know that the inhabitants of Deir el-Medina felt that burning could be a suitable punishment.

The Harem Conspiracy

Nothing could be viewed as a more direct assault against *Ma'at* than an attack on the keeper of Order, the king. After more than 32 years on the throne, Ramesses III was spending time in his southern palace, in the storied city of Thebes. Unaware of intrigue in his own harem, things seemed placid. However, Teya, one of his wives, was plotting rebellion. Her plan, supported by others in the harem, some military leaders, and many other officials who had been brought into collusion, was to kill the old king and incite enough rebellion among the people to replace the intended heir with her son, Pentawere. The conspirators attacked the king, but they failed to incite a

---

[36] Norman de Garis Davies, *Two Ramesside Tombs at Thebes*, New York: Metropolitan Museum of Art, 1927; see especially MMA photographs 1887-8.

[37] Norman de Garis Davies and Nina M. Cummings Davies, *The Tomb of Nefer-hotep at Thebes With Plates in Color by Nina de Garis Davies*, New York: Metropolitan Museum of Art, 1933, p. 42 and pl. 20.

[38] J. Gwyn Griffiths, "The Tekenu, the Nubians and the Butic Burial", *Kush* 6, 1958, 112.

[39] G.L. Harding, "Recent Discoveries in Jordan", *Palestine Exploration Quarterly* 90-1, 1958-9, 15-18.

[40] J. Basil Hennessy, "Thirteenth Century B.C. Temple of Human Sacrifice at Amman", in E. Gubel and E. Lininski (ed.), *Phoenicia and Its Neighbours*, Leuven: Peeters, 1985, p. 90.

[41] Hennessy, "Thirteenth Century B.C. Temple of Human Sacrifice at Amman", p. 95; V. Hankey, "Vases and Objects made of Stone", *Levant* 6, 1974, 160-78; and V. Hankey, "A Late Bronze Age Temple at Amman Airport: Small Finds and Pottery Discovered in 1955", in S. Bourke and J.P. Descoeudres (eds.), *Trade, Contact, and the Movement of Peoples in the Eastern Mediterranean: Studies in Honour of J. Basil Hennessy*, Mediterranean Archaeology Supplement 3, Sydney: Meditarch, 1995, pp. 175-85.

[42] See "Amman Jordan", in Gregory D. Mumford, "International Relations between Egypt, Sinai, and Syria-Palestine during the Late Bronze Age to Early Persian Period Dynasties 18-26: ca.1550-525 B.C.", PhD dissertation, University of Toronto, 1998, 2815-53, for a summary of the evidence and arguments.

[43] Hennessy, "Thirteenth Century B.C. Temple", p. 95.

[44] Hennessy, "Thirteenth Century B.C. Temple", p. 97.

[45] Hennessy, "Thirteenth Century B.C. Temple", p. 97

[46] Hennessy, "Thirteenth Century B.C. Temple", p. 104.

[47] Besides Mumford's chapter cited above, he expressed this argument in personal conversation and correspondence while he prepared an article entitled "A Re-assessment of the Amman Airport Structure: Date-range and Function", forthcoming.

[48] Ostracon IFAO 680, as in Jaroslav Černy, "Nouvelle Série de Questions Adresées aux Oracles," in BIFAO 41 (1942): 14. I am grateful to Dr. John Gee for pointing out these examples to me.

[49] Ostracon IFAO 854, as in Jaroslav Černy, "Troisième Série de Questions Adresées aux oracles," in BIFAO 72 (1972): 52.

larger rebellion. The conspirators were quickly apprehended. We cannot be certain, but it appears that the king brought the perpetrators to meet their fate as he lay dying.

While the attempted assassination of Ramesses III must have been a nightmare for those involved, it is a playground for Egyptological historians. Undoubtedly there had been other assassination attempts and successes. Here and there, we find bits of evidence of assassinations, but this type of event would have been so disruptive of Ma'at that the Egyptians dared not include it in lasting inscriptions. Were it not for the accidental preservation of legal documents, we would know nothing of assassination attempts. However, when Teya and her harem cohorts rose up against the last of the great new-kingdom pharaohs—possibly mortally wounding him—details from the trials of those involved were recorded, and some portions of the record survived thousands of years to tell their grisly, intricate tale.

These documents preserved a tremendous amount of information regarding the death penalty in the Ramesside phase of Egyptian history. The story-line and the debate over whether or not Ramesses III died as a result of this attempt are outside the scope of this investigation. Instead, we will concentrate on the types of punishment inflicted, and the reasons for those punishments. We learn about the conspiracy trials and punishments largely from four documents: Papyrus Lee, Papyrus Rollin, Papyrus Varzy, and the Turin Judicial Papyrus.[50] The first three are brief summaries of small parts of the investigation and trial. The latter is a long account of who was investigated and their ensuing punishments. The information gathered from these is somewhat supplemented by two other papyri, Papyrus Rifaud I and Papyrus Rifaud II, both of which have been lost in modern times and are preserved only in poorly made hand copies, which make much of the text unusable.

It is important to note that Ramesses III exempted himself from involvement in the issue. He declares, "As for all this that has been done, they have done it. All that they will do shall fall upon their heads, for I am consecrated and exempted forever."[51] Whether Ramesses exempted himself to avoid political turmoil from the powerful families of the people involved or to go to the afterlife untarnished by the proceedings is unclear. In any case, Ramesses commissioned and empowered the investigations, but claimed no responsibility for them. Nevertheless, the trials doubtlessly involved killing that was specifically sanctioned by the state.

The trial proceedings outline different groups of criminals and different types of punishments, though the punishments do not seem to relate to the type of criminal.

First, six men and six women were arraigned for inciting rebellion. It was said of all twelve that after being found guilty, "they [the officials] caused his punishment to overtake him [or them]."[52] Were the Turin Judicial Papyrus our only available document, we would be sorely pressed to determine the nature of this punishment. Papyrus Lee makes the punishment more clear; it allows us to identify one of these men—*Payry*, son of *Ruma*[53]—with a more specific description of his punishment. This latter document relates that this culprit had been examined in regard to the crimes, and "he had fully committed them together with the other great criminals like him, the abomination of every god and every goddess. The great punishment of death was applied to him [*iw=tw iri n=f sb3yt ʿ3y n mwt*], which the gods said, 'Do them to him.'"[54] From this we can deduce that the Turin Papyrus's phrase "they caused his punishment to overtake him," is a euphemism for a death penalty. Thus we surmise that these twelve conspirators were killed, in an unknown manner, for their efforts to incite rebellion in the form of a conspiracy against the king.[55] Besides these 12, we learn of 10 men who had learned of the plot but had failed to report it (also sometimes phrased as having concealed it). These men likewise had their punishment overtake them, meaning they were executed.[56] These 22 people constitute the first group of prisoners interrogated.

After the first set of examinations, another group of six men were accused of collaborating with the original group of conspirators. After being found guilty, they were left alone in the court, where each took his own life. It is specified that no one had harmed them.[57]

The third group to be tried contained one man who had been in collusion, and three who had known of the conspiracy but had not reported it. All of these took their own lives.[58] A fourth group were officials who had apparently been wined and dined by the prisoners during the juridical process. The record reads that they had "forsaken the good instructions given to them; the women had gone; they reached them at the place where they were; they caroused with them and with Pays.[59] All four

---

[50] Published in Théodule Devéria, "Le Papyrus judiciaire de Turin et les papyrus Lee et Rollin", *Journal Asiatique* 10, 1867; Papyri Lee and Rollin reproduced in Hans Goedicke, "Was Magic Used in the Harem Conspiracy Against Ramesses III?" *JEA* 49, 1963, pls. 10 and 11.

[51] See also A. deBuck, "The Judicial Papyrus of Turin", *JEA* 23, no. 2, 1937, 154. This translation has been immensely helpful in arriving at my own.

[52] Turin Judicial Papyrus, IV.2 and 3–V.3, as in Théodule Devéria, *Le Papyrus Judiciaire de Turin et Les Papyrus Lee et Rollin*, Paris: Impériale, 1868. Similar translation in deBuck, "Judicial Papyrus of Turin", 154–5. Compare Breasted, *ARE* 4, 214–17, who translates "they brought his punishment upon him."

[53] Goedicke, "Was Magic Used in the Harem Conspiracy Against Ramesses III?" pp. 80–1, notes r and s.

[54] As in Goedicke, "Was Magic Used in the Harem Conspiracy Against Ramesses III?", 78.

[55] Although Susan Redford, *The Harem Conspiracy: The Murder of Ramesses III*, DeKalb, IL: Northern Illinois University Press, 2002, pp. 124–7, 131, believes that burning was the most likely form of punishment inflicted, we have no evidence to this effect. Chapters 9 and 10 of the study will demonstrate that her reasoning that this was the form of punishment used on rebels does not necessarily hold up, because impalement was a more popular form of punishment in the Ramesside Era and because many forms were used for rebels.

[56] deBuck, "The Judicial Papyrus of Turin", pp. 154–5.

[57] Turin Judicial Papyrus, VI.6. See also deBuck, "The Judicial Papyrus of Turin", p. 156.

[58] Turin Judicial Papyrus, V.6–10.

[59] Turin Judicial Papyrus, VI.1. Compare deBuck, "The Judicial Papyrus of Turin", p. 156; and *ARE* 3, 219.

of these men were punished by having their noses and ears cut off. One of them, a butler, took his life.[60] A final man was brought in for being "connected" with the guilty. He was sternly scolded.

We know nothing of the fate of Teya, the original conspirator, nor of the other women of the harem. Because they cavorted with the prison keepers, we know they were in custody, but decorum must have prevented the publication of their fates, perhaps being a royal wife protected them from having their fates recorded. It is unlikely that they were not killed, and thus an unknown number of the harem were probably executed in an unknown manner.

It should be noted that one conspirator is listed as having been executed in the Turin Judicial Papyrus, but he is listed as having killed himself in Papyrus Rollin.[61] The most likely reason for this is scribal confusion. However, it may also be due to an intended punishment being recorded in one text, and then a surprise suicide being recorded in another. Another possibility is that all of the executions were in fact forced suicides.

Several issues from this incident must be addressed. The first is the question of why the people involved had to die. It is obvious that an assault on the king was against the incarnation of correct social Order, and was thus a direct attack on Ma'at. While presumably being an active conspirator carried a greater degree of culpability, both actively participating and failing to report the conspiracy were great enough to bring about a death penalty. Hence we can assume that even a failure to act against the *Isfet*-enclave of conspirators was an attack on Ma'at, probably because failing to report the conspiracy implied complying with its ideas. In the Turin Judicial Papyrus, each person accused before the council is described as a "great enemy." This description is an apt term for one who literally made himself an enemy of Order. Papyrus Lee contains the most specific wording of how the Egyptians themselves viewed this attack on Order. It has already been noted that such conspiracy was "the abomination of every god and every goddess." Furthermore, the conspirators were "great abominations of the land."[62] This offense against the land and the gods, and an attempted attack on Ma'at brought about divine condemnation, for it was the gods who declared that the punishment should be carried about.[63]

The suicides of this case bring up two questions. First, why would one commit suicide, and second, why were some allowed to do so while some were executed? Papyrus Rollin provides insight into the former question. There it is recorded that when one criminal was found guilty, "offenses worthy of death, and a great abomination for the land was that which he had done. When he saw that which he had done were great offences worthy of death, he killed himself for his own sake."[64] The text would have us believe that upon this criminal's realization of the atrocity of his crime—including its abominable effect on the whole country—he wanted to take his own life. Of course, the reality of individual situations may have been less simple than this. For example, the butler who had not been condemned to die but had lost his ears and nose, but then committed suicide, may have had several motives. The realization of the odiousness of the crime may have played a part. Perhaps he could not bear the thought of living with the shame of the involvement, or maybe with the ignominy of his defacement. Or the pain of his mutilation could have been literally too great for him to live with. Whatever the real reasons, our text records the ideologically orthodox explanation that the crime was such an abomination that suicide was the only course one would take when he realized the grossness of the crime.

Excursus on Suicide versus Execution

The differentiation between those who were executed and those who were allowed to commit suicide is more complex. Even the inquiry reveals a presumption that it was better to commit suicide than to be killed by another. Bedell postulates just this idea, that it was more honorable to commit suicide.[65] She also argues that because of this, suicide was reserved for those of a higher rank.[66] The evidence does not bear this out. Among those executed were butlers, a chief of the chamber, an overseer of the royal harem, a scribe of the king's harem, several inspectors of the royal harem, a scribe of the White House, an overseer of the White House, a captain of the archers in Nubia, and several members of the harem.[67] Among those who committed suicide were a captain of the army, a few scribes of the house of sacred writings, an overseer of the [house] of Sekhmet, butlers, a royal son, a deputy of the harem, and a scribe of the royal harem. While the prince was notably of a higher status than others, most of the ranks are essentially equal between the groups. It is especially hard to espouse Bedell's argument when a matching group of butlers, scribes, and harem officials were among both those who were executed and those who committed suicide.

Bedell also feels that suicide was allowed to some because it was unfitting for someone of a higher rank to be condemned to death by someone of a lower rank.[68] Again the equality in the ranks of the two groups bespeaks problems with this assumption. Additionally, several members of the court were of equal or higher rank than many of those who committed suicide. It could be hypothesized that the deciding factor was the nature of a person's involvement in the conspiracy. This idea is also insupportable. From both groups, we find people who were actively involved in the conspiracy and those who

---

[60] Turin Judicial Papyrus, VI.2.
[61] Lorton, "The Treatment of Criminals in Ancient Egypt", p. 34.
[62] See Papyrus Lee 2.4.
[63] See Papyrus Lee 1.7.
[64] Papyrus Rollin, lines 4–5.
[65] Bedell, "Criminal Law in the Egyptian Ramesside Period", p. 169.
[66] Bedell, "Criminal Law in the Egyptian Ramesside Period", p. 169.
[67] Titles adopted are those used in Breasted's translation.
[68] Bedell, "Criminal Law in the Egyptian Ramesside Period", p. 167–8.

heard about it and failed to report it. There may be some merit to Redford's idea that many of the executed were of foreign extraction, but she presents little evidence for this.[69] She also aptly notes that some of those who were not executed were accused of using magic in the conspiracy, and fear of their magical abilities may have caused them to be treated differently.[70] However, this accounts for only some of those who were not executed. McDowell has summed up the conundrum well: "The two groups appear to have been equally culpable and of equally high rank, and both included active conspirators as well as others who merely knew of the conspiracy and failed to report it."[71] Assmann hypothesizes that judges preferred suicide to execution because the immortal soul of the executed could call for an accounting of its executioners in the hereafter.[72] Perhaps the people left to commit suicide were those whose guilt was less certain, and thus the executioners did not have to face the possibility of paying for a wrongful execution in the next life.

We must also address the issue of the names which were recorded in the Turin Judicial Papyrus. Many of these were obviously changed names. For example, names such as *p3-b3k-k3 mn,* the blind servant; *p3-nšn,* the rebellious one; and *msd-sw-rꜥ,* Re hates him, are surely not names given at birth. These names not only say something about the perceived character of traitors, but by changing the names of the convicted, the scribes moved the traitors one step closer to complete obliteration.[73] Because the name of a person was one of the essential elements for his or her survival in the afterlife, losing one's name amounts to a type of debaptism, or *damnatio memoriae*, effectively erasing these elements of Isfet from the afterlife. In these cases, both physical and compositional violence served Order by eliminating Chaos.

Perhaps the execution of Ba'y during the reign of Siptah also had to do with a plotted insurrection, though some have thought that Ba'y had slept with the king's wife. Ultimately, we know neither why nor how he was executed, just that that pharaoh had "killed the great enemy Ba'y."[74]

The Great Tomb Robberies

After Ramesses III died, the dynasty began a slow, consistent decline. Toward the end of the Ramesside Era, the rulers were hollow shadows of their powerful predecessors. One of the ways this was manifested was their inability to properly police sacred lands. As a result, many royal tombs were pillaged. Many royal mummies were rescued by desperate, covert measures to hide the bodies, but the tombs were eventually all emptied of goods, with the exception of Tutankhamun's. Rampant looting of temples was also part of the crimes committed by these *tomb robbers*. Undoubtedly such activities were manifestations of Chaos triumphing over Order. Many of the robberies happened during a spate of corruption, greed, desecration, and deceit toward the end of the Ramesside Era. When the robberies were discovered, mayors pointed fingers at each other, workmen, officials, ancient police, and temple guards were all implicated. Investigations were put off, counter-accusations were made, and resources were diverted in a complicated collection of overt and covert actions. The robberies spanned a number of years, which sped past while the problem was supposedly under investigation. Eventually many were tried for their crimes. Undoubtedly, many more received protection and never stood before a tribunal.

From the several documents dealing with the Great Tomb Robberies, such as Papyrus Amherst, Papyrus Abbott, Papyrus Mayer, and Papyrus British Museum 10052, we learn much about the penalties connected to perjury and tomb robbery. While a twisted and intriguing story lies behind the evidence we will examine, we must restrict our investigation to the details which are pertinent to the topic at hand.

During the many interrogations conducted as more and more tomb robberies came to light, many oaths were administered.[75] Most of these were oaths to tell the truth during the questioning, and thus contained penalties for perjury within the oath. Lorton has examined these in detail. He notes that eight oaths invoke the penalty of being mutilated and sent to Kush for penal servitude.[76] Nine oaths describe impalement as the potential punishment, though four of these are informal oaths uttered during testimony.[77] Though Lorton tries to find a pattern in the penalties attached to perjury, there does not seem to be a consistent trend.[78] The case is further complicated by the nature of the punishment of the crime. As will be outlined below, impalement was the punishment to be meted out to tomb robbers. Therefore, calling for impalement in the oath may imply that if the testator is lying, then he must be guilty of tomb robbery, and would thus be executed by impalement. Elsewhere we do not find impalement in perjury oaths.[79] We must thus conclude that either the death penalty for perjury was

---

[69] Redford, *Harem Conspiracy*, p. 129.
[70] Redford, *Harem Conspiracy*, p. 130.
[71] McDowell, *Crime and Punishment*, p. 317.
[72] Jan Assmann, *The Mind of Egypt: History and Meaning in the Time of the Pharaohs*, trans. Andrew Jenkins, New York: Metropolitan Books, 2002, p. 147.
[73] See Georges Posener, "Les Criminels Débaptisés et les Morts sans Noms", *RdE* 5, 1946, for a discussion on this phenomenon. Also see Richard Parkinson, *Cracking Codes: The Rosetta Stone and Decipherment*, Berkeley: University of California Press, 1999, pp. 140-2; Lorton, "The Treatment of Criminals in Ancient Egypt", p. 30; Goedicke, "Was Magic Used?", p. 84; and McDowell, *Crime and Punishment*, p. 317, for discussions on this particular case.
[74] IFAO 1864, as in Pierre Grandet, "L'exécution du chancelier Bay. O. IFAO 1864," in *BIFAO* 100 (2000): 339-345.

[75] See John A. Wilson, "The Oath in Ancient Egypt", *JNES* 7, 1948; Klaus Baer, "The Oath *sḏf3-tryt* in Papyrus Lee, 1", *JEA* 50, 1964; and Scott N. Morschauser, "The End of the *Sḏf3-Tryt* 'Oath'", *JARCE* 25, 1988, for discussions on the oaths administered in such cases.
[76] Lorton, "The Treatment of Criminals in Ancient Egypt", p. 33.
[77] Lorton, "The Treatment of Criminals in Ancient Egypt", 33-6.
[78] McDowell, *Jurisdiction at Deir el-Medina*, p. 224, independently agrees.
[79] See Lorton, "The Treatment of Criminals in Ancient Egypt", p. 33-8; McDowell, *Jurisdiction at Deir el-Medina*, p. 224; and Wilson, "Oath in Ancient Egypt", which lists scores of oaths and their penalties.

different here due to the nature of the crime, or that mentioning impalement was a reference to the penalty for tomb robbery, which the person would indubitably be guilty of if the person were lying during trial.

It is abundantly apparent that the penalty for royal tomb robbery during this time period was impalement. It is also clear that this was common knowledge at the time. One man accused of tomb robbery uses as his defense the reasoning that he "saw the punishments, oh, that were done to the thieves in the time of the Vizier Khaemwese. Is it that I go to seek death when I know it?"[80] Another man maintained that he had warned a friend not to become involved in tomb robbing. He testified, "I quarreled with him, and I said to him, you will be put to death for the thefts which you committed [in] the Necropolis."[81] A man accused of robbing the Great Tombs of the kings replied, "Far be it from me, far be it from me! The Great Tombs! If they put me to death on account of the tombs of Iteru, they are the tombs in which I was."[82] Apparently, the man knew that robbing from the Great Tombs was certain death, and that robbing other tombs could lead to the same punishment. Non-royal tombs had been plundered and were considered in this investigation. The robbers of non-royal tombs were also condemned to die.[83]

We know that a number of men—it is difficult to tell how many—were sentenced to death. The condemnations came from the *knbt*, but the robbers apparently were referred to the king for a final decision. This is discernible in many cases, but is most transparent in Papyrus Amherst, where it is stated that the vizier and his commission put the condemnation in writing and sent it to the king for approval.[84] Ramesses III's deferral of responsibility for punishment during the Harem Conspiracy investigation and the evidence just cited are usually used to argue that death penalties could only come from the king. As both Peet and McDowell have pointed out, these two incidents are scant evidence for such a conclusion. Both of these cases involve unusual circumstances and the direct purview of the king.[85] The king likely did have to give final approval for an execution, but the data is insufficient to draw a strong conclusion.

As stated above, we do not know whether some of the men condemned to death were executed, because we have no documents about the king's decision regarding their death sentence. We can assume that the sentences were confirmed. This conclusion is supported by other evidence. Because these investigations were in reality a sequence of examinations over a number of years, we find in the record of one investigation that some robbers had already been killed. At least seven men had been put *ḥr tp ḫt*.[86] At this point in our study, we can be sure that this phrase means that the men were impaled.[87]

The robbers investigated and punished in the papyri dealing with the Great Tomb Robberies were not exclusively tomb robbers. Goods were also stolen from temples, sometimes by temple officials themselves.[88] All of these goods clearly belonged to the state or the gods. The goods were all integral parts of processes designed to maintain Ma'at, both in this life and in the next. Thus, the robbers were, in effect, obstacles to Ma'at. The inclusion in the investigation of temple officials who stole temple goods rings an according note with the interpretation of the Instructions of Amenemope presented above. Such embezzlement is the perfect example of not giving property to its temple owners, and did in these cases result in execution, as the teachings implied. However, the Nauri Decree did not specify that execution was necessary for all thefts from the temple; though a subtle yet important difference may be that the Nauri Decree concerned property from a temple estate, and not from the temple itself.

Those who were exonerated during the trials were "given breath by the king." While to some extent, all men received breath at the king's behest, this phrase, coupled with idea that possible death was the king's decision, leads to the conclusion that those accused of robbing sacred sites had their lives put into the hand of the king. The investigators that the king appointed would determine the accused' guilt or innocence, and then it was up to the king to let the accused live or die. And so, amidst such chaotic times, Egypt's grand era of greatness and Order quietly diminished and dwindled until it waned almost into nothingness. The kings became incapable of upholding Order, and it fell to others to attempt to defeat Chaos. However, as will be seen in the next chapter, the attempts to defeat Chaos often actually strengthened it. It would be some time before Egypt regained any vestige of unified power. This time, many of those who vied for control in Egypt were Libyans whose families had lived in Egypt for generations. Perhaps the Egyptians themselves felt the Chaos as Egyptologists feel it when studying this period. Modern scholars call it the Libyan Anarchy.

---

[80] Papyrus British Museum 10052, 8.19–20, as in T. Eric Peet, *The Great Tomb-Robberies of the Twentieth Egyptian Dynasty*, Oxford: Clarendon, 1930, vol. 2, pl. 30. See also McDowell, *Jurisdiction at Deir el-Medina*, pp. 192, 223; and Bedell, "Criminal Law in the Egyptian Ramesside Period", p. 147.

[81] P.B.M. 10052, lines 4.9–10, as in Peet, *Great Tomb-Robberies*, pl. 27.

[82] P.B.M. 10052, 8.3–5, as in Peet, *Great Tomb-Robberies*, pl. 30.

[83] See J. Capart, A.H. Gardiner, and B. Van de Walle, "New Light on the Ramesside Tomb-Robberies", *JEA* 22, 1936, 171.

[84] P. Amherst 3.9, as in Peet, *Great Tomb-Robberies*, pl. 5.

[85] Peet, *Great Tomb-Robberies*, pp. 26–7; McDowell, *Jurisdiction at Deir el-Medina*, p. 223.

[86] Papyrus Mayer A.13B, as in Peet, *Great Tomb-Robberies*, pl. 24.

[87] For other discussions of the execution of Great Tomb Robbers, see also Lorton, "The Treatment of Criminals in Ancient Egypt", pp. 31–2; and McDowell, *Jurisdiction at Deir el-Medina*, p. 223.

[88] Ogden Goelet, "A New Robbery Papyrus: Rochester Mag 51.346.1", *JEA* 82, 1996, 107.

Ramesside Evidence of Sanctioned Killing

Violence	Weak Evidence	Plausible Evidence	Strong Evidence	Very Strong Evidence
Seti I decrees at Kanais that future kings who interfere with his decree will burn	X			
Seti I decrees at Kanais that future people who interfere with his decree will burn	X			
Impalement decreed for herdsmen, cattle keepers, or hound keepers who embezzled from the Osireion estate or diverted cattle to be offered to another god				X
Impalement decreed for officials of other temples who embezzle or interfere with proceeds (prohibited in Nauri Decree)		X		
Impalement of a great number of Libyan prisoners of war by Merneptah				X
Burning of a great number of Kushite prisoners of war by Merneptah				X
Ramesses III slays captured Libyans with ritual trappings				X
Ramesses III slays captured foreigner and the foreigner's father				X
Capital punishment for adultery		X		
5 tekenu sacrifices associated with burials			X*	
Ongoing process of execution of dependant poor for unknown reason				X
Ongoing practice of executing officials who falsify documents				X
Ongoing process of execution for "building up" or "raising desire" in a temple				X
Ongoing process of executing those who falsify oracles or otherwise use a temple office for personal gain		X		
Stealing state property demands capital punishment			X	
Recommendation of death for thief of state copper chisel				X
Death for diverting corvée labor	X			
Egyptian involvement in human sacrifice in Amman	X			
Execution of 22 people involved in Harem Conspiracy (plus Harem women?)				X
Mandated suicide of 10 people involved in Harem Conspiracy (plus Harem women?)				X
Impalement of 7 people for tomb robbery				X
Death decreed for many others for tomb robbery				X
Death decreed for temple official who helped embezzle temple goods				X
Ongoing decapitation as demonstrated by funerary literature		X		
Ongoing burning as demonstrated by funerary literature and oracles		X		

* Case borders between plausible and strong evidence

Chapter 8

THE CONSTANCY OF KILLING AMIDST ANARCHY
(Dynasties 21, 22, 25, and 26)

Then his majesty spoke again in the presence of this great god, "O my good lord, will you slay the guard?" The great god nodded.

—*Stela of Sheshonq*

The great general and prince Osorkon forced his body to contain his rage, for now the end was in sight. At last, after the vile and miserable group of Theban nobles who had dared rebel against Osorkon had sought refuge in the sacred precincts of Karnak, he had captured them. They had caused him to violate the sanctity of the great temple itself in order to crush their rebellion. While keeping a watchful eye on the small chapel in which the rebels were now imprisoned, the prince carefully supervised the lighting of the ritual braziers. Turning to his second-in-command, he gave the order: "Tonight, at the time of the evening sacrifice and the going forth of Sothis, we will bring the mace down upon these vile rebels. Then we will cast them on the braziers, and in order to cleanse the chapel of their filth, we will burn it. Burn them all!"

The history of Egypt after the end of the Twentieth Dynasty is difficult and chaotic. No period poses such a problem for Egyptological historians as does this period. The story of the Third Intermediate Period and Twenty-sixth Dynasty is one of fragmentation, rival kingdoms, conflicting internal and external pressures, and a paucity of textual evidence. Evidence of sanctioned killing during Dynasties 21–6 lacks real cohesion. Hence the evidence presented in this chapter will be grouped more diachronically and regionally, since the politico-cultural scene underwent many changes during this period.

Dynasty 21

The capital of the volatile Twenty-first and Twenty-second Dynasties was the city of Tanis. Accordingly, this Delta town became the home of temples, the royal palace, and royal tombs. While excavating a Tanis temple, Montet uncovered a foundation deposit that included human remains. He concluded that human sacrifice had been part of the temple founding rituals.[1] Griffiths felt that Canaanite influence may have introduced this ritual,[2] though there is no evidence for this. Follow-up studies have cast doubt on whether the remains were found within the actual foundation, for if the remains were not in the foundation, they may not represent human sacrifice.[3] Still, the conclusions of the original excavator cannot be completely disregarded; hence, ritual slaying at the founding of a Tanis temple should be regarded as a possible example of sanctioned killing supported by plausible, yet somewhat weak, evidence.

One of the most famous texts from Dynasty 21 is the Banishment Stela. This stela records, among other things, questions posed to Amun through one of his statues, and the god's answers as indicated by the statue's movements. Toward the end of the inscription, the high priest asks whether Amun desires the slaying of a murderer. "Then the great god nodded greatly, greatly."[4] While we know nothing of the enactment of Amun's proclamation, we do know that murder was specifically

---

[1] Pierre Montet, *Les enigmes de Tanis*, Paris: Payot, 1952, p. 36.
[2] John G. Griffiths, "Menschenopfer", in *LA* 4, 64.
[3] See Jean Yoyotte, "Héra d' Héliopolis et le Sacrifice Humain", *Annuaire—Ecole pratique des hautes aetudes, Section-sciences religieuses*, 1980–1, p. 35.
[4] Heinrich Karl Brugsch, *Reise nach der grossen Oase El Khargeh in der libyschen Wüste; Beschreibung ihrer Denkmäler und wissenschaftliche Untersuchungen über das Vorkommen der Oasen in den altägyptischen Inschriften auf Stein und Papyru*, Leipzig, Germany: J.C. Hinrichs, 1878, pl. 22, line 23.

designated as a capital offense in this case. No definite manner of execution was stipulated, neither was any reasoning provided for the punishment. While murder appears to have been infrequent,[5] as will be seen below, at times homicide was apparently punished with death. However, we know nothing of how murder was regarded before this time period, so we cannot determine whether Amun's decree on this stela was an introduction of a new practice or a reaffirmation of an old one. As we shall see, the principles of this decree outlining capital punishment for murder were acted upon, whether because of this specific ruling or not.

Another oracular decree of Amun was recorded by Sheshonq (grandfather of Sheshonq I, sometimes called Sheshonq the Elder)[6] on a red granite stela in Abydos. The stela records Sheshonq's actions after learning that the priests in charge of his son's mortuary establishment had been appropriating the proceeds for themselves. He appealed to the king, who in turn appealed to Amun via an oracle. After Amun proclaimed the guilt of the priests, the god dictated their sentence:

> Then his majesty spoke again in the presence of this great god: "O my good lord, will you slay the guard,[7] the administrator, the scribe, the inspector, every one who was sent on any commission to the field, those who stole anything of his from the offering-table of Osiris the great chief of Mê, Namlot the triumphant, son of Mehetnusekhet, who is in Abydos; all the people who plundered from his divine offerings, his people, his cattle, his garden, his every oblation, and all of his beneficent things...."
> The great god nodded.[8]

The capital punishment thus decreed by Amun agrees with both the Teachings of Amenemope and the death sentence of an embezzling temple official connected with the Great Tomb Robberies discussed in chapter 7.[9] This case presents clear evidence that misuse of priestly office for personal gain, especially embezzlement, was considered a capital crime. However, we know from the Nauri Decree that not all such fraudulent use of proceeds demanded death. It is difficult to determine whether there was a rhyme or reason for applying capital punishment in some cases and not in others. Perhaps in the current case, Sheshonq's political power mandated greater penalties. Still, Seti I could easily have done the same, and he did not. We may safely conclude that in the case recorded on this stela capital punishment was the condemnation. Further generalizations are imprudent.

Dynasty 22

Some generations after Sheshonq, one of his descendants committed to writing an act of sanctioned killing on a large scale. Midway through the reign of Takelot II, he appointed his crown prince, Prince Osorkon, to be general of the entire army, Governor of the South, and High Priest of Amun.[10] Thebes did not accept Osorkon's rule well, and within a few years the city rebelled. Osorkon dealt with this uprising harshly; after putting down the rebellion, the prince called for the prisoners to be brought to him: "Then they were brought to him immediately, like a bunch of pinioned ones (*mi ḥtr dnḥw*) Then he struck them down for him (*ʿḥʿ.n sḫr=f n=f st*) causing them to be carried like goats on the night of the Feast of the Evening Sacrifice in which braziers are lit (*mi ʿrw grḥ ḥt h3wy rkḥ ʿhw im*) like braziers at the going forth of Sothis (*mi ʿhw prt spdt*). Every man was burned with fire at the place of his crime."[11]

Several salient issues arise from this inscription. First, an indeterminate number of "rebels" (*sbiw*) were obviously killed. It is unknown whether they were killed by a blow from Osorkon and then burned, or whether they were struck by a nonfatal ritual blow and then burned alive. Leahy, while acknowledging that either interpretation is valid, believes that since "each man" was burned, they may have been dealt a ritual blow, perhaps as kings did in smiting scenes, and then individually burned alive.[12] Kitchen argues that they were killed first.[13] If the rebels were indeed substitutes for a regular sacrifice, they were likely slain and then burned, as was probably done to goats and other animal sacrifices. In either case, we again see the likelihood that the victims were first struck by a knife or mace and then burned.

More important is the ritual context in which the act occurs. Whatever the method of death, the inscription makes two references to ritual activities. It was performed "on the night of the Feast of the Evening Sacrifice" in a manner similar to the lighting of braziers "at the going forth of Sothis," the Dog Star. The inscription also makes two references to braziers. Furthermore, two similes compare the criminals to sacrificial animals. They were pinioned like sacrificial birds and then carried like goats.[14]

---

[5] John Laurence Gee, "The Requirements of Ritual Purity in Ancient Egypt", PhD dissertation, Yale University, 1998, 260.

[6] See Kenneth A. Kitchen, *The Third Intermediate Period in Egypt (1100–650 B.C.)*, 2nd ed. with supplement, Warminster, England: Aris & Phillips, 1995, pp. 100–22, for a discussion of the names and rulers of this period.

[7] The word is illegible—only the military determinative is left.

[8] Auguste Mariette, *Abydos: Choix de Monuments*, vol. 2, Paris: Nationale, 1880, pl. 36; my translation is indebted to that of Breasted, *ARE* 4, 329.

[9] See chapter 7, "Various Capital Offenses" and "The Great Tomb Robberies".

[10] See Kitchen, *The Third Intermediate Period*, p. 330, for a more detailed discussion.

[11] Bubastite Portal, Annals of the High Priest Osorkon, inscription of Year 11 of Takelot II, cols. 35–6, as in Harold Hayden Nelson, *Reliefs and Inscriptions at Karnak*, Chicago: University of Chicago Press, 1936, pls. 16, 18, 19; see also Ricardo Caminos, *The Chronicle of Prince Osorkon*, Rome: Pontificium Institutum Biblicum, 1958, p. 48.

[12] Anthony Leahy, "Death by Fire in Ancient Egypt", *Journal of the Economic and Social History of the Orient* 27, no. 2, 1984, 202 and n. 42.

[13] Kitchen, *The Third Intermediate Period*, p. 331.

[14] As was noted in chapter 5, Dennis D. Hughes, *Human Sacrifice in Ancient Greece*, New York: Routledge, 1991, p. 4, discusses the problem of the terminology of human sacrifice in the study of Greek religion and scholars' semantic wrestle, which parallels the terminology problem outlined in this study. He concludes that when humans are sacrificed in the place of animals, or when the slaying of humans is described using language identical to that of animal sacrifice, the act should undoubtedly be referred to as *human sacrifice*. While his point is

By using three pairs, the text's author ensured that the ritual connections could not be overlooked. Osorkon clearly treated these criminals like sacrificial animals, and their fate was the same.[15] Leahy opines that the uprising had been a strike against Ma'at, especially since it had been against the man who was concurrently prince and High Priest of Amun; the ritualistic punishment was designed to erase that threat.[16] The comparison to goats is apropos to this interpretation, since goats were sometimes sacrificed as symbols of disorder.[17] Also, as we have previously discussed, burning completely destroyed the person, in the mortal realm and all others. Such complete destruction secured Ma'at's integrity. Additionally, we know that some temple sacrifices were consumed by fire, especially in the Late Period.[18] Thus, it seems likely that Osorkon replaced goats with human rebels in a sacrifice designed to completely destroy a disorderly element.

Interestingly, there may even be archaeological evidence for this act. Osorkon made it plain that each man was burned "in the place of his crime." Excavators working outside of Karnak's enclosure wall found on the southeast corner a columned hall destroyed by fire. Carbon dating places the ashes from this layer in the same time period as the Theban uprising.[19]

Prince Osorkon's acts are vividly and unmistakably portrayed. There can be no doubt that he killed a large number of people nor that he did it with ritual intent. In Osorkon's chronicle of the event, he also calls for the fire of Mut to consume those who do not obey the king's orders promulgated by Osorkon.[20] This threat, presumably, notified all who might think of rebellion in the future that they would meet the same fate as those he had already burned. Such a warning, with its obvious reference to real burning, illuminates other threats of action from supernatural beings in royal decrees. If Osorkon's threat could have real consequences, was it the same with others? We cannot know, but it seems likely.

The reference to the "going forth of Sothis" rings an according note with fragment 86 of Manetho.[21] Manetho, an Egyptian historian, writes that at one point humans had been sacrificed during the dog days (the going forth of Sothis). Yoyotte points out this parallel[22] and argues that fragment 85 may concern an ongoing practice of ritualized capital punishment at Heliopolis during the Third Intermediate Period.[23] He believes that Osorkon may have continued this practice in Thebes. Whether Osorkon was following Heliopolis custom or not, his slayings clearly took place in a ritual context.

Davies writes that servant burials are attested from this time period.[24] He includes no further information and no citations. My research has not revealed any evidence for such. Thus, unless more data is forthcoming, this remains a spectral allegation.

It must be acknowledged that the rulers of Dynasty 22 were Libyan and could have brought foreign customs which influenced the killing outlined above. However, both of the cases just presented fit so well with patterns of Egyptian practice already established that we must conclude that these Libyans were acting in an Egyptian manner. Their actions are not singular, but they instead invite comparison with their wholly Egyptian predecessors and neatly place themselves in a continuum of Egyptian actions. Clearly, the sanctioned killing just outlined is in keeping with Egyptian practice as presented thus far in this study.

Dynasty 25

The Napatan rulers of Dynasty 25 engaged in several activities that impinge upon our topic. The Napatans came from Kush, conquered Egypt, then returned to their Kushite capital. Soon, however, they began ruling from within Egypt. They were thoroughly Egyptianized, though it is difficult to ascertain what Kushite practices they brought into their methods of rule. Therefore, we will compare each incident with previous Egyptian practice in order to ascertain whether the new evidence fits a previously established pattern.

After gaining control of Egypt, King Piankhy erected a victory stela, which records a crucial event. Quickly thrusting forward in a pattern that had begun long before him, King Piankhy emphasized purity a great deal in his stela. This emphasis can be seen in his appeal to the people of Memphis. After marching to Memphis, King Piankhy made his appeal at least partially in response to the growing power of his rival ruler Tefnakht in the Twenty-fourth Dynasty. Before arriving at Memphis, Piankhy celebrated the Feast of Amun and Opet at Karnak and Luxor. Next, he besieged Hermopolis. A few defenders were killed by archers and slingers during the siege, yet eventually Hermopolis capitulated, and Piankhy took control with little bloodshed. Upon learning of Hermopolis's surrender, Herakleopolis surrendered without a fight. The town of Per-sekhemkheperre originally planned to oppose Piankhy, but upon his warning they acquiesced without fighting or loss of life.

---

well made, I will continue using the term *ritual slaying* to avoid the pitfalls outlined in chapter 1, "The Terminology of Sacrifice."

[15] Harco Willems, "Crime, Cult and Capital Punishment (Mo'alla Inscription 8)", *JEA* 76, 1990, 50–1, makes the same point more briefly.

[16] Leahy, "Death by Fire", p. 201.

[17] Byron E. Shafer, "Temples, Priests, and Rituals: An Overview", *Temples of Ancient Egypt*, Byron E. Shafer (ed.), Ithaca, NY: Cornell University Press, 1997, p. 25; see also Book of the Dead, chapter 18.

[18] Shafer, "Temples, Priests, and Rituals: An Overview", p. 25.

[19] Donald Redford, *The Excavation of Kom elpAhmar and Environs*, The Akhenaten Temple Project 3, Toronto: Akhenaten Temple Project, 1994, p. 14–15.

[20] Caminos, *The Chronicle of Prince Osorkon*, p. 73; Leahy, "Death by Fire", p. 201.

[21] Gerald P. Verbrugghe and John M. Wickersham, *Berossos and Manetho*, Ann Arbor: University of Michigan Press, 2000, p. 169.

[22] Yoyotte, "Héra d'Héliopolis", p. 98. For a larger discussion on this fragment of Manetho, see J. Gwyn Griffiths, "Human Sacrifices in Egypt: The Classical Evidence", *ASAE* 48, 1948.

[23] Yoyotte, "Héra d'Héliopolis", pp. 101–2. For Manetho fragment 85, see Verbrugghe and Wickersham, *Berossos and Manetho*, p. 165.

[24] Nigel Davies, *Human Sacrifice in History and Today*, New York: William Morrow, 1981, p. 37.

Mer-Atum and Iti-tawy responded similarly. The only violence to occur in these towns was some kind of sacrifice performed in Mer-Atum, but a lacuna prevents us from knowing what kind of sacrifice.

Next, Piankhy approached Memphis. In order to convince the people of Memphis that capitulation was in their best interest, Pianky told them to look at what had happened in the south: "Not one was slain there, except the rebels (*sbiw*) who had blasphemed god. They were executed as malcontents (*ḫ3k-ibw*)."[25] We possess no further knowledge about the blasphemers to which Piankhy refers. Perhaps *blasphemer* was the label he applied to traitors who had planned to resist Piankhy or had allied themselves with Tefnakht. Since Piankhy considered himself so closely allied with Amun, defying Piankhy would be considered blasphemy. Later in his reign, Piankhy refused to allow uncircumcised fish-eaters into his palace because they were impure. In light of this event, Piankhy could have considered blasphemy any action that was ritually impure. Clearly, in the face of relatively peaceful victories, the killings must have taken place in a noncombat setting. For unknown reasons, Piankhy felt that some people deserved to die, so the blasphemers were executed.

The execution of rebels while a ruler (re)asserts power is very much in line with what we have seen in Egypt thus far. Senusret I engaged in similar activity in Tod. Merenptah executed both Libyan and Nubian insurgents. Prince Osorkon's measures against Theban insurrectionists also fit the pattern. Piankhy's actions against blasphemers appears to follow earlier Egyptian rulers. His motivation for selecting certain people may have been due to his Napatan background, though it may also have been the rising concern with purity. Since we do not know what his motivation was, we cannot discern its degree of Egyptian nativity; however, the act itself is clearly not of a foreign nature.

Piankhy also decreed the possibility for death as he tried to take firm control of the entire kingdom. As the rulers of lower Egypt gathered before him, he made it clear that plotting to withhold taxes/tribute was worthy of death (*mwt=f n mwt=f n it=f*).[26] While the exact meaning of this line, especially the last part of the phrase, has been debated, it is clear that death was the intended penalty.[27] As is so often the case, we do not know if this was ever enacted. But at least at this time it was considered a capital offense.

Piankhy's Piankhy's successor Shabako committed a similar slaying of Tefnakht's successor Bocchoris.[28] We are unsure why Shabako left his Napatan home to establish himself as a resident ruler in Egypt. Because of Shabako's actions against Bocchoris, we can assume that Bocchoris's rising power in the Twenty-fourth Dynasty was part of the reason. A fragment of Manetho's history, preserved by Syncellus, records that Shabako "captured Bokhkhoris and burned him alive."[29] We know nothing of how or why. Still, as Leahy notes, the Manethoan account has been largely accepted by scholars.[30] We may assume, as Leahy does, that Bocchoris was viewed as a vassal in rebellion.[31] The burning comports with both the actions of Piankhy and the actions of those whom Piankhy seems to be imitating, as outlined above. The inclusion of burning makes Shabako's act an even closer parallel, since Senusret, Merenptah, and Prince Osorkon all burned those who had rebelled against their rule. The burning of the parvenu Bocchoris appears to have almost certainly happened, and it fit in the Egyptian tradition.

A private donation stela from the reign of Shabako states that anyone who harmed the donated fields would fall to the sword of the king and was destined to be involved with Sakhmet, though a break in the text makes it impossible to tell what this involvement was.[32] Since the donation had been given to a temple, and since Shabako was pictured on the stela, we may assume that the land in question had come under state protection. Of course, we cannot know whether anyone ever damaged the fields and received the said punishment. What is more important is the idea that such lands were protected by a threat of execution under the auspices of the king. From this we learn both that royal execution, like the kind mentioned in inscriptions from the First Intermediate Period, continued at this late date and that damaging property protected by the state potentially carried a death sentence.

The mention of Sakhmet could be construed to shift the stela's threats into the supernatural sphere; conversely, the reference to the king's sword seems to belong distinctly to this world. More plausible is the idea that, as has been attested so many times, the stela represents an appeal for punishment in both spheres to ensure penalty. This particular case actually sheds some light upon earlier similar inscriptions, since the state would almost certainly protect its lands in an earthly manner. The certainty that this stela makes a concrete reference to state action makes it all the more likely that earlier inscriptions were appealing for action in both spheres. It should also be apparent that the inscription under discussion matches known Egyptian practice perfectly well, and it is extremely unlikely that its elements related to capital punishment are due to Napatan influence.

The date of the Shabako Stone's composition is somewhat in question, but it appears to have originated in

---

[25] Nicolas-Christophe Grimal, *La stèle triomphale de Pi(ankh)y au Musée du Caire, JE 48862 et 47086–47089*, Cairo: Institut Français d'Archéologie Orientale, 1981, p. 95, line 86.

[26] Piankhy Stela, line 111.

[27] See Anthony Spalinger, "The Military Background of the Campaign of Piye (Piankhy)," SAK 7 (1979), p. 288; Hans Goedicke, *Pi(ankh)y in Egypt*, Baltimore: Halgo, 1998, 129-31; and, for the most recent and explicit treatment of the phrase and what it means, see Dan'el Kahn, "I Swear to Pay (Only Part of) My Taxes: Padiese's Oath to Piankhy," *JARCE*, 42, 2005-2006, p. 105-108.

[28] Bocchoris is also known as Bakenranef.

[29] Verbrugghe and Wickersham, *Berossos and Manetho*, p. 147; see also W.G. Waddell, *Manetho*, Cambridge, MA: Harvard University Press, 1980, p. 167; and Leahy, "Death by Fire", p. 201.

[30] Leahy, "Death by Fire", p. 201.

[31] Leahy, "Death by Fire", p. 201.

[32] Emil Brugsch-Bey, "Mittheilungen von Emil Brugsch-Bey", *ZÄS* 34, 1896, 84.

the Twenty-fifth Dynasty. Toward the end of the text, we are informed that "life is given to he who acts peacefully; death is given to those who commit criminal acts."[33] While this phrase appears in a highly abstract text about the creation of man, it still probably reflects the attitudes of its day, indicating that at least some criminals were killed.

Tantamun put Necho to death. This was almost certainly because he saw Necho as someone who had rebelled against him.

The last relevant evidence for this time period comes from a stela found in the Nubian capital of Napata, the native city of the rulers from the Twenty-fifth Dynasty. This stela reports that Amun, probably via an oracle, ordered some priests to be burned to death because they had either murdered or plotted to murder an innocent man.[34] This inscription dovetails into the patterns we have already discerned. Capital punishment for murder has already been attested in the immediately preceding periods, though evidence is unknown before then. The divine decree for justice to be acted out by mortal men is another trend well attested and on the rise. Burning was one of the most well-established modes of sanctioned killing. We do not know whether Amun's demands were met, but we can be sure of two things: the practice is Egyptian, and the decree provides a window to juridical procedures, regardless of its successful enforcement. Clearly the Twenty-fifth Dynasty rulers engaged in sanctioned killing as much as did their Egyptian predecessors.

Dynasty 26

The Twenty-sixth Dynasty saw the final known example of the *tekenu* burial. Theban Tomb 36 depicts the rite.[35] The existence of this depiction does not simply demonstrate one more example of this somewhat likely case of ritual slaying involved with burial; indeed its existence nearly 1200 years after the first attestation of the tekenu ritual implies that this practice was more prevalent than its attestations denote. The longevity of such a rite is unlikely if it were employed sporadically and selectively. While it is true that the Twenty-sixth Dynasty witnessed an intentional attempt to return to the ways of the past,[36] it is improbable that they would have been able to recover a rite that had not been in use for hundreds of years. It is, instead, far more plausible that this rite took place with more continuity and frequency than tomb depictions and excavations indicate. It is, however, also plausible that the owner of this tomb archaized his decorations by copying from earlier tombs scenes that had no meaning for him. However, the rest of his tomb decoration is not archaized, making it less probable that such was the case with this one relief.

Another type of sanctioned violence is highlighted in the so-called Petition of Petiese, preserved on Papyrus Rylands IX. This records the petition of Petiese, a man of some influence,[37] concerning the murder of two of his grandsons during the time of Psamtek I. After apprehending two of the priests who had committed the crime, Petiese brought the case before the king. It is recorded that "Pharaoh caused that the law be enacted on the two priests."[38] Here it is unclear which law was enacted upon the priests. Some ideas about the possible punishment comes from a later portion of the text. Petiese, apparently appeased by the death of two priests in requital of the death of his two grandsons, returned to the town of the crime. In an effort to make peace, Petiese vowed to do no more punishing, telling the rest of the guilty that of "the injury which you have committed, I have caused its equivalent to be done to you. Is it right to cause Amun to strike down the remainder of these youths and let this town become an enemy?"[39] Thus, Petiese later declines the suggestion of throwing the criminals into a brazier ($w^c\ {}^cḫ$).[40] This suggestion strongly implies that burning was the form of death inflicted upon the two priests whom Pharaoh had punished. Furthermore, Petiese's assurances that he would not slay all the youth involved in the murder provides firm evidence that killing them was his right. This incident continues the pattern we have seen for the execution of criminals, especially murderers, as well as the pattern for burning rebels.

A similar story is told from the Twenty-sixth Dynasty. The composition date of the text is uncertain, but its terminal dates lie between the Twenty-sixth Dynasty and the fourth century BCE.[41] In this fragmentary tale, a group of men have killed one Djedseshep under the direction of a prophet of Horus. For this murder, Pharaoh commands "that he [the prophet of Horus] would be set upon the brazier with his family and his compatriot . . . placing a man who was the prophet of Horus, Lord of Letopolis, upon the brazier."[42] We even know the place of the execution, since a later character retells all that happened to his "fellows upon the brazier which had been done at the door of the palace."[43]

---

[33] Shabaka Stone, line 57.
[34] Cairo JE 48865 as in Nicolas-Christophe Grimal, *Quatre steles napatéennes au Musée du Caire*, Cairo: Institut Francais d'Archeologie Oriental, 1981, p. 38, lines 15–17 and p. 39, lines 4–5. See also Leahy, "Death by Fire", p. 202.
[35] J. Gwyn Griffiths, "The Tekenu, the Nubians and the Butic Burial", *Kush* 6, 1958, 112.
[36] See Peter Der Mannuelian, *Living in the Past: Studies in Archaism of the Egyptian Twenty-Sixth Dynasty*, New York: Keagan Paul International, 1994; and Anthony Spalinger, "The Concept of Monarchy during the Saite Epoch: An Essay of Synthesis", *Orientalia* 47, 1978, for some of the evidence for this trend.
[37] See Robert K. Ritner, "The End of the Libyan Anarchy in Egypt: P. Rylands IX cols. 11–12", *Enchoria* 17, 1990, 101–8, for a discussion of his position.
[38] P. Rylands IX 11/19, as in F. Lloyd Griffith, *Catalogue of the Demotic Papyri in the John Rylands Library, Manchester, with Facsimiles and Complete Translations*, London: University, 1909. Also Claude Traunecker,"Les deux enfants du temple de Teudjoï" in Gabolde (ed.), *Hommages à Jean-Claude Goyon*, Cairo, BdE 143, 2008.
[39] P. Rylands IX, 12/16–17. My translation is indebted to Griffith's.
[40] P. Rylands IX, 13/11. See also Leahy, "Death by Fire", 202 and n. 52.
[41] H.S. Smith and W.J. Tait, *Saqqâra Demotic Papyri*, London: Egypt Exploration Society, 1983, pp. 61–2.
[42] P. Dem. Saq. I, 14/3-4, as in H.S. Smith and W.J. Tait, *Saqqâra Demotic Papyri*, London: Egypt Exploration Society, 1983, pp. 8, 40.
[43] P. Dem. Saq. I, 14/36, pp. 9, 41. The place of execution runs contra to the conclusion reached by Laure Bazin, "Enquête sur les Lieux

While the story is fictional, it draws upon elements familiar to its Egyptian audience. As Leahy argues, the actions depicted are wholly Egyptian, and the definite article before the brazier suggests that not only was the audience familiar with the practice of burning criminals, but they were also familiar with the brazier itself.[44] Additionally, the story adds to the evidence for murder being a capital crime because its reading depends upon Egyptian familiarity with the punishment. This piece of literature provides a clear reflection of Egyptian practices, a reflection that dovetails perfectly with the pattern established thus far in this study.

Similarly, a stela from this dynasty demonstrates the tradition of burning, probably cultic burning, as punishment for interfering with funerary activity. This stela threatens those who damage it with being judged in the temple of Herakleopolis. The condemned person is destined for the knife; his body parts will become a burnt offering ($ḥ^cw=f\ m\ sbi\ n\ sḏ.t$), since he is now destined for the brazier of Osiris.[45] It could be argued that these threats are meant completely for the supernatural realm. However, the temple of Herakleopolis exists on this earth. Moreover, while the events threatened do have similarities with funerary literature, they also have similarities with worldly events, as demonstrated in this study. At this point in our investigation, burning criminals in a cultic setting is well established. The use of a knife before cultic burning recalls Senusret I's actions at Tod and Prince Osorkon's actions at Thebes. While the majority of stelae do not threaten mortal punishments, this particular stela joins the list of those herein presented that impinge upon the worldly realm. It is not known if the punishments of the stela were intended for real enactment. The actual realization of the threat is unlikely. Nevertheless, it likely draws from its real-life milieu.

The events of this period strengthen conclusions we have already drawn. From this time period, we learn of the fate of murderers. Capital punishment for murder may be a new development. It is certainly curious to witness the sudden rise in reports regarding murder. This rise may be due to more societal unrest in the midst of less centralized control; alternatively, the lack of earlier evidence could stem from a prohibition against recording such incidents during earlier eras, due to a fear of the record constituting a disturbance of Ma'at. If this is true, we must ask why this prohibition would have evaporated. Other than this curious new development, the evidence available from this period matches perfectly the evidence that preceded it. We now have a large body of evidence for sanctioned killing that must be analyzed.

D'Exécution dans l'Égypte Ancienne," in *Égypte, Afriqe et Orient* 35 (2004), 31-40.
[44] Leahy, "Death by Fire", p. 200.
[45] Griffith, *Rylands Library*, pl. 40, lines 7–9; see also Willems, "Crime, Cult and Capital Punishment", p. 42–3.

Third Intermediate Period and Twenty-Sixth Dynasty Evidence of Sanctioned Killing

Violence	Weak Evidence	Plausible Evidence	Strong Evidence	Very Strong Evidence
Ritual killing in connection with foundation of Tanis temple	X*			
Death decreed by oracle for murderers in Banishment Stela				X
Death decreed by oracle for priests who had embezzled funerary proceeds				X
Burning of many Theban rebels by Prince Osorkon in a ritual setting				X
Servant burial in Twenty-second Dynasty	X			
Slaying of blasphemous rebels by King Piankhy				X
Death decreed for tax evasion				X
Burning alive of Bocchiris by Shabako				X
Tantamun puts Necho to death				X
Death decree for those who would harm temple lands				X
Ongoing practice of death for those who damage state property		X		
Death by burning decreed for priests who murdered				X
Ongoing process of the death penalty for murderers			X	
Ritual tekenu slaying at Twenty-sixth Dynasty burial			X**	
Ongoing practice of tekenu slayings for burials		X		
Death by burning decreed for two priests who murdered Petiese's grandsons				X
Literary tale reflects real practice of burning murderers				X
Death by burning decreed for those who interfere with funerary establishment			X	
Death by burning in a ritual setting decreed for interference with a funerary establishment			X	

* Case borders between weak and plausible
** Case borders between plausible and strong

Chapter 9

A TIME TO KILL:
THE APPROPRIATENESS OF VIOLENCE

I will cause you to be turned to ashes, as one who does not exist.

—*The Shipwrecked Sailor*

Poring over the fascinating details of mounds of data is not enough. Thus far we have looked at small plots of land, occasionally taking a step back to see how one plot affected another, but we have not looked at this land from a higher vantage point, attempting to survey all of our fields together. Without taking our microexamples and applying them to the macro, gaining the big picture, we have left too much undone. Therefore, it is now time to analyze our data, to find the larger story of Egyptian attitudes and practices regarding sanctioned killing. In order to see the frequency of sanctioned killing and to trace trends over time, the known evidence will be analyzed in several manners, using charts to illustrate the data. We will look at the number of evidences by period.

While performing our analyses, we should keep in mind that greater numbers for later periods do not necessarily demonstrate greater actual frequency. Instead, the greater evidence largely reflects the greater number of sources available. Still, an overview of violence for each time period can help identify trends and demonstrate consistencies. In order to compensate for the chronological differences in textual sources available, figure 9.2 was created as a control group. This table represents the number of pages dedicated to each time period in Breasted's monumental work, *Ancient Records of Egypt*. While many more sources have been discovered since Breasted undertook his work in the early part of the last century, it is safe to posit that the ratio of texts per period has not changed significantly. With this control-group table, we may compare the number of records of sanctioned killing in a time period to the amount of records of any kind available from that period. Furthermore, each table is accompanied by another table that represents only the violence known from textual sources, allowing us to compare the tables more closely with the control group.

In order to track trends diachronically, we will chart the number of evidences by period. We will also examine the types of violence inflicted, both by period and overall. Likewise, we will analyze the actions that brought about sanctioned violence, both by period and overall. These analyses will maintain the evaluation of *plausible evidence*, *strong evidence*, and *very strong evidence*. The categories will be cumulative; for example, the total for violence supported by *plausible evidence* will also include violence that is supported by *strong* and *very strong* evidence. This will allow the reader to see a graphic representation of the total possible number of events. Violence supported only by weak evidence is not charted.

Some events fall into more than one category. The primary example is the conjunction of killing in a ritual context and the formal execution of enemies. Not all ritual slaying was of enemies, and not all execution of enemies was in a ritual context, so two separate categories must be created. Nevertheless, some enemies were slain in a ritual context. These enemies will be counted in both categories in the charts that demonstrate the number of evidences of each category, but they will not be counted twice in the charts that demonstrate the overall number of evidences for violence.

For known slayings, each person killed is represented with one to five units. The maximum of five units has been set because there were many incidents in which we do not know how many people were killed, only that it was a large number. Likewise, ongoing trends are assigned five units. Hence, the numbers indicated in the charts are not designed to reflect actual numbers of incidents—we have no way of knowing these—but instead they will help to demonstrate trends. Care should be taken not to employ these charts for anything other than their intended purpose of demonstrating trends.

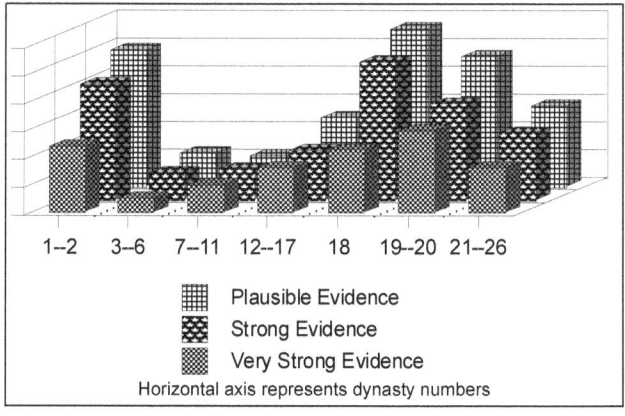

Figure 9.1a – Evidences of Violence by Period

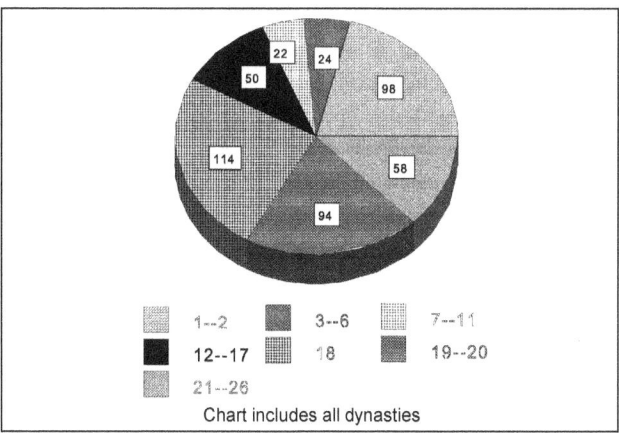

Figure 9.2a – Evidences of Plausible Violence by Dynasty

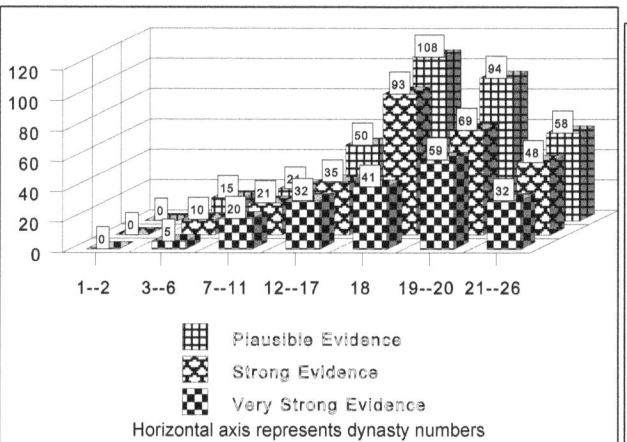

Figure 9.1b – Evidences of Violence
by Period as Learned from Textual Sources

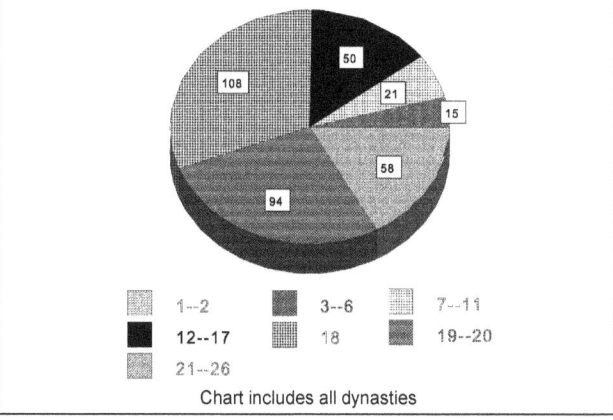

Figure 9.2b – Evidences of Plausible Violence
by Dynasty as Learned from Textual Sources

As the charts are examined, the reader must remember that the evidence we have found can be but the tip of the iceberg. Certainly we have not uncovered even a majority of the incidents of sanctioned killing. Still, the date we have should be discussed and understood. With these things in mind, the following presentation of data is very revealing.

In some ways, the information in the preceding tables is more consistent than the rise and fall of the bars indicate. As mentioned above, we must always be mindful of the changes in the amount of sources available to us. By comparing trends to chart 9.2, we can examine the evidence presented in the tables as compared to the total amount of textual evidence available. For instance, figure 9.1a represents the number of known evidences of sanctioned killing by period. The general trend of frequency is consistent both in the control group of figure 9.2 and in figure 9.1a. The one exception is the incidental spike in the Early Dynastic Period, which represents archaeological finds somewhat unique to that period. Because of their non-textual nature, these archaeological finds are not accounted for in our control group. This is amply demonstrated in figure 9.1b, which documents only those evidences attested in textual sources. Thus, figure 9.1b matches the control group more precisely.

Because the rise and fall of known incidents mentioned in documents matches so well the known number of documents from each period, we can conclude that in all likelihood the frequency of sanctioned killing remained largely consistent over time. This comparison may be skewed somewhat by large events such as the Harem Conspiracy and the Great Tomb Robberies, which generated both a rise in killings and a rise in documents. While several documents were produced in the Twentieth Dynasty as a result of these events, they are too small in number to significantly impact the recorded trend. Additionally, the earlier periods may also have produced a greater number of documents than we have, but for one reason or another, these sources have not survived. For example, the biographical inscription of Weni speaks of a harem conspiracy in the Old Kingdom. He records nothing of its outcome, but executions and accompanying documents quite possibly surrounded this conspiracy only in the twentieth-dynasty intrigue. Inevitably, the lack of known evidences of sanctioned killing in earlier periods parallels the dearth of known textual sources. Therefore, to iterate, it is likely that the frequency of sanctioned killing remained somewhat consistent over time.

A greater variety of information can be gained from the tables that examine the types of and reasons for sanctioned killing over time. Comparing figure 9.3,

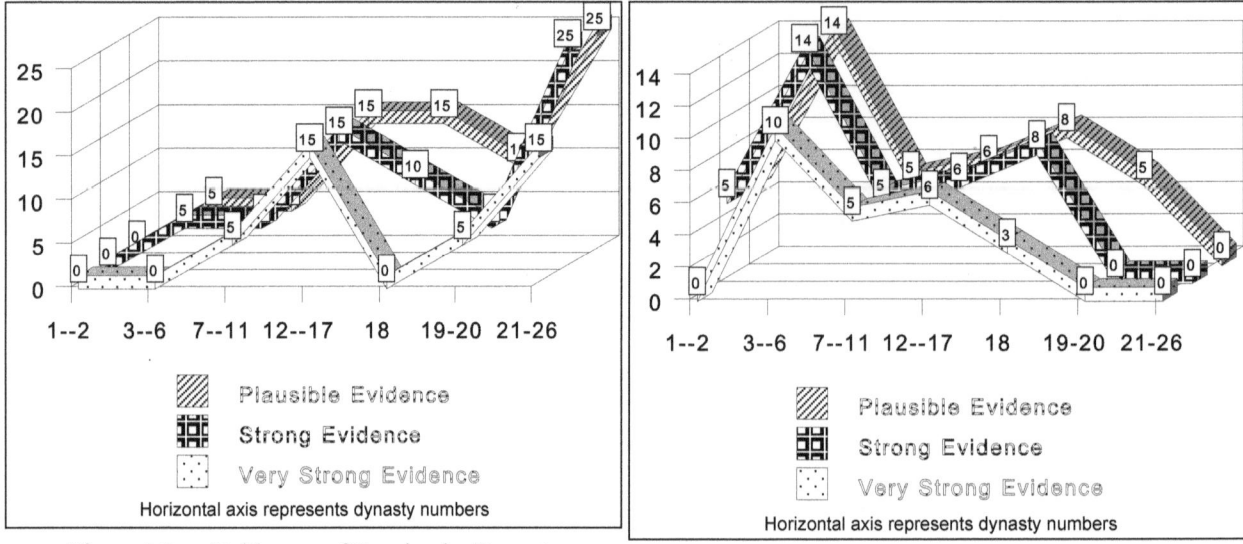

Figure 9.3a – Evidences of Burning by Dynasty

Figure 9.4a – Evidences of Decapitation by Dynasty

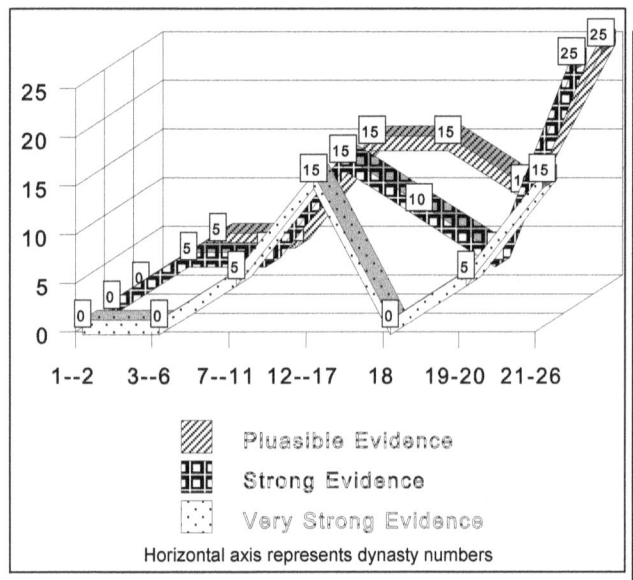

Figure 9.3b – Evidences of Burning by Dynasty as Learned from Textual Sources

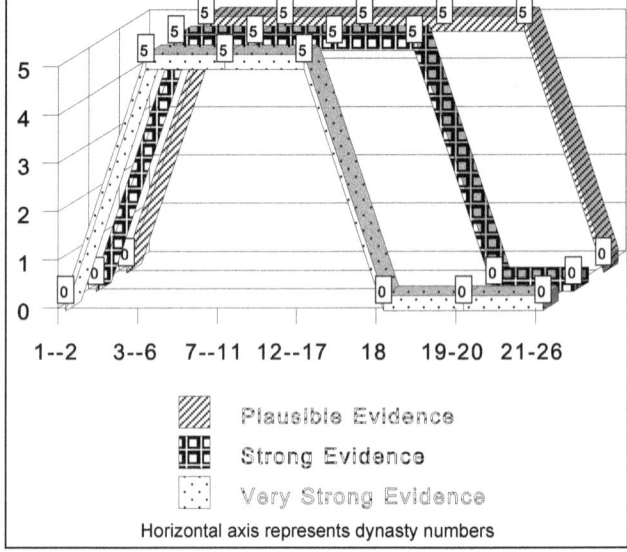

Figure 9.4b – Evidences of Decapitation by Dynasty as learned from textual sources

which examines incidents of burning, with figure 9.1b and 9.2 shows that there is some similarity but also a great deal of divergence. Hence, figure 9.3 may actually reflect changes in the practice of burning over time. Burning is relatively unattested in the earlier periods. We must be careful, since this is an argument of silence. Probably the practice was more prevalent than our evidence indicates. For example, if the Cannibal Hymn really does indicate a system of burning criminals, and if this ritual was spawned in the earlier periods, then there may have been a great deal of burning. What is significant is the spike in burning activity during the Middle Kingdom. We must be aware that this may be due to the accident vof preservation. Preservation is largely determined by the medium of the text, which was often determined by the purpose behind the creation of that text. Hence, acts such as Senusret I burning desecrators at Tod, which were meant to be known and lasting, were inscribed on stone and have thus survived to this day. We are certainly unaware of many violent acts that were not recorded on such a durable medium. Nevertheless, the trend of known violence indicates that the practice of burning may have become more popular during the Middle Kingdom and thenceforth remained a consistent method of inflicting sanctioned killing.

Figure 9.4a and 9.4b, charting incidents of decapitation, also diverge from the control pattern of figure 9.2. Here we see that, at least according to the evidence at hand, decapitation was most popular in the early periods and gradually became less used. This actually matches the other figures well because they show a rise in other types of killing. Yet, it appears that decapitation was a part of sanctioned killing throughout most of the history of ancient Egypt.

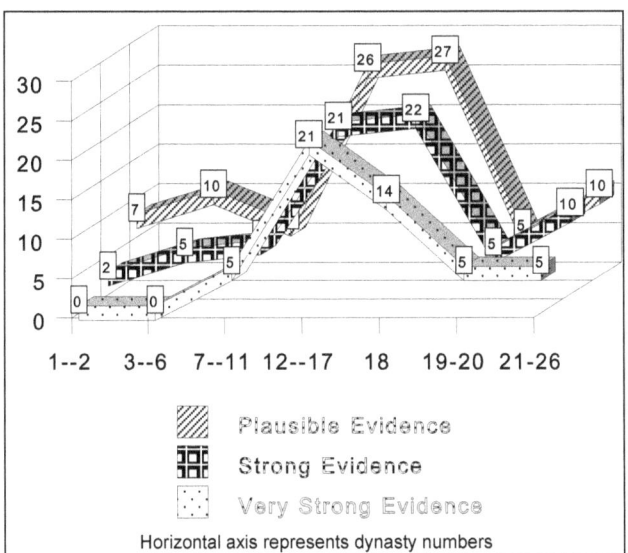

Figure 9.5a – Evidences of Killing in a Ritual Context by Dynasty (Ritual killings in funerary setting not included, they are included in another chart)

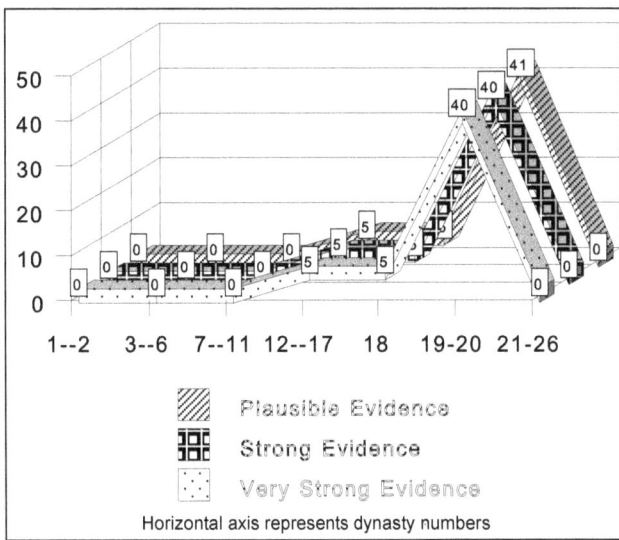

Figure 9.6a – Evidences of Impalement by Dynasty

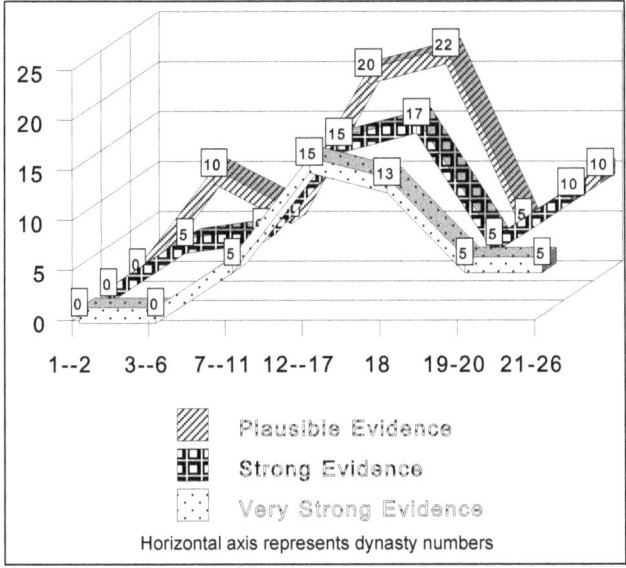

Figure 9.5b – Evidences of Ritual Killings by Dynasty as Learned from Textual Sources (Ritual killings in funerary setting not included, they are included in another chart)

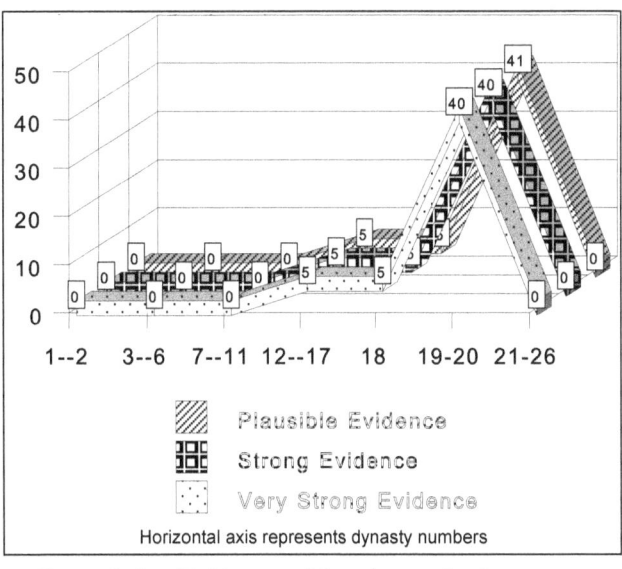

Figure 9.6b – Evidences of Impalement by Dynasty as Learned from Textual Sources

Figure 9.5a does match the control group represented in figure 9.15 fairly well. A comparison of figure 9.5b and figure 9.2 reveals that, for the most part, our knowledge of sanctioned killing in a ritual context matches the availability of documents. As stated above, this indicates that the practice remained somewhat consistent over time. The evidence leads to a firm conclusion that ritual slaying was part of Egyptian society. This idea will be revisited in the next chapter, in which we will examine the smiting scene.

The practice of impalement, represented in figure 9.6, stands in stark contrast to the control group. With the exceptions of Senusret I's Tod inscription and the account of Akhenaten's Nubian campaign, this practice is unattested except in the Ramesside Era. While it is unlikely that the practice was avoided prior to Seti I, the trend is so drastic that we must conclude that impalement was relatively unused except under the Ramessides. In fact, it was apparently the Ramessides' punishment of choice. The reasons for this are unclear.

Killing in association with burial practice, most likely in a ritual context, is represented in figure 9.7. The comparison of figure 9.7b and the control group demonstrates that the practice matches fairly well, though the spike in Dynasty 18 is somewhat more dramatic. The practice of sacrificial servant burial, attested in the earliest dynasties and known from archaeological sources, does seem to have fallen into disuse. However,

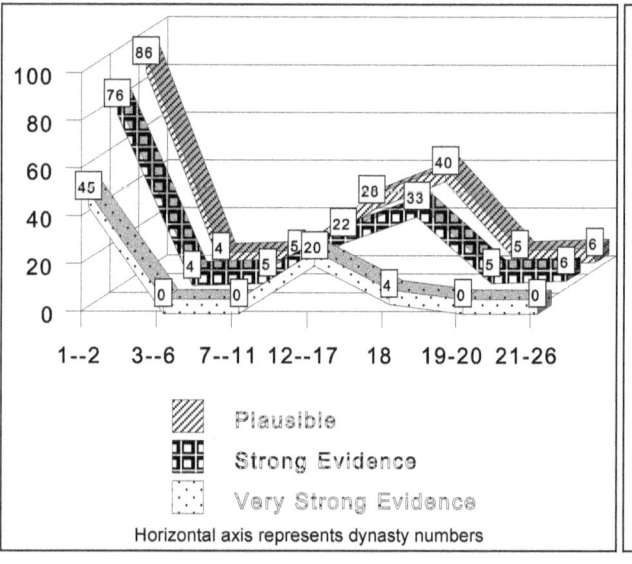

Figure 9.7a – Evidences of Killing Associated with Burial Practice by Dynasty

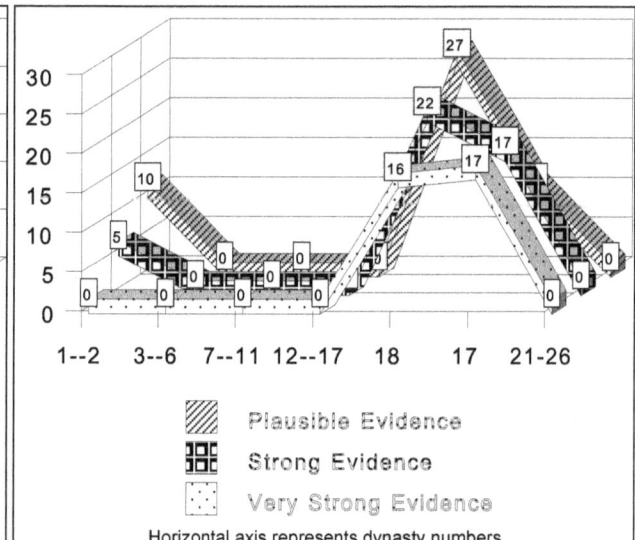

Figure 9.8a – Evidences of Formal Execution of Enemies by Dynasty

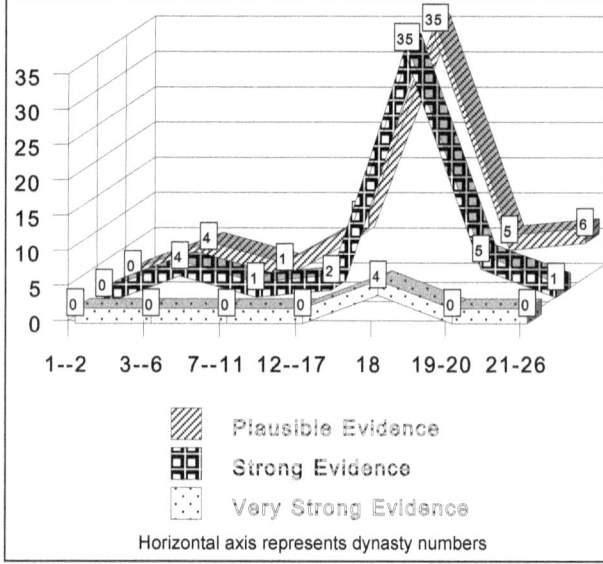

Figure 9.7b – Evidences of Killing Associated with Burial Practice by Dynasty as Learned from Textual Sources

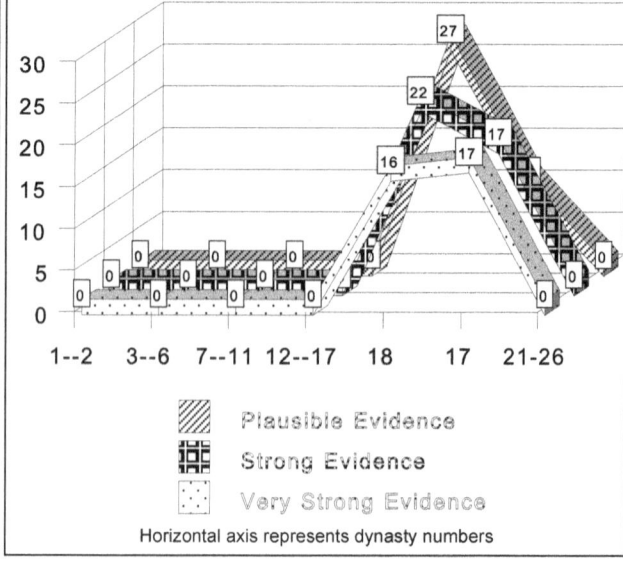

Figure 9.8b – Evidences of Formal Execution of Enemies by Dynasty as Learned from Textual Sources

the decrease after Dynasty 18 is steeper than that of the control group, and the numbers in this dynasty primarily represent the *tekenu* ritual. If the tekenu ritual were not a sanctioned killing in association with burial practice, then it would not correspond to the control group. Funerary slayings may have remained consistent over time, but the case for this stands on less than firm ground. Further research into the tekenu rite is required to truly understand the nature of such practices.

Other than an early-dynastic spike, the formal execution of enemies represented in figure 9.8 also largely corresponds to the control group. This spike may be due to a change in the decorum of what could be presented in royal art, which may have eschewed the frequent depiction of executing enemies that the early-dynastic kings employed. The early-dynastic evidence is not represented in figure 9.8b. Figure 9.8b, representing what we know of the practice from textual sources, somewhat mirrors the control group. This again indicates a roughly consistent employment of this practice over time.

Figure 9.9, which graphs the execution of those who rise up against the state in some manner, conveys very little information. Pictured is a spike in occurrences in the Ramesside Era. This spike is almost completely due to the Harem Conspiracy and the Great Tomb Robberies. It is unlikely that these were unique occurrences in Egyptian history; instead, the discovery of papyri reporting the aftermath is unusual. The propriety of recording such events may have changed over time as well. It is reasonable to suppose that those who rose against the state were always executed. For example, Amenemhet I was very likely assassinated, and it is

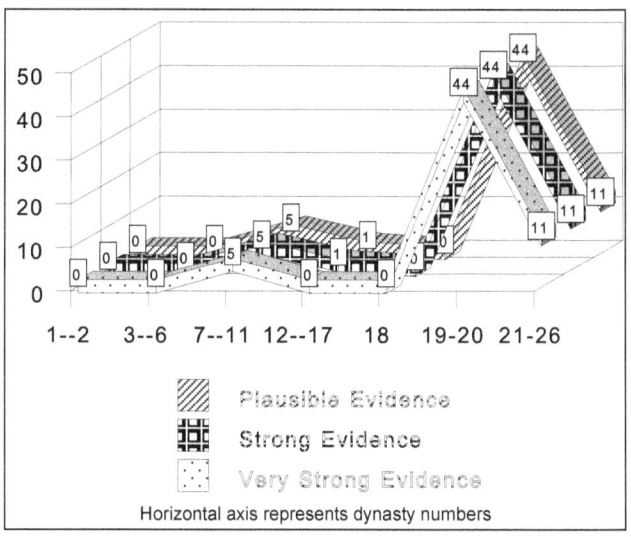

Figure 9.9a – Evidences of Execution of those who Uprise by Dynasty

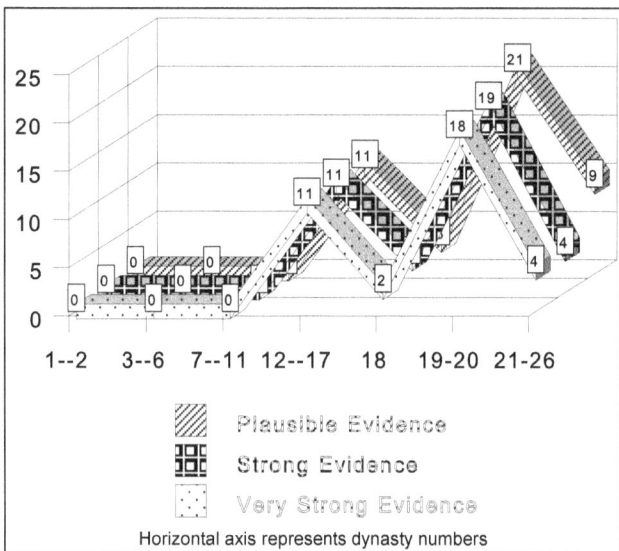

Figure 9.10a – Evidences of Death for Damaging or Stealing State Property by Dynasty

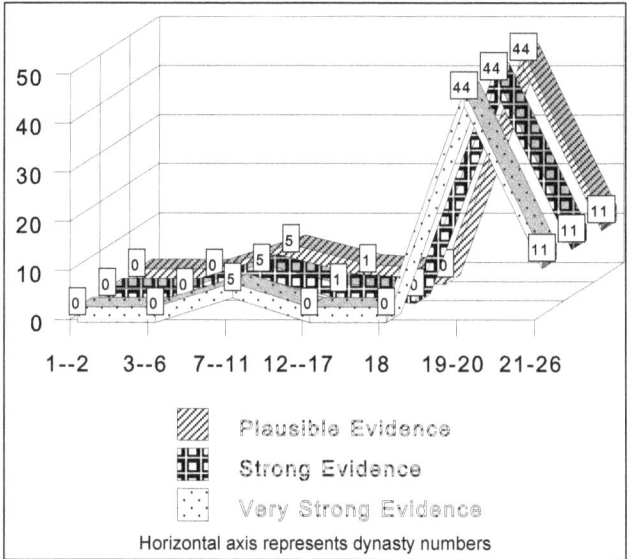

Figure 9.9b – Evidences of the Execution of those who Uprise by Dynasty as Learned from Textual Sources

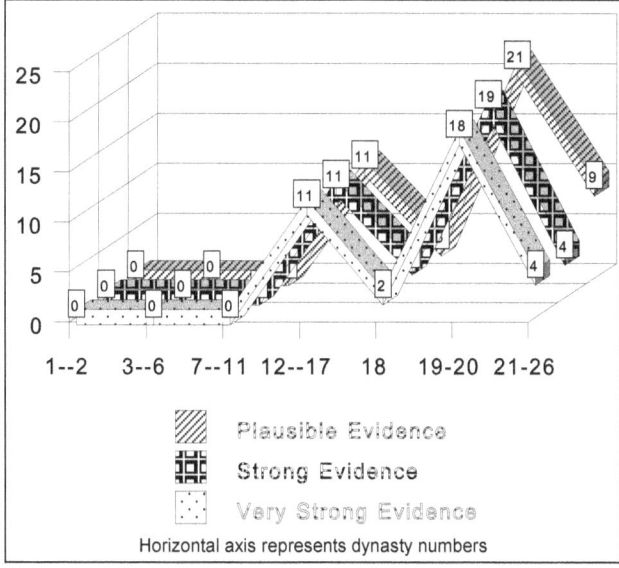

Figure 9.10b – Evidences of Death for Damaging or Stealing State Property by Dynasty as Learned from Textual Sources

unthinkable that his son, Senusret I—whom we know was not opposed to violence—would have let the incident pass without some kind of retribution. But we have no evidence that he got retribution. The graph may represent our knowledge of such events more than it represents a change in policy toward those who rebel.

Capital punishment for damaging or stealing state property is reflected in figure 9.10. The middle-kingdom rise, the eighteenth-dynasty dip, and the Ramesside spike may represent changes in the practice of considering this a capital crime. Middle Kingdom rulers likely reacted to patterns of the First Intermediate Period by creating more stipulations to protect state property from local leaders and individuals. The Ramesside rulers may have had a similar reaction to the Great Tomb Robberies and to the unstable conditions that prevailed toward the end of the Eighteenth Dynasty. The Seventeenth and Eighteenth Dynasties do not seem to have continued such punishment during the interim periods. We know from a seventeenth-dynasty stela that at least one incident of stealing a sacred temple relic was punished by removal of name and office but not by death.[1] The numbers in figure 9.10 probably represent actual changes in sanctioned killing, but the reasons for such changes can presently only be hypothesized.

Figure 9.11 is so dramatic that it almost certainly reflects a change in opinion about what made one worthy of death. The Ramesside spike does not come from a single source or type of source. The idea of killing people who are false in office does not appear before or after this era,

---

[1] Cairo Stela 30770.

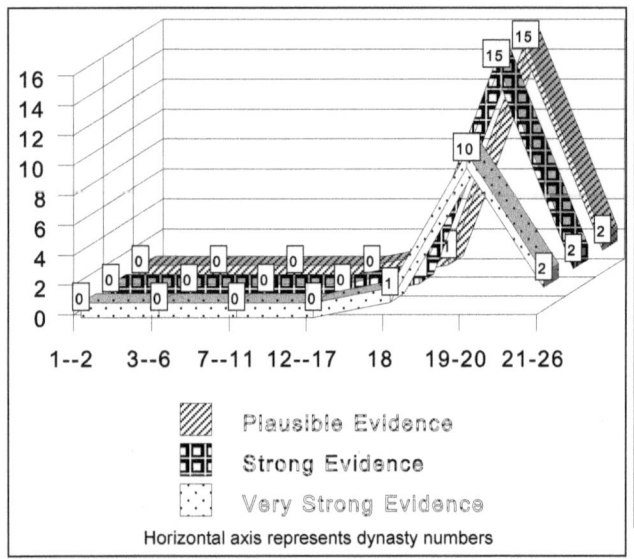

Figure 9.11a – Evidences for Death for Those Who are False in Office by Dynasty

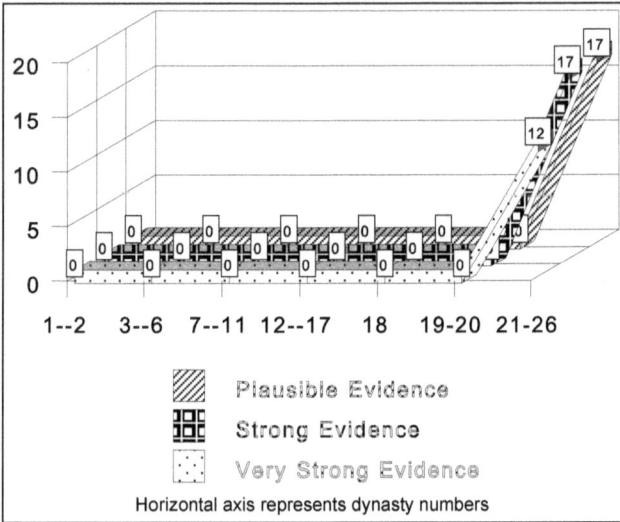

Figure 9.12a – Evidences of Death for Murder by Dynasty

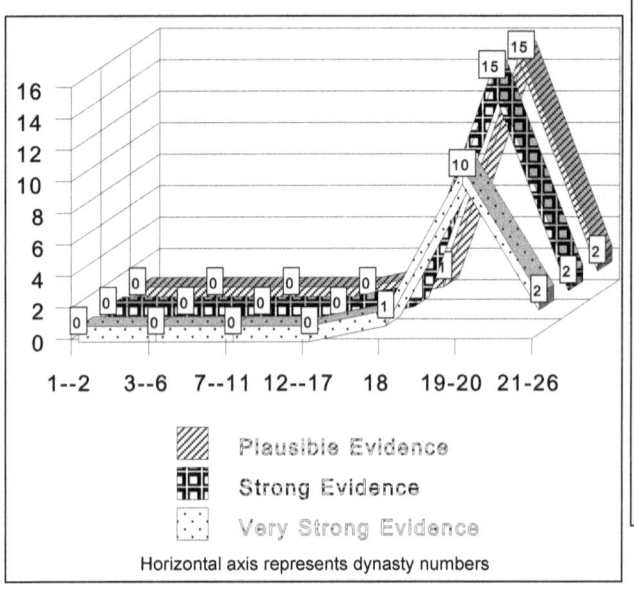

Figure 9.11b – Evidences for Death for Those Who are False in Office by Dynasty as Learned from Textual Sources

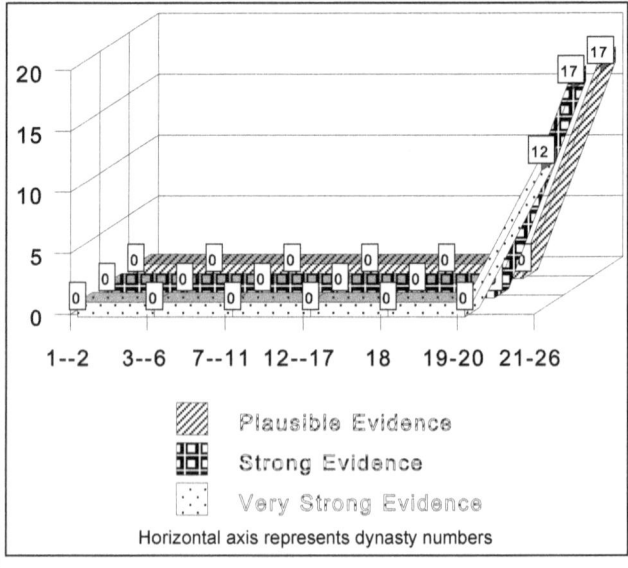

Figure 9.12b – Evidences of Death for Murder by Dynasty as Learned from Textual Sources

with the exception of the decree of Horemheb, who was in many ways a precursor to the Ramesside Era. The evidence indicates that this idea was unique to this time period, or that it was at least more heavily emphasized during this time period.

Similarly, the knowledge we have that murder was considered a capital offence, as represented in figure 9.12, comes exclusively from the Third Intermediate Period. Such a dramatic flux ostensibly reflects a real change in practice. It may instead be due to a change in the practice of recording such chaotic episodes. We have very little evidence for the occurrence and punishment of murder before this period. Still, it is difficult to conceive that the topic of murder would not have been manifested in some way. We must be careful in applying an argument of silence, yet the evidence is strong for a change regarding this practice during the Third Intermediate Period.

From all of these figures, we can gather some basic information. The practice of sanctioned killing seems to have remained largely consistent throughout time, but the preferred manner of inflicting death changed. Burning appears to have been a common practice but was used with greater frequency in the Middle Kingdom and in Dynasties 19–26. Decapitation also seems to have been a consistent method of sanctioned killing, but it was more popular in the earlier periods. Killing in a ritual context was apparently consistent throughout time. Impalement was essentially only employed during the late Eighteenth Dynasty and the Ramesside Era. Some form of killing in association with burial practice, while changing over time, appears to have remained a regular feature of

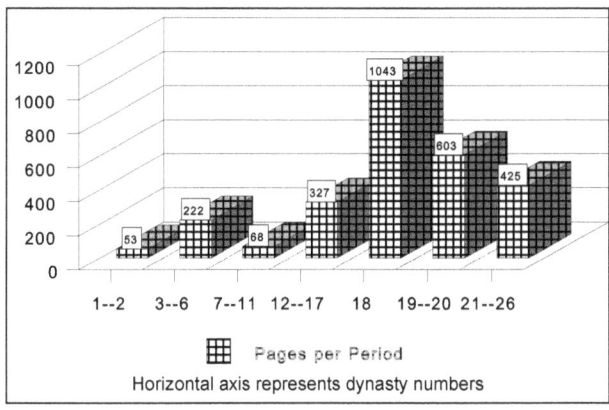

Figure 9.13 – Evidences for Pages in Breasted by Dynasty

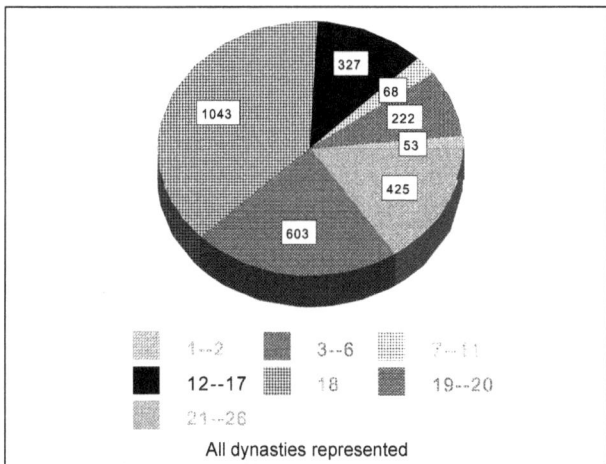

Figure 9.14 – Evidences for Pages in Breasted by Dynasty

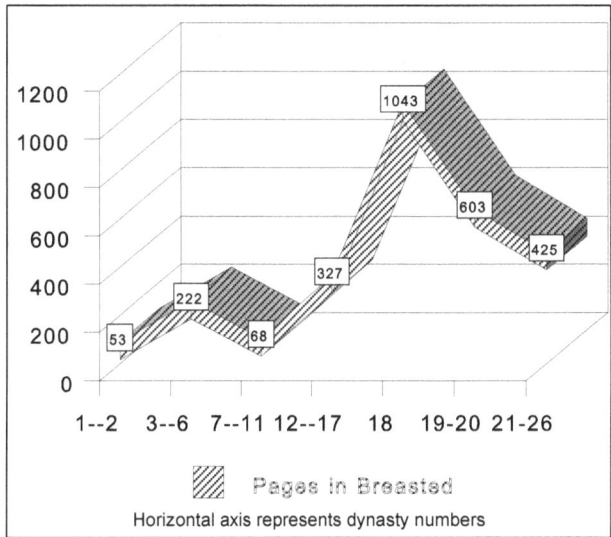

Figure 9.15 – Evidences for Number of Pages in Breasted by Dynasty

Egyptian culture. This regularity is also true of the formal execution of enemies. Additionally, we can assume that those who rose up against the state were always executed, but our evidence on this point is not completely clear.

Capital punishment for stealing or damaging state property varied over time, and death for murder was perhaps an exclusive feature of the Third Intermediate Period.

A Time to Kill

We have concluded that sanctioned killing was a regular and consistent feature of Egyptian society throughout the Pharaonic Era, and we have concluded that some forms of killing changed over time, while others were used consistently. Additionally, we have seen that specific reasons for engaging in sanctioned killing changed somewhat over time. However, we have not yet investigated the appropriate occasions for sanctioned killing in ancient Egypt. Some textual evidence indicates that some occasions were inappropriate for formal violence, but other occasions mandated it. We have already reviewed one of the earliest stipulations against such violence in the Instructions for Merikare. Here the ruler was warned, "Do not strike down, it does not empower you. Punish with beatings, with captivity, and thus will the land be established."[2] Stated exceptions will be discussed below, but here it is plain that the king should generally eschew killing.

From the same general time period as the Merikare text but much farther south, a local ruler, our familiar friend Ankhtifi, writes, "No power in whom there is the heat of strife will be accepted, now that the destruction of all forms of evil which men hate has been accomplished."[3] Here the ruler explicitly says not only that violence will not be tolerated but also that it is evil.

The middle-kingdom Tale of Sinuhe contains a hymn to the king, which informs us that the king did not need to employ violence to conquer: "A lord of kindness is he, great of sweetness. He conquered through love. His city loves him more than its appendages; it rejoices in him more than its god."[4]

In the New Kingdom, Horemheb also decries violence. A stela contains an edict from Horemheb, and the edict is likely a stone copy of a royal decree.[5] Herein the king describes the edict as an attempt to expel "*isfet* and destroy falsehood. His majesty's plans were a potent refuge, repelling violence."[6]

---

[2] P. Leningrad 1116A and P. Moscow 4658, lines 47–8, as in Joachim Friedrich Quack, *Studien zur Lehre für Merikare*, Wiesbaden: O. Harrassowitz, 1992. See also Aksel Volten, *Zwei altägyptische politische Schriften. Die Lehre für König Merikare (Pap. Carlsberg VI) und die Lehre des Königs Amenemhet*, Copenhagen: Einar Munksgaard, 1945.

[3] Mo'alla Inscription no. 2, as in Jacques Vandier, *Mo'alla. La tombe d'Ankhtifi et la tombe de Sébekhotep*, Cairo: Institut français d'archéologie orientale, 1950, p. 163.

[4] P. Berlin 3022, lines 65–7, as in Friedrich Vogelsang and Alan H. Gardiner, *Literarische Texte des Mittleren Reiches*, Leipzig: H.C. Hinrichs'sche, 1908, Table 7a.

[5] *ARE* 3, 23.

[6] Line 11, as in Kurt Pfluger, "The Edict of King Haremhab", *JNES* 5, no. 4, 1946, pl. 1. See also Benedict G. Davies, "Fascicle VI", in *Egyptian Historical Records of the Later Eighteenth Dynasty*, Barbara Cumming and Wolfgang Helck Warminster (eds), England: Aris &

Spell 125 of the Book of the Dead is particularly important because of its statements concerning things people had not done. One of these was the confession that the owner of the spell had not been violent (*n pr-ʿ=i*).[7] Also included in the negative confession are the closely related protestations "I have not slain," "I have not ordered to slay," and "I have not slain men."[8] Significantly, spell 125 was the first to appear on the wall of a king's tomb.[9] However, Merenptah's representation of this spell on his tomb wall was probably not the first time the text appeared in a royal tomb. Several spells from the Book of the Dead were inscribed on the gilded shrines of Tutankhamun. Since this was the only tomb found with its shrines still intact, we do not know if other pharaohs did the same, but it is likely that they did. Since spell 125 remained the most important portion of the Book of the Dead in royal tombs from the time of Merenptah on,[10] we can justifiably posit that if earlier kings had included spells from the Book of the Dead on any of their funerary accouterments, this spell would have been included. Royalty's consistent use of this text would indicate that they felt killing and ordering killing was inappropriate.

After reading kings' claims that they eschewed violence, we must immediately admit that most of these statements are made concomitantly with descriptions of appropriate violence. For example, the Instructions for Merikare explicitly describe when to avoid violence and when not to. The section quoted above, after warning that Merikare should not kill, revealingly continues: "Except for the rebel (*sbi*) whose plans are discovered, for god knows those who plot treason, god smites his obstacles in blood."[11] Elsewhere this text records, "He who is silent toward the violent diminishes the offerings. God will attack the rebel for the sake of the temple."[12] Both of these passages end with the image of god attacking the rebel, but the forepart of both make it clear that the king's actions are being discussed. This issue has been addressed above,[13] and we can be sure that the purview is the king's godlike conduct. The same is true for a portion of the text that reads, "The talker [who spreads dissension] is a trouble-maker. Repulse him, kill [him] (*sm3[sw]*),[14] blot out his name."[15]

Though Ankhtifi will not accept power of strife, in the same text he threatens violent punishments for desecrating his tomb.[16] In the same hymn in which Sinuhe describes Senusret I as one who conquers by love, he also describes him as a "vengeful smasher of foreheads;"[17] one who subjugates countries, slaying with only one blow;[18] and one who will strike Asiatics and trample sand dwellers."[19] These are only a few of the violent deeds ascribed to Senusret I. Similarly, in the same decree in which Horemheb speaks of repelling violence, he also decrees death for those who are false in office.[20]

Although spell 125 of the Book of the Dead occurred in royal tombs, it is obviously not valid for the kings of Egypt, who certainly both killed and ordered people to be killed. The protestation of not having committed violence, *n pr-ʿ=i*, is a term that the kings themselves expressly contradict. John Gee has noted that the expression "to be violent" (*pr-ʿ*) was used almost exclusively for sanctioned activities from the reign of Senusret I onward; Gee musters many examples of kings using this phrase to describe themselves.[21] While the list is too large to be presented here, a few examples are illustrative.

The term was applied to Thutmosis III several times, as on the Gebel Barkal Stela, where he was described as one "whose equal is not found, a violent warrior on the battlefield."[22] Another king who was described as violent several times was Tutankhamun. His tomb contains an assertion that he was "violent (*pr-ʿ*) like Montu who dwells in Thebes."[23] At Kanais, Seti I describes how he enlarged the borders of Egypt: the land was broadened "with violence every time."[24] Ramesses III describes himself at Medinet Habu as "a violent ruler, lord of the two lands."[25]

These examples are neither all the attestations of the use of these rulers using the term *pr-ʿ*, nor are they the only rulers who used it. The characterization of the pharaoh as violent continued from Senusret I throughout the Ptolemaic rulers.[26] Gee summarizes by writing, "The expression *pr-ʿ* is used mainly of the king, and in the context of war when the king is subjecting enemies and rebels without any pejorative connotations."[27] Clearly the king's protestations of not having done *pr-ʿ* in spell 125 did not refer to their royal duties.

What are we to make of these seemingly contradictory ideas? Could the king be simultaneously nonviolent and

---

Phillips, 1982. Also in Jean-Marie Kruchten, *Le Décret d'Horemheb*, Brussels, Editions de l'Université de Bruxelles, 1981.

[7] John Laurence Gee, "The Requirements of Ritual Purity in Ancient Egypt", PhD dissertation, Yale University, 1998, 263, discusses this term and provides many different scholars' translations. The term *pr-ʿ* does seem to be best rendered "violent."

[8] Gee, "The Requirements of Ritual Purity in Ancient Egypt", 255–6, again provides a discussion and alternate translations of these phrases.

[9] Erik Hornung, *The Ancient Egyptian Books of the Afterlife*, David Lorton (trans.), Ithaca: Cornell University Press, 1999, p. 13.

[10] Hornung, *The Ancient Egyptian Books of the Afterlife*, pp. 13–14.

[11] P. Leningrad 1116A, lines 47–50.

[12] P. Leningrad 1116A, line 110.

[13] See chapter 4, "The Instructions for Merikare".

[14] Volten, *Zwei altägyptische politische Schriften*, 8–9, restores "him." Parkinson, *Voices from Ancient Egypt*, 217, restores "his children."

[15] P. Leningrad 1116A, lines 23–24.

[16] See chapter 4, "The Tomb of Ankhtifi".

[17] P. Berlin 3022, line 55.

[18] P. Berlin 3022, lines 61–2.

[19] P. Berlin 3022, lines 61–2.

[20] See chapter 6, "The Death Penalty"; Davies, "Fascicle VI"; and Pfluger, "Edict of King Haremhab", p. 265.

[21] Gee, "Requirements of Ritual Purity", p. 264.

[22] G.A. Reisner and M.B. Reisner, "Inscribed Monuments from Gegbel Barkal: Part 2: The Granite Stela of Thutmosis III", *ZÄS* 69, 1933, 27; and Gee, "Requirements of Ritual Purity", p. 266.

[23] *Urk.* 4, 2059; Gee, "Requirements of Ritual Purity", p. 266.

[24] *KRI* 1, 66; Gee, "Requirements of Ritual Purity", p. 268.

[25] *KRI* 5, 69; Gee, "Requirements of Ritual Purity", p. 268.

[26] See Gee, "Requirements of Ritual Purity", pp. 163–74.

[27] Gee, "Requirements of Ritual Purity", p. 271.

violent? Perhaps the answer is demonstrated in the use of the term *pr-ꜥ* in various texts. As was mentioned above, after Senusret I, this term was usually used to describe the activities of the state and as such was always portrayed in a positive light. In a few instances, the term was applied to non-state activities, and in these cases, *pr-ꜥ* was viewed negatively.[28] This dichotomy can be extrapolated to the figure of the king. According to decorum, the king was a gentle person, kind to the point that cities followed him out of love. Yet in fulfilling his royal duties, the king had to use violent means. The ideology of kingship included and demanded violence, vis-à-vis the need for nonviolence in individuals.[29]

An abundance of texts both describe the king's violence and give a reason for his violence. A small sample will be presented here. The stela of Sehetepibre, from the time of Senusret III, records that the king "is Bast protecting the Two Lands. He who adores him will escape his arm. He is Sekhmet toward him who transgresses his command. He is calm to those who are satisfied."[30] Here it is clear that in protecting Egypt and in enforcing his commands the king can be very violent but not toward those who respect him. This is reinforced further in the same stela, where the complete destruction of those who rebel is threatened: "There is no tomb for him who rebels (*sbî*) against His Majesty, and his corpse shall be cast into the waters."[31]

A text from a little earlier in the Middle Kingdom, the Words of Neferti, also refers to the king's appropriate violence: "Rebels (*sbîw*) are destined for his [the king's] rage, and the malcontent (*ḥ3k-ibw*) to his awe. The uraeus at his fore pacifies the malcontent (*ḥ3k-ibw*)[32] for him."[33] While this passage does not refer to an actual violent incident, it does address when and why the king should be violent: when rebels or malcontents are present and in order to restore *Ma'at*. "Ma'at will return to its seat, Isfet is driven out."[34] Hence, the king must be violent against these rebels and malcontents in order to dispel Chaos and reestablish Order.

In her mortuary temple at Deir el-Bahri, Hatshepsut describes—almost certainly pseudepigraphically—being charged by her father at her accession. He instructed, "You will be powerful in the Two Lands; you will seize the malcontent."[35] Here *seizure* clearly has mortal implications. Ramesses II's treaty with the Hittites included a clause: if Ramesses's subjects turned against him, then the Hittites would help him kill the rebels.[36] This clause exemplifies a formal stipulation for sanctioned violence and its impetus.

We have already reviewed another example of a king who avoided killing everyone except a specific group. Piankhy recorded, "Not one was slain there, except the rebels (*sbîw*) who had blasphemed god. They were executed as malcontents" (*ḥ3k-ibw*).[37] The text implies being ill-hearted—or a malcontent (*ḥ3k-ibw*)—would lead one to become a rebel (*sbî*). Furthermore, Grimal notes that the term *wꜥ3* anciently meant rebellion against the king but by the Coptic Era had come to mean "blasphemy." Since Piankhy coupled *wꜥ3* with the idea of being against god, the word should translate as "blasphemy."[38] Grimal is correct about the word's history, but in Pianky's era, the term *wꜥ3* probably retained its rebellious connotations. Its use would have strongly implied that the blasphemers had rebelled against both god and king.

Violence was also sanctioned against foreign enemies. Examples of this sanction are voluminous; they will be discussed in the next chapter. However, from the examples just provided we can see a definite pattern. The king was justified in, or more correctly, was charged with using violent means to put down rebellion. Texts such as Merikare's make this kingly duty extremely explicit. To be sure, the previous examples do not constitute a complete list of the texts that describe when the king could, should, and would be violent, and certainly some texts that describe sanctioned kingly violence do not mention rebellion. Nevertheless, most texts that deal with sanctioned violence connect it to rebellion. This connection stems from ancient Egyptian theology: because rebellion is the chaotic behavior of one who should be following Ma'at, rebellion embodied Isfet. "To act against the king was to risk the stability of the cosmos,"[39] by becoming an element of Isfet.[40] "Attempts to overthrow the established political order, embodied in the person of the king, echoed parallel mythological

---

[28] Gee, "Requirements of Ritual Purity", p. 271, table 6.2.

[29] Katarina Nordh, *Aspects of Ancient Egyptian Curses and Blessings: Conceptual Background and Transmission*, Stockholm: Gotab, 1996, p. 47 and Joyce A. Tyldesley, *Judgment of the Pharaoh: Crime and Punishment in Ancient Egypt*, London: Weidenfeld & Nicolson, 2000, p. 70, independently made this assertion as well.

[30] Stela of Sehetepibre as in Karl Piehl, *Inscriptions Hiéroglyphiques Recueillies en Europe et en Égypt*, Leipzig: J.C. Hinrichsche, 1895, vol. 3, pl. 6.

[31] Stela of Sehetepibre as in Karl Piehl, *Inscriptions Hiéroglyphiques Recueillies en Europe et en Égypt*, Leipzig: J.C. Hinrichsche, 1895, vol. 3, pl. 6.

[32] *Wb* 3, 363, defines this as an ill-disposed person, or an enemy. Rainer Hannig, *Grosses Handwörterbuch Ägyptisch-Deutsch: (2800-950 v. Chr.): die Sprache der Pharaonen*, Kulturgeschichte der antiken Welt; Bd. 64, Mainz: P. von Zabern, 1995, p. 631, lists "enemy." Raymond O. Faulkner, *CD*, 201, writes "disaffected persons."

[33] P. Lenningrad 1116B, lines 64–5, as in Wolfgang Helck, *Die Prophezeihung des Nfr. Tj*, Wiesbaden: O. Harrassowitz, 1970, pp. 53–4.

[34] P. Lenningrad 1116B, lines 68–9.

[35] *Urk.* 4, 256.

[36] Ibram E. Harari, "The Historical Meaning of the Legal Words used in the Treaty Established Between Ramesses II and Hattusili III in Year 21 of the Reign of Ramesses II", in *Studies in Egyptology Presented to Miriam Lichtheim*, Sarah Israelit-Groll (ed.), Jerusalem: Magnes, 1990, p. 434.

[37] Nicolas-Christophe Grimal, *La stèle triomphale de Pi(ankh)y au Musée du Caire, JE 48862 et 47086–47089*, Cairo: Institut français d'archéologie orientale, 1981, line 86.

[38] See Grimal, *La stèle triomphale de Pi(ankh)y*, p. 110n305.

[39] Emily Teeter, "Ma'at", in *The Oxford Encyclopedia of Ancient Egypt*, Donald B. Redford (ed.), London: Oxford University Press, 2001, p. 319.

[40] See also Wolfgang Boochs, "Religöse Strafen", in *Religion und Philosophie im Alten Ägypten*, Ursula Verhoeven and Erhart Graefe (ed.), Leuven: Peeters, 1991, p. 58, who writes that offenses directed toward the king or state concerned both the legal system and the divine cosmic order.

assaults on Ma'at. Rebellion was thus inevitably a crime with strong religious connotations."⁴¹ As it is put in the Teachings for Merikare, "Indeed, he who rebels against you [the king] damages heaven."⁴² One tomb owner demonstrated the counter-relationship between Ma'at and rebellion: "I did Ma'at for the lord of the two lands, at night as at day, for I, I have been aware that he lives on her [Ma'at]. My abomination is the speech of rebels."⁴³ Clearly, rebellion against the king harmed the makeup of the cosmos itself. Such was the case largely because Egyptians absolutely relied on the king to establish Ma'at for both the gods and mankind. Because both groups depended on the king to uphold Ma'at, interfering with the king's ability to perform his duties was a crime against the entire cosmos. Rebellion against the king was rebellion against mankind, the gods, the cosmos, and Ma'at.⁴⁴ Hence, rebellion thoroughly identified its perpetrator with Isfet, a perpetrator who must be stopped by the most effective and immediate means available to the king.

The textual evidence presented earlier in the chapter, which designates rebellion as an appropriate occasion for sanctioned killing, coupled with the theological reasoning just outlined, leads to the conclusion that rebellion was the leading reason for sanctioned killing. This hypothesis can be tested by examining the known incidents of sanctioned killing as delineated in this book. Many of our examples do not explain why the victim was killed. Nevertheless, many examples do reveal something about the rationale behind the action, so these examples will be explored in the next section.

A Reason to Kill

In our effort to verify the hypothesis that rebellion was the chief motive for sanctioned killing, we will very briefly examine each type of sanctioned killing. The first- and second-dynasty sacrificial servant burials do not support the hypothesis, which is not surprising since they seem to be a different type of killing. These slayings did not destroy Isfet but did uphold Ma'at. Apparently, sacrificial servant burials provided the king in the afterlife with the social standing he deserved, and thus they preserved social Order. Tekenu burial is such an enigma that no conclusions can be drawn about it. Even if the ritual did include killing a human, we have no idea of the ritual's purpose nor of how the victims were selected.

While the Narmer Palette does not specifically explain why the prisoners depicted thereon were beheaded, we can surmise much about the motivation. Whether the kingdom had already been united, was united when the palette was created, or was soon to be united, a sort of manifest destiny was part of Narmer's portrayal.

Obviously, Narmer considered himself the king of both lands because he wears both crowns. If he already ruled the Nile Delta, or considered it his destiny to do so, then anyone who fought him in the delta would, by definition, be a rebel. Thus, we can conclude that the Narmer beheadings were a response to rebellion.⁴⁵

On the other hand, the labels of Aha and Djer, which possibly depict ritual slayings, present no evidence about why the depicted event was taking place, and so little is known that nothing can be surmised. Still, Bernadette Menu has proposed that people who had revolted were the victims in the rites depicted on these labels and perhaps alluded to on the labels of other rulers.⁴⁶ While Menu specifically proposes revolt in the delta, these men could also have been prisoners from wars abroad. If they were foreigners, by modern definition they could not be rebels. This view is antithetical to the ancient Egyptian's views on the subject. Liverani has amassed a great amount of evidence that proves that in Egyptian thought all the world belonged to Egypt.⁴⁷ Even newfound lands were properly ruled by the Egyptian king.⁴⁸ Any foreigners who did not acknowledge Egypt's hegemony were rebels and were described thus in Egyptian texts.⁴⁹ Of course, this concept is contrary to modern Western reality, but the ancient Egyptians ideologically and practically viewed the world this way.

In a similar vein, the cage found at Giza, which may have held prisoners intended for ritual slaying while they were transported on a boat, does not contain specific evidence about the reasons for its use. However, its new-kingdom descendants are specific. The possible ritual slayings that Thutmosis I, Amenhotep II, and Tuthankamun performed with similar cages were expressly of foreigners who had rebelled against Egyptian hegemony (*sbiw* in the texts associated with Thutmosis I and Amenhotep II). Hence, we may surmise from circumstantial evidence that the Giza cage was created for slaying rebels.

After the conclusion of successful battles, Merenptah killed great numbers of Libyans and Kushites. These groups were under Egyptian hegemony and were specifically labeled *rebels*.⁵⁰ Akhenaten similarly designated the Nubian prisoners of war whom he killed as

---

⁴¹ Anthony Leahy, "Death by Fire in Ancient Egypt", *Journal of the Economic and Social History of the Orient* 27, no. 2, 1984, 201.
⁴² P. Lenningrad 1116A, line 113.
⁴³ *Urk*. 4, 1795.
⁴⁴ Boochs, "Religöse Strafen", p. 58, independently arrives at a similar assertion.

⁴⁵ See also David O'Connor, "Egypt's View of 'Others'", in *Never Had the Like Occurred: Egypt's View of Its Past*, John Tait (ed.), Walnut Creek, CA: Left Coast, 2003, p. 157.
⁴⁶ Bernadette Menu, "Mise á mort cérémonielle et prélèvements royaux sous la 1ère Dynastie (NÂRMER-DEN)", in *Archèo-Nil*, 2001, vol. 11, p. 175.
⁴⁷ Mario Liverani, *Prestige and Interest: International Relations in the Near East ca. 1600–1100 B.C*, Padua, Italy: Sargon, 1990, pp. 51–5, very convincingly demonstrates this.
⁴⁸ Liverani, *Prestige and Interest*, p. 127.
⁴⁹ Liverani, *Prestige and Interest*, p. 127
⁵⁰ Besides the texts, see B.W.B. Garthoff, "Merenptah's Israel Stela: A curious case of Rites de Passage?", in *Funerary Symbols and Religion: Essays Dedicated to Professor M.S.H.G. Heerma van Voss on the Occasion of his Retirement from the Chair of the History of Ancient Religions at the University of Amsterdam*, Jacques H. Kamstra, H. Milde, and K. Wagtendonk (eds), Kampen, Netherlands: Kok, 1988, p. 23, in which he demonstrates that Mernptah identified rebels with Apophis. See also chapter 11, "The Egyptian Return".

plotters of rebellion (*sbit*).⁵¹ Akhenaten's threat to put a vassal's family to the ax was also a response to the foreign ruler's perceived rebellion.

The remains of six executed people from the Old Kingdom are completely silent about why the people were executed and thus do not give us any information on the question we try to answer in this section. The same is true of the depiction of decapitation presented in the tombs of Mereruka and Khentika. The depiction in Mentuherkhepeshef's tomb of Nubians being strangled is similar, but their status as foreigners classifies them as rebels and representatives of Isfet.

Execration rituals, whether or not they included human sacrifices, were specifically against rebels (*sbiw*). We should remember that these rituals were connected to the "rebellion formula"; putting down rebellion (whether of Egyptians or foreigners) was the entire purpose of the rites.⁵² Hence, the human execration rite at Mirgissa fits the pattern of sanctioned killing of rebels, as does the human execration rite at Avaris.

If the Cannibal Hymn referred to an actual rite of killing people, it is difficult to know what set certain people apart for this "honor." Our only clue comes from the hymn's Coffin Text descendant, which tells us that those who were killed were evildoers, or criminals. This information is not very specific. The evil, or crimes, that the victims may have committed is not outlined, and we are left only to guess. Such sacrificial victims, if indeed there were any, were possibly not seen as rebels. The victims could just as easily have rebelled against the king or against Ma'at. The case is too ambiguous to add to or to take away from our hypothesis.

We can learn two things from the many inscriptional threats of the First Intermediate Period and later. First, whether or not they could be punished in the mortal realm, tomb desecrators were identified as rebels. Some of the inscriptions state this explicitly. For example, Assiut Tomb IV threatens, "Any rebel (*sbi*) and any malcontent (*ḥȝk-ib*), who will commit wrong (*pnʿyt*)."⁵³ Other inscriptions employed such terminology as well.⁵⁴ Thus, those who violated tombs were seen as rebels—

probably not in rebellion against the king directly, but against Order, which the king upheld.

The second concept to be learned from inscriptional threats stems from the proposition that these inscriptions paralleled the juridical sphere: the subjects of inscriptional threats resemble those whom the king killed as criminals and rebels. This rings an according note with the Cannibal Hymn. As for the threat associated with the tomb of Ankhtifi, Willems has made a convincing argument that anyone who desecrated the tomb was identified as a rebel.⁵⁵ The stela usurped by Neferhotep I, which specified burning for those who trespassed on sacred land, does not contain any terminology germane to our discussion. Its only description of the violator is he who trespassed the sacred land. Since the offense was both against the king, who had set up the decree, and against a god, whose sacred land was protected by the decree, the trespass would presumably be seen as rebellion against god and king. However, this is highly circumstantial and somewhat circular. Though such trespassing could be compared to the desecration of tombs, this case fails to support the hypothesis that rebellion was the primary reason for sanctioned killing. Further evidence from this time period comes from the Instructions for Merikare, which explicitly states that rebels are the very people who should be killed.

When enacting a great ritual slaying at the Temple of Tod, Senusret I continually used the term *ḥrwy*, or enemy. This word especially denotes an enemy to the king,⁵⁶ a rebel. The abstract form of this noun is defined as war, rebellion, or revolt;⁵⁷ hence, Senusret I emphasized repeatedly that the sacrificial victims were rebellious enemies of the king. The great slaughter carried out by Prince Osorkon was wholly concerned with rebels (*sbiw*)—the rebellion of Thebes that occasioned the entire episode. As already noted, Piankhy slew only "the rebels (*sbiw*)."⁵⁸ Similarly, Shabako reportedly burned Bocchoris, who was attempting to rule in a rival dynasty. Without question, Bocchoris was burned because of his rebellion.

Papyrus Westcar outlines the consequences for adultery as being burned to death or being killed by crocodile. Ptahohotep and the Instructions of Ani indicate similar consequences. Adultery does not appear to be a form of rebellion, though it does go against the social Order. The Shipwrecked Sailor is threatened with burning because he did not obey the snake-god's command to speak, a refusal that could be construed as rebellion. This text is so fictional, though, that it proves largely irrelevant. The Intefiqer graffito reveals that he "put fire to their homes, as is done to a rebel (*sbi*) against the king."⁵⁹ This passage

---

⁵¹ This phrase is from the Amada account, as in *Urk.* 4, 1963. See also Alan R. Schulman, "The Nubian War of Akhenaton", in *L'Égyptologie en 1979. Axes prioritaires de recherches*, Paris: Centre National de la Recherche Scientifique, 1982, vol. 2, pp. 302–3, esp. n. 27.

⁵² See also Harco Willems, "Crime, Cult and Capital Punishment (Mo'alla Inscription 8)", *JEA* 76, 1990, 47, who writes about execration as dealing with rebellion; see also Edda Bresciani, "Foreigners", in *The Egyptians*, Sergio Donadoni (ed.), Chicago: University of Chicago Press, 1997, p. 222.

⁵³ Elmar Edel, *Die Inschriften der Grabfronten der Siut-Gräber in Mittelägypten aus der Herakleopolitenzeit: eine Wiederherstellung nach den Zeichnungen der Description de l'Egypte*, Abhandlungen der Rheinisch-Westfälischen Akademie der Wissenschaften Bd. 71, Opladen: Westdeutscher Verlag, 1984, pp. 120–7, fig. 15. See also Willems, "Crime, Cult and Capital Punishment", p. 37.

⁵⁴ Willems, "Crime, Cult and Capital Punishment", p. 42. See also David Lorton, "Legal and Social Institutions of Pharaonic Egypt", in *Civilizations of the Ancient Near East*, Jack M. Sasson (ed.), New York: Charles Scribner's Sons, 1995, p. 348.

⁵⁵ Willems, "Crime, Cult and Capital Punishment", pp. 44–6.

⁵⁶ *Wb* 3, 325.

⁵⁷ Hannig, *Grosses Handwörterbuch Ägyptisch-Deutsch*, p. 615, defines it as "controversy, war, rebellion, revolt."

⁵⁸ Grimal, *La stèle triomphale de Pi(ankh)y*, line 86.

⁵⁹ Zbyněk Žába, Fritz Hintze, and Miroslav Verner, *The Rock Inscriptions of Lower Nubia (Czechoslovak concession)*, ústav Československý egyptologický (ed.), Prague: Charles University, 1974,

is very specific about rebels' fates and Intefiqer's actions. If Kamose did drown Teti's wife, then her drowning was also a punishment against rebellion, since Kamose specifically states that Teti—and his wife, by association—was a rebel (*sbi*). The royal slave who ran away was condemned to death because his desertion could be viewed as rebellion, though this is not strong evidence.

While stealing was not a capital offense, stealing royal property, or perhaps property used for royal tombs, apparently was a capital offense. While modern societies would not typically see theft as rebellion, it may have been considered as such in the Egyptian zeitgeist. Stealing from the sacred sphere was probably a capital offense, or even considered rebellion, because it attacked correct Order. We can suppose that the unauthorized conscription of corvée laborers from their properly appointed service to a specific god was also rebellion. Similarly, Horemheb may have ordered the death sentence for venal officials who rendered false rulings. These false rulings were considered rebellion because the venal officials were entrusted with upholding Ma'at, and they had rebelled against the very concept they represented. Still, these are weak cases.

It is difficult to understand why Seti I commanded death in the Nauri Decree for a keeper of cattle, a keeper of hounds, or a herdsman who had embezzled or misoffered cattle. Perhaps a betrayal of his trust in those who were supposed to care for the animals constituted a sufficient breach of Order that capital punishment was inevitable. Even so, the criminals were not rebels any more than were other offenders listed in the same decree.

The Instructions of Amenemope outline possible death for being false in office and for some type of failure on the part poor people. We know too little of the latter situation to even speculate about the reason for death in this instance, though it is difficult to imagine any motive construed as rebellion. The former is similar to the death sentence imposed for being false in office decrees as issued in Horemheb's edict and the Nauri Decree. Capital punishment in these cases does not appear to be specifically for rebellion but was perhaps for rebellion against Ma'at. However, all crimes could be considered rebellion against Order, but not all crimes merited capital punishment. Capital punishment for murder was evidenced throughout the Third Intermediate Period. Murder was considered to be rebellion against the gods, who had said that mankind should not hurt one another. Murder may well have been identified with the original murder, Seth's murder of Osiris.

The death decree for speaking against Hatshepsut certainly targeted rebellion, since speaking against Hatshepsut's precarious position would have endangered her position as ruler.

The Harem Conspiracy was obviously rebellion against the king in its purest form. One of the perpetrators was even given an alternate name that meant "the one of the rebellion" (*p3-nšn*).[60] The Great Tomb Robberies were also obviously rebellious acts. The robberies both desecrated tombs and attacked the royal family.

This very brief survey of known incidents and reasons for sanctioned killing is revealing. While not every incident discussed in this study was mentioned specifically above, every type of killing was. Of a few examples, we know nothing of the reasons for the killing. Murder, adultery, theft of royal property, being false in office, tomb desecration, and interference with funerary or temple cult are all reasons for being put to death. All of these, except the first two, could be construed as rebellion but do not correlate strongly. Criminals may have been burned because they rebelled, though one could expect that *rebels* would then be specified instead of *criminals* (though O'Connor argues that criminals were a type of rebel).[61] All other known reasons for sanctioned killing specifically involve rebellion. This data set makes two conclusions inescapable: first, rebellion was not the only reason for sanctioned killing, but second, rebellion was the most common reason for sanctioned killing. These conclusions confirm the earlier conclusions drawn from the texts that outline the times sanctioned violence was appropriate. Significantly, when Kemboly outlines the origins of violence in Egypt, every case specifically involves rebellion.[62] While violence could serve Ma'at for a number of reasons, the overwhelmingly greatest reason was to destroy the ultimate manifestation of Isfet: rebellion.

---

p. 99, inscription no. 73. Also translated in Richard B. Parkinson, *Voices from Ancient Egypt: An Anthology of Middle Kingdom Writings*, Norman, OK: University of Oklahoma Press, 1991, pp. 95–6; and Donald B. Redford, "The Tod Inscriptions of Senwosret I and Early 12th Dynasty Involvement in Nubia and the South", *JSSEA* 17, no. 1/2, 1987, 45.

[60] Hans Goedicke, "Was Magic Used in the Harem Conspiracy Against Ramesses III?", *JEA* 49, 1963, 84.

[61] O'Connor, "Egypt's View of 'Others'", pp. 175–6.

[62] Mpay Kemboly, "Violence and Protection in Early Egyptian Funerary Texts", Master's thesis, Oxford University, 2000, 17–20.

Chapter 10

FOREIGNERS AND *ISFET*

Whose slaughter brought death to thousands of Bowmen who had come to invade his borders. Who shoots an arrow as Sakhmet. He felled thousands who ignored his might. The tongue of his majesty restrains Nubia, and his utterances make Asiatics flee.

—Hymns to Senusret III

Chaotic Foreigners

In order to more fully understand the concept of rebellion, we must further explore the prototypical rebel: the foreigner. The case of the foreigner in ancient Egypt is complex. This imbroglio arises, in part, due to a dual portrayal of foreigners in Egyptian sources. As has been pointed out, foreigners as presented in pragmatic texts do not match their literary counterparts.[1] As Loprieno has precisely and convincingly demonstrated, there is a dichotomy in the view of foreigners as presented in *topos*-dominated genres as opposed to *mimetic* depictions.[2] While the *mimesis* view of foreigners is not germane to the current topic and will therefore be left untreated, the *topos* presentation is of great concern to us.

There may have been pragmatic sociopolitical reasons for the creation of the foreigner *topos*. Often a significant part of the process of unifying one group is the perception of an aggressive "other."[3] Frequently this unification comes at the cost of spilling the blood of the "other."[4] This may have played a role in Egyptian unification at various times,[5] but more importantly for our purposes, the classification of a dangerous "other" came to be a dominant theme in the *topos* of foreigners. The depiction of foreigners centered on the king upholding *Ma'at* in the face of foreigners presenting a threat to his work. Foreigners were seen as inherently chaotic and were thus an enemy to Ma'at. From the earliest to the latest periods of its history, Egypt thought of itself as surrounded by foreign enemies, a concept that served as a symbol of chaos continually attempting to impinge upon order.[6] These enemies were in continual rebellion against Ma'at.[7] The anti-culture of foreigners was the perfect representation of *Isfet*.[8]

This *topos* view can be traced through time in Egyptian texts. The earliest religious corpus, the Pyramid Texts, attest to the idea. In one group of spells, the qualitative difference between Egypt and others is highlighted. First, the eye of Horus, representing several distinct qualities of Egypt, is told that he will not obey Westerners, Easterners, Southerners, or Northerners.[9] Next, it is made explicit that desired doors will not open for any of these groups but only for Horus, who saved the doors and the eye from the destructive forces of Seth (literally "save them from every ill which Seth did to them"), so that he

---

[1] Antonio Loprieno, "Slaves", in Sergio Donadoni (ed.), *The Egyptians*, Chicago: University of Chicago Press, 1997, p. 187. See also David O'Connor, "Egypt's View of 'Others'", in John Tait (ed.), *Never Had the Like Occurred: Egypt's View of Its Past*, Portland: Cavendish Publishing, 2003.

[2] Antonio Loprieno, *Topos und Mimesis. Zum Ausländer in der ägyptischen Literatur*, Ägyptologische Abhandlungen, Wiesbaden: Otto Harrosowitz, 1988, vol. 48.

[3] Walter Burkert, "The Function and Transformation of Ritual Killing", in Ronald L. Grimes (ed.), *Readings in Ritual Studies*, Upper Saddle River, New Jersey: Prentice-Hall, Inc., 1996, p. 62.

[4] Ronald L. Grimes, *Beginnings in Ritual Studies*, Columbia: University of South Carolina Press, 1995, p. 228.

[5] This position is strengthened by the voluminous cases wherein bound foreigners are associated either with the *sm3 t3wy* scene or are tied by the heraldic plants which form an integral part of the scene. The latter case seems to be present in the vast majority of depictions of bound foreigners from mid-Eighteenth Dynasty through the Twenty-sixth Dynasty. See Kerry Muhlestein, "Binding Foreigners with Heraldic Plants." *Proceedings of the IXth International Congress of Egyptologists*, (Leuven: Peeters Publishers, 2007), 1335-1341.

[6] G. Belova, "The Egyptians' Ideas of Hostile Encirclement", in C.J. Eyre (ed.), *Proceedings of the Seventh International Congress of Egyptologists*, Orientalia Lovaniensia Analecta, Leuven: Uitgeverij Peeters, 1998, p. 145.

[7] B.W.B. Garthoff, "Merenptah's Israel Stela: A curious case of Rites de Passage?", in Jacques H. Kamstra, H. Milde, and K. Wagtendonk (eds.), *Funerary Symbols and Religion: Essays Dedicated to Professor M.S.H.G. Heerma van Voss on the Occasion of His Retirement from the Chair of the History of Ancient Religions at the University of Amsterdam*, Kampen, the Netherlands: J.H. Kok, 1988, p. 23.

[8] See also Loprieno, *Topos und Mimesis*, p. 23.

[9] Pyr. 1588.

could set them in order (*grg=tm*).¹⁰ Here Horus, who represented Egypt, is pitted against Seth, who represented unpredictable foreign lands.¹¹ Horus is portrayed as bringing about order, while Seth is undermining his work. The spell continued by having the king speak, repeating his acts as they had already been outlined and stating that it was he who made the settlements, he who erected them (*sꜥḥꜥ=sn*), he who warded off untoward elements, he who put them in order *(grg=tm)*, and he who restored them.¹² As a part of this description, the king repeated that Egyptians should not obey Westerners, Easterners, Northerners, and Southerners and that doors would not open for these groups.¹³ This text creates a conspicuous dichotomy between orderly Egypt and her rulers and disorderly Seth, represented by all those who were from anywhere but Egypt.¹⁴

Also from the Old Kingdom, the Execration Texts and Rebellion Formula described above are illustrative of the perception of chaotic foreigners.¹⁵ To reiterate, these texts were primarily concerned with foreign individuals, peoples, and areas, which represented a "rebellious" (*sbiw*) and chaotic group. This rite was used for thousands of years in an effort to ward off the chaos intrinsic to foreign peoples. One specific spell will illustrate, being directed against "all Nubians, all soldiers, all messengers, all allies, and all confederates of all foreign lands who will rebel (*sbi.ti=sni*), who are in the land of Wawat, of Djatju, Irtjet, Iam, Ianekh, Maset, Ka'u, who will rebel (*sbi.ti=sni*), who will plot, who will fight, who will talk of fighting, or who will talk of rebelling (*ddw sbi=sn*) against Upper and Lower Egypt [will be destroyed] for all time."¹⁶ The characteristic of rebellion was thought to be so much a part of the constitution of the foreigner that this type of proactive, prophylactic magic was practiced against them throughout the entire span of Egyptian history.

From a little later in history, the Instructions for Merikare also contain descriptions of foreigners as chaotic. Outlining that which is typically said of the foreigner, the text reads:

> The poor Asiatic
> he truly suffers in the place where he lives
> sparse in water, poor in trees
> where many paths lead, and the mountains make hardships
> he never stays in one place
> and hunger will always push his feet

> he has struggled since the time of Horus
> never able to win, yet never defeated
> since he never announces his days of battle
> just like a thief, afraid of the arm of the troops.¹⁷

This passage describes characteristics that were the antithesis of the Egyptian ideal. Elsewhere, the text again lists qualities of the Asiatic: "The Asiatic is like a crocodile on its bank. It snaps from a solitary path. It does not take from a busy village."¹⁸ As Loprieno has said of these passages, "The focus is the *morally* despicable behavior of the foreigner: his attitude is marked all around [+*izf.t*]-d.h. [-*mꜣꜥ.t*]."¹⁹

The near contemporary Prophecy of Neferti also outlines the chaotic nature of foreigners:

> A strange bird will breed in the Delta
> Its nest made beside the people,
> The people let it approach through need.²⁰
> Then those delightful things perish,
> The fish ponds are full of fish-eaters,
> Full of fish and fowl.
> All happiness has vanished,
> The land is bowed down in distress
> Because of those who eat provisions.
> Asiatics roaming the land.
> Enemies have arisen in the East,
> Asiatics have come down to Egypt.²¹

These chaotic conditions, apparently brought about by the presence of foreigners, could only be corrected in one way: a new king would arise, who would reunite the two lands. As a part of this,

> Those who fall into evil
> Those who plan rebellion [*kꜣy sbiw*]
> Bring down their own speech in fear of him
> Asiatics will fall to his slaughter
> Libyans will fall to his flame
> Rebels [*sbiw*] are destined for his rage²²
> and the hostile [*ḫꜣkw-ib*] for his awe
> the Uraeus at his fore pacifies the hostile [*ḫꜣkw-ib*] for him

---

¹⁰ Pyr. 1593–95.
¹¹ Leonard H. Lesko, "Ancient Egyptian Cosmogonies and Cosmology", in Byron E. Shafer (ed.), *Religion in Ancient Egypt*, Ithaca: Cornell University Press, 1991, p. 93.
¹² Pyr. 1595–99.
¹³ Pyr. 1596–1606.
¹⁴ Edda Bresciani, "Foreigners", in Sergio Donadoni (ed.), *The Egyptians*, Chicago: University of Chicago Press, 1997, p. 222.
¹⁵ See chapter 3, the section on Execration Texts.
¹⁶ Text and reconstruction in Georges Posener, *Cinq figurines d'envoûtement*, Cairo: Institut français d'archéologie oriental du Caire, 1987.

¹⁷ P. Leningrad 1116A and P. Moscow 4658, as in Joachim Friedrich Quack, *Studien zur Lehre für Merikare*, Wiesbaden: O. Harrassowitz, 1992. Also used is Aksel Volten, *Zwei altägyptische politische Schriften. Die Lehre für König Merikare (Pap. Carlsberg VI) und die Lehre des Königs Amenemhet*, København: Einar Munksgaard, 1945.
¹⁸ P. Leningrad 1116A.
¹⁹ Loprieno, *Topos und Mimesis*, p. 26; translation by author.
²⁰ Richard Parkinson, *The Tale of Sinuhe and Other Ancient Egyptian Poems*, Oxford: Oxford University Press, 1997, p. 136, translates "through want." Loprieno, *Topos und Mimesis*, 27, translates "from their emergency," though in this line he substitutes O. Petrie 38 for P. Leningrad 1116B. I read it also as "out of," or "through need."
²¹ P. Leningrad 1116B, lines 29–33, as in Wolfgang Helck, *Die Prophezeihung des Nfr.tj*, Wiesbaden: O. Harrassowitz, 1970.
²² This rendering is according to Tablet Cairo 25224 and Gardiner-Cerny Ostraca 101,2 and 98,1.

The walls of the ruler are built
Asiatics will not be allowed into Egypt
They will ask for water as a supplicant
to allow their flocks to drink
Ma'at will return to its seat
Isfet is driven out [*isft dr.tỉ²³ r rwty*].²⁴

These lines clearly polarize the presence of foreigners and the existence of Ma'at. Isfet is driven away and Ma'at takes its place only when foreigners are expelled and prevented from returning. It is difficult to more clearly equate foreigners with chaos.

The inherent, chaotic nature of foreigners is also portrayed in the Eighteenth Dynasty, as in a message to the viceroy of Kush stating that "the people of Takshi [in Syria] are of no account, and of no use" and that he should "not trust Nubians, beware their people and their magic."²⁵ In the Nineteenth Dynasty, a scribe was chastened for his lack of learning and was told that even "monkeys listen to words, and they are brought from Kush."²⁶

Clearly, foreigners, in programmatic sources, were viewed as representatives of Isfet. While an everyday view may not have depicted this official decorum, undoubtedly the official paragon of chaos was the foreigner.²⁷ It is to be expected, then, that the foreigner would take the prime place in rituals aimed at destroying Isfet.

The Smiting Scene

These conclusions lead to a necessary reexamination of the prototypical scene involving the subjugation of foreigners: the smiting scene. This scene consists of the king grasping one or more enemies by the hair with one hand, with the other hand depicted in the act of bringing some type of weapon upon the head of the foreigner. This scene is prevalent from the earliest periods of Egyptian history through the Roman era.

The earliest-known example of this scene dates to the late Naqada I Phase, ca. 3600 BCE. A C-ware vessel has been found, which depicts a large figure grasping smaller individuals, and holding what appears to be a mace (see fig. 10.1).²⁸ This early example of the smiting scene pre-dates the famous Narmer Palette by roughly half a millennium. In the past, the smiting scene of Narmer's

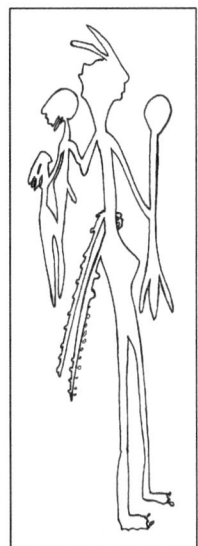

Figure 10.1 – Naqada Ware Smiting Scene

day had been thought of as a depiction of a real ritual, with later scenes consisting of an ideological motif possessing no actual referent.²⁹ Ensuing the discovery of this earlier example of the smiting scene, this traditional interpretation has merely been set back five hundred years. Current postulation is that the Naqada I depiction may have represented an actual ritual and that by the time of Narmer, this ritual was likely out of practice, and the smiting scene was part of a program of ideological decoration.

Why this rush to push back the date of the referent of the smiting scene? What is the evidence for the motif representing and not commemorating a corresponding current event?

Part of the answer to these questions lies in the smiting depictions themselves. One of the most striking examples comes from a relief first attested during the reign of Sahure. In this Abusir representation, a victory was depicted, which included a smiting scene and the names of conquered leaders. These same names, including the names of individual Libyan rulers, were reproduced by Neferirkare (also in Abusir), by Pepi I and Pepi II in Saqqara, and by Taharka at Kawa.³⁰ Neferirkare was the successor of Sahure and may have copied his predecessor partially out of a desire to commemorate his own possible participation in the victory. The Saqqara depictions were approximately two hundred years and one dynasty later. The conclusion is inescapable that these reliefs, while perhaps commissioned because of real battles, were contentual copies of earlier reliefs. The same is also true of the Twenty-fifth Dynasty replication.

---

²³ The stative rendering of this verb is according to C25224. P. Lenningrad 1116B reads *dr si*.
²⁴ P. Lenningrad 1116B, 61–69.
²⁵ *Urk.* 4, 1344.
²⁶ P. Bologna 1094, 3.9, as in *LEM*, 3.
²⁷ Egyptians who rebelled against order could be assigned a type of foreign identity. See Nathalie Beaux, "Ennemis Étrangers et Malfaiteurs Égyptiens. Signification du Châtiment au pilori", *BIFAO* 91, 1991, 33–53; and O'Connor, "Egypt's View of 'Others'", p. 156.
²⁸ Günter Dreyer and others, "Umm el-Qaab", *MDAIK* 54, 1998, especially figures 12 and 13. I am grateful to Jocham Kahl for making me aware of this depiction.

²⁹ See, for example, Whitney Davis, *Masking the Blow: The Scene of Representation in Late Prehistoric Egyptian Art*, Berkeley and Los Angeles: University of California Press, 1992, pp. 130, 172.
³⁰ See John A. Wilson, "The Royal Myth in Ancient Egypt", *Proceedings of the American Philosophical Society* 100, 1956, 439–42; and Alan Schulman, "Narmer and the Unification of Egypt: A Revisionist View", *BES* 11, 1992. Many others have pointed out this repetition as well.

Similar duplication is found among the reliefs of Ramesses II and Ramesses III. One of the latter's smiting scenes at Medinet Habu and its list of defeated enemies is a direct copy of the former's reliefs at Abu Simbel. There are a few variations, such as changing "Hatti" to "every land" in part of the inscription; yet concurrently the lists indicate that Ramesses III fought the Hittites, which he did not. The contentual emptiness of the imitated smiting scenes brings into question the veracity that such scenes represented real events.[31] Clearly, Ramesses III did not smite the Hittite leaders that his reliefs indicate; neither did Taharka ritually slaughter the exact same Libyans as Sahure.

The reality of smiting-scene referents is further called into question by reliefs that include unrealistic elements. On a shield, Tutankhamun is pictured smiting his enemies, represented by two lions, which he holds by their tails.[32] Ramesses VI is shown smiting an enemy while a lion strides between the prisoner's legs.[33] Another king is pictured smiting a Nubian as a lion bites the captive.[34] None of these depictions has a plausible referent in reality. The same is true of depictions of the king smiting numerous complacent prisoners at the same time. Also serving to call into question the reality of any such smiting scenes are the depictions of the king as a sphinx or griffin slaying enemies.[35]

Furthermore, in Sinai there are reliefs of kings, such as Djoser, Snefru, and Khufu, smiting representatives of the local inhabitants. It is improbable that any of these kings traveled to the Sinai, casting doubt upon the reality of that which is represented in the relief. It is possible that foreign leaders were taken to the Nile Valley, where they were slain, and the representations were made at Sinai. But such an explanation is hardly convincing. It is far more plausible that these smiting scenes commemorated a victory by the king's armies, similar to the obvious meaning in reliefs such as the one depicting Ramesses II smiting a group of prisoners whose heads protrude from their city walls.[36]

The copied reliefs and the unrealistic scenes indicate that at least these depictions were more concerned with representing an ideological reality than they were with representing a historical one. This ideological focus, at the apparent cost of history, has led most Egyptologists to believe that the smiting scene was consistently concerned with ideology and never with an actual smiting.

According to this prevailing view, smiting scenes often represented authentic conquests but not actual ritual slaughter of people by the king. Hall has written that "the scene of smiting the enemy is a way of commemorating a victory."[37] Wilkinson writes that the smiting scene "which was doubtless originally based on the actual execution of prisoners seems to have come to be a purely representational device in which the king's raised mace became a gesture signifying the concept of the destruction of foes."[38] The statements of these two scholars represent the *communis opinio* of Egyptology.

The assumption that the smiting scene was always concerned with ideology is justifiable. But are we equally safe in assuming that it was never representative of an actual ritual slaying? The fallacy of presuming ideological representations to be completely bereft of a historical referent should be avoided. While the representations cited above, and doubtless countless others, do indeed seem to be void of a ritual referent, are we then justified in assuming that all smiting scenes are similarly ahistorical?

There is some evidence that such presuppositions are not warranted. The foremost has been presented by Schulman. In his heterodox monograph *Ceremonial Execution and Public Rewards*,[39] he presents nineteen private stelae from the late-Eighteenth through the early-Twentieth dynasties that he believes are representations of actual ritual slaughter. He painstakingly outlines the scenes of these stelae, noting their apparent temple setting. Further, he coherently delineates the case that private stelae were much less likely to present kingship dogma than they were to portray the crowning achievement of a person's life, such as being allowed to attend a royal ritual. Schulman writes that these scenes can be taken either as "a symbolic and propagandistic illustration of the royal myth, or as an actual depiction of a real event. I believe that the latter was the case, and that on these stelae, we are looking at a specific ceremonial sacrifice which was performed in a specific temple at a specific point in time."[40]

Was Schulman right?

Schulman's ideas have met resistance. We have already noted an Egyptological opposition to anything associated with "human sacrifice," an idea that Schulman's hypothesis swims against. Ward has been one of Schulman's critics. To his great credit, he has been forthright about the underlying assumptions on which he bases his disagreement with Schulman. He writes:

---

[31] For example, Schulman, "Narmer and Unification", p. 82, after pointing out such duplications, writes that we must "question the historical value of all of the later examples of this tableau."

[32] Emma Swan Hall, *The Pharaoh Smites His Enemies: A Comparative Study*, Münchner ägyptologische Studien; Heft 44, München: Deutscher Kunstverlag, 1986, fig. 42.

[33] Hall, *The Pharaoh Smites His Enemies*, fig. 79.

[34] Hall, *The Pharaoh Smites His Enemies*, fig. 80. Davis, *Masking the Blow*, 133, postulates that the lions may represent either the ruler or an aspect of the ruler.

[35] See Joachim Sliwa, "Some Remarks Concerning Victorious Ruler Representations in Egyptian Art", *Forschungen und Berichte* 16, 1974, 105–7.

[36] Hall, *The Pharaoh Smites His Enemies*, fig. 57.

[37] Hall, *The Pharaoh Smites His Enemies*, p. 3.

[38] Richard H. Wilkinson, *Symbol & Magic in Egyptian Art*, New York: Thames and Hudson, 1994, p. 194. See also Jan Assmann, *The Mind of Egypt: History and Meaning in the Time of the Pharaohs*, Andrew Jenkins, (trans.), New York: Metropolitan Books, 2002, pp. 150–1.

[39] Alan R. Schulman, *Ceremonial Execution and Public Rewards. Some Histoical Scenes on New Kingdom Private Stelae*, Orbis Biblicus et Orientalis, Göttingen: Universitätsverlag Freiburg Schweiz Vandenhoeck & Ruprecht, 1988, vol. 75.

[40] Schulman, *Ceremonial Execution*, p. 41–2.

I must admit that my reluctance to embrace the idea of Egyptian kings practicing human sacrifice to show gratitude to their gods after winning a war stems partially from my own view of the Egyptian character. They could be as brutal in battle as any of their contemporaries; no society in history has been immune from the collective and individual barbarity that makes brutes of otherwise ordinary people when they go off to war. But it is quite a different thing to postulate the planned, public execution of captured prisoners by grateful rulers as a "thank you" to deities who have cast their blessings of victory over the land. One expects this of the Assyrians, not the Egyptians. This just does not seem to me to be part of the Egyptian national character, nor is there reason to believe they thought their gods required human sacrifice in any context.[41]

While Ward's frankness is to be commended, there are several problems with his argument. First, he argues against the rituals being a type of thank-offering to the gods.[42] While Schulman proposed this as the reason for the slaying, it seems more likely that such ritual slaying would have been more in the form of prophylactic rites, as were the execration rituals, than as a thank-offering. This idea will be discussed more fully below, but if it is true, it makes much of Ward's disagreement irrelevant.

Further, Ward does not believe that ritual slaying was within the Egyptian national character. He says of Schulman that "for the public human sacrifice he postulates, only the small group of twenty-one[43] stelae collected in this study have a direct bearing on the problem at hand."[44] Ward notes the Amada Text of Amenhotep II, but dismissing this as a dissimilar event, he avers that "a major objection, then, to Schulman's theory is that there is no supporting literary evidence."[45] Here Ward not only employs an argument of silence, but he utilizes it in the midst of evidential clamor. This study has noted repeated examples of ritual slaying, meaning that there is literary evidence far beyond Schulman's stelae that bears upon the subject.

Ward eventually admits, "I can accept Schulman's theory that a public ceremony did take place from time to time in which the king 'slew' an enemy in the presence of a cult statue of a deity, but was this an actual execution? I think not, since it would be a unique example in Egyptian cultural history of human sacrifice which, if I understand the Egyptians at all correctly, was a concept foreign to their mentality."[46] Here Ward admits that Schulman's evidence does seem to point to a ritual, but he would like to avoid placing a human as the focus of the ritual because of a lack of confirming pattern elsewhere. Now that a confirming pattern has been established, it seems much more sensible to avoid creating a substitute and to follow the natural conclusions of Schulman's evidence.

Ward is certainly not alone in disagreeing with Schulman. Müller-Wollermann has also questioned the veracity of Schulman's arguments.[47] Her first stricture is somewhat problematic. She notes that Schulman uses a classification of stelae typology that does not enjoy a *communis opinio*, because no such consensus exists.[48] She then proceeds to employ a typology that would similarly hold no such consensus. Furthermore, her reclassification of certain stelae from commemorative to votive[49] only affects Schulman's arguments if we impose a strict diversification of purpose to these stelae. Such a division of purpose is an academic exercise; we find little evidence that the Egyptians themselves maintained such box-like classifications. What Müller-Wollermann reclassifies as a votive stela is not necessarily devoid of all commemorative elements. The argument that some of Schulman's stelae were votive and thus could not contain a commemorative component cannot be sustained. Thus, Müller-Wollermann's argument is based on a classification typology that has nothing more to strengthen it than Schulman's, and even if it were true, the arguments based upon this typology employ underlying assumptions that cannot be maintained.

Additionally, Müller-Wollermann plies what even she terms to be a conclusion *ex silentio*.[50] Willems writes of Müller-Wollermann's attempt to use this argument: "Her criticism does not carry much weight. In rejecting the possibility of ritual executions, she disregards much of the textual evidence, while she fails to adduce parallels for her interpretation of the iconography of the stelae."[51] As noted in our discussion of Ward's disagreements, the silence of their effete argument has been broken.

Some substantive criticisms come from Ahituv, who, in his review of Schulman's book, notes that Schulman's thesis is attractive and reasonable.[52] Concurrently, he draws attention to some issues he believes undermine the thesis. Ahituv points out that stela number 18 contains two possible inconsistencies. Schulman himself noted that while the text reports the prisoners being slain are chiefs of Kush, the prisoners pictured were Semites (see fig. 10.1). He explains the contradiction by writing, "We may well assume that the artist who prepared this stele was influenced by what must have been a stock scene in

---

[41] William Ward, "Review of Ceremonial Execution and Public Rewards", *JNES* 51, 1992, no. 2, 153.
[42] It should be noted that Sliwa, "Some Remarks Concerning Victorious Ruler Representations", p. 103, believes this is a scene which "takes place in the presence of a god, presumably it is a sacrifice in his honour."
[43] The number of stelae Schulman evaluates is 19.
[44] Ward, "Review of Ceremonial Execution", p. 153.
[45] Ward, "Review of Ceremonial Execution", p. 153.
[46] Ward, "Review of Ceremonial Execution", p. 154.
[47] Renate Müller-Wollermann, "Der Mythos vom Ritus 'Erschlagen der Feinde'", 1988, vol. 105.
[48] Wollermann, "Der Mythos vom Ritus 'Erschlagen der Feinde'", pp. 69–70.
[49] Wollermann, "Der Mythos vom Ritus 'Erschlagen der Feinde'", pp. 71–2.
[50] Wollermann, "Der Mythos vom Ritus 'Erschlagen der Feinde'", p. 74.
[51] Harco Willems, "Crime, Cult and Capital Punishment (Mo'alla Inscription 8)", *JEA* 76, 1990, 50n122.
[52] Shmuel Ahituv, "Review of *Ceremonial Execution and Public Rewards*", *Israel Exploration Journal* 41, 1991, no. 4, 304.

his repertoire and gave no really careful attention to whether or not the nationality of the victims was in harmony with what the accompanying text recorded."[53] There is some merit to this notion. Schulman also opines that perhaps the Asiatics were pictured in order to give a northern balance to the inscriptional southern victory in Kush.[54] However, Ahituv asseverates that an inscription with a real referent cannot possess any element that lacks complete realism. He writes, "Realism cannot be divided: the representation on the stelae is either realistic, adhering to the real events in the life of the deceased, or not, using artistic motifs for their own sake."[55] Of this statement we must ask: why? Why can a real event not be depicted using stock artistic representations? What was to prevent an artisan from inscribing the wrong term, or from drawing the type of enemy that was most familiar to him or that he was most accustomed to draw? It is certainly true that in Western culture we would not intentionally mix elements of accuracy with inaccuracy. Is it safe to impose this ideal on those who created ancient Egyptian stelae? (Are the terms *accurate* and *inaccurate* even appropriate from an Egyptian point of view?) What are the grounds for doing so?

Moreover, no one has entertained the idea that the scribe could have accidentally written the wrong foreign group. This touches directly on Ahituv's second criticism of this stela. We have no record of any military activity of Ramesses II in Nubia close to the date of the stela.[56] Concurrently, we do not know of an Asiatic campaign from this year either. However, a smiting ritual did not necessarily have to be associated with a particular battle. If the ritual were not a thank-offering, which will be argued below, then such a ritual did not necessarily need to coincide with a known military campaign. When an occasion for the ritual arose, it is quite possible that leaders would be brought from captivity for participation in such rites. The inconsistency between the text and the depiction could arise because of the use of a stock scene, because of a scribal error, or because both a Kushite and an Asiatic were slain, leaving the stela creator trying to depict both by using picture and text to accomplish his purposes. None of these propositions are completely satisfactory, but all are plausible. While the complications of this stela do undermine the thesis somewhat, it is by no means inexplicable, nor does it amount to dismissive evidence.

Ahituv writes of another element which weakens Schulman's hypothesis. Schulman presents a stela that was stylistically dated to the Ramesside Era but that pictured Thutmosis IV. He explains this by postulating the presence of a statue of Thutmosis IV deified. Ahituv notes that this is "hardly convincing"[57] and thus remains problematic. Yet other of Ahituv's arguments are less tenable. He doubts Schulman's idea because "we have no evidence from Egypt to support it."[58] What evidence would he expect, other than descriptions such as that associated with Amenhotep II? Did he expect pictures such as a prisoner being transported via ship in a cage, or stelae such as those Schulman presents? Furthermore, he dismisses evidence such as the depiction of a Syrian in a cage by contrasting it with the practice of bringing Syrian nobility as hostages to Egypt.[59] The two practices are in no way mutually exclusive. There is no tenable argument which could make the case that if foreign rulers were brought to Egypt as hostages that no foreign leaders could ever be ritually slain.

Ahituv writes that "even if we do not accept all his [Schulman's] conclusions, we must surely free ourselves from long-established conceptions about the purely symbolic nature of various scenes on Egyptian monuments, and consider other approaches."[60] Even while admitting this, Ahituv maintains that Schulman's hypothesis "is still unproven."[61] While Ahituv is certainly correct that Schulman's hypothesis is unproven, there is more evidence for actual ritual enemy slayings than has been heretofore discussed. Besides examples of ritual slaying noted thus far in this study, we will look at several other small pieces of evidence for a real referent in smiting scenes.

Evidences for Smiting

On a square-bezeled ring from the reign of Amenhotep II, a smiting scene is pictured. In this scene, the captive attempts to relieve the pressure of the gripped hair-lock with one arm and hand. The other arm rests on his knee and does not have a hand (see fig. 10.2). The ring is of exceptional craftsmanship and is made of silver (more valuable than gold at the time), and thus it seems unlikely that the hand was accidentally omitted. It is the only piece of art in ancient Egypt in which a hand seems to be deliberately excluded.[62] While the representation seems odd, there is a likely explanation. The taking of hands as trophies of battle was a well-known practice in ancient Egypt. While this was usually practiced on the dead, we do know of instances when captives were punished by the removal of a hand.[63] Alternatively, perhaps a prisoner is pictured who had been born without a hand. The salient point is that any explanation for this artistic inconsistency finds itself rooted in a concrete referent. The uniqueness

---

[53] Schulman, *Ceremonial Execution*, p. 50.

[54] Schulman, *Ceremonial Execution*, p. 96n140.

[55] Ahituv, "Review of *Ceremonial Execution and Public Rewards*," p. 303.

[56] Ahituv, "Review of *Ceremonial Execution and Public Rewards*," p. 303.

[57] Ahituv, "Review of *Ceremonial Execution and Public Rewards*," p. 303.

[58] Ahituv, "Review of *Ceremonial Execution and Public Rewards*," p. 303.

[59] Ahituv, "Review of *Ceremonial Execution and Public Rewards*," p. 304.

[60] Ahituv, "Review of *Ceremonial Execution and Public Rewards*," p. 305.

[61] Ahituv, "Review of *Ceremonial Execution and Public Rewards*," p. 304.

[62] Hall, *The Pharaoh Smites His Enemies*, pp. 1–2.

[63] Merneptah's Amada stela, *KRI* 4, 1, line 8, tells us that after capturing Nubians, bringing them to Egypt, and burning some, "the remainder, their hands were cut off because of their crime" (*spy šꜥd drwt ḥr nꜣ ii=sn btꜣw*). See also chapter 7, the section on Royal Inscriptions.

Figure 10.2 – Ring of Amenhotep II

of the scene indicates that it pictured a unique event, not an ideological idea. This, then, seems to be one case of a historical smiting.

Another artistic element points toward the reality of at least some smiting scenes. Originally, the mace was the weapon always used in smiting scenes.[64] Occasionally, this weapon was supplemented with an axe-mace in earlier periods, but this practice was rare until Ramesside times.[65] Beginning with the New Kingdom, a curved sword began to replace the mace as the weapon used for smiting.[66] At times, other weapons are utilized, such as Ahmose plying a dagger.[67] If the smiting scene were truly a stock scene, employed ideologically, the change of weapons would be less likely. Instead, it seems concomitant with a change in the weapons actually wielded by kings, and such a change was reflected in the art. While it is possible that the artists changed their stock to reflect their modern era, it is more probable that the artists were attempting to depict a real change while maintaining essential stylistic elements. This is not necessarily so, but it is the most plausible explanation.

In one of the stelae Schulman presents, the smiting king is given the epithets "Lord of Festivals" (nb ḥbw)[68] and "Master of Ritual" (nb iri ḫt).[69] While these may have been applied for a variety of reasons, it is conceivable that they were inscribed because pictured above was the king involved in a festival ritual.

At Karnak, Ahmose's judgment hall is described: "Asiatics come with fearful step to stand in his judgment hall. His sword is in Khentihennefer [determined by a bound prisoner: ⌂]. His war cries are in the lands of Fenkhu."[70] The mention of fearful Asiatics in the hall in conjunction with the king's sword among some type of bound people may imply that the sword might be used on some of the bound people, perhaps even within the hall. As will be shortly noted, this fear was not without reason.

As was mentioned above,[71] at Medinet Habu, Ramesses III records that in his fifth-year Libyan war, after destroying the enemy, "their leaders were carried off and slain. They were cast down and were made as pinioned."[72] The text makes it plain that the battle was over and that the leaders were carried away before they were slain. Additionally, the reference to being pinioned echoes sacrificial terminology and is reminiscent of Osorkon's ritual slaying of rebels. Combined, these elements seem to indicate that some of the smiting scenes at Medinet Habu may have been representations of actual ritual smitings. This is important given the fact that some Medinet Habu smiting scenes are copies of Ramesses II's Abu Simbel or Karnak scenes and are often used as argument against an actualization of the depictions.

The idea that some of the smiting scenes may represent actual ritual smitings is strengthened by two other passages from Medinet Habu. In one, Amun informs Ramesses III that he has brought enemy prisoners before him so "that you may grant breath to him whom you like among them, and that you may slay whom you desire."[73] Here it is made explicit that while the king could let some prisoners live (probably the vast majority, as slave labor), he very well might kill some. This idea is confirmed in an aforementioned incident, wherein the father of a captured chief came to Ramesses III to ask for his son's life. Apparently, because of a divine revelation of their ill intent (literally "the god knows what is in the belly"),[74] the king "came down upon their heads like a mountain of granite" (ḥm=f h3w ḥr tp=sn mi ḏw n m3t).[75] Presumably the pronoun "their" refers to the chief and his father.[76] Coming down on their heads like a mountain of granite seems to denote that something very hard came upon their heads very quickly. What could match this description better than a mace being used to smite these men on the head? Thus, it seems that these were two men to whom Ramesses did not give the breath of life but instead whom he ritually slew. If this event is not unique to Ramesses III, then it would explain why foreigners approached the judgment hall of Ahmose with a fearful step.

---

[64] Hall, *The Pharaoh Smites His Enemies*, pp. 1–16.
[65] Hall, *The Pharaoh Smites His Enemies*, p. 15.
[66] Hall, *The Pharaoh Smites His Enemies*, pp. 16–42, esp. 19.
[67] H. Schaefer, "Das Niederschlagen der Reinde", *Wiener Zeitschrift für die Kunde des Morgenlandes*, 1957, vol. 54, 175.
[68] Schulman, *Ceremonial Execution*, fig. 18, right side, line 1.
[69] Schulman, *Ceremonial Execution*, fig. 18, right side, line 3.
[70] *Urk.* 4, 18.
[71] See chapter 7, the section on Royal Inscriptions.
[72] *KRI* 5, 25, line 54. See also William Franklin Edgerton and John Albert Wilson, *Historical Records of Ramses III. The Texts in Medinet Habu Volumes I and II*, Chicago: University of Chicago Press, 1936, plates 27–8.
[73] *KRI* 5, 97, lines 6–7.
[74] *KRI* 5, 70, line 28.
[75] *KRI* 5, 70, lines 28–9. See also Shlomit Israeli, "*t3w n ꜥnḫ* ["breath of life"] in the Medinet Habu War Texts", in Irene Shirun-Grumach (ed.), *Jerusalem Studies in Egyptology*, Wiesbaden: Harrassowitz Verlag, 1998, p. 280.
[76] Breasted, in *ARE* 3, 58, n. b, independently agrees with this assessment.

Circumstantial evidence lies in the name of a feast outlined at Medinet Habu. Ramesses III inaugurated a new festival, known as the festival of "slaying the Libyans."[77] The smiting of pinioned Libyan leaders just mentioned above may have taken place at this new festival.

Moreover, we know of many examples of Egyptian kings slaying their enemies after having subdued them. Amenhotep II slew seven princes after his victorious battle against their forces. In what is apparently a separate event, he also slew several leaders at his accession. Akhenaten impaled 225 prisoners of war after his Nubian battle. Merneptah impaled a group of enemy Libyans after having brought them under his control, and burned Nubians whom he had subdued. Ramesses III slew Libyan leaders whom he had captured. Prince Osorkon did likewise with rebels against whom he waged battle. Pianky and Shabaka also ritually slew enemies they had already conquered. It is important to note a significant feature of the burning engaged in by Osorkon and Senusret I: these two rulers struck their captives with a blade of some sort before burning them, with the evidence being most strong in the case of Prince Osorkon. The most plausible scenario for these ritual slayings is that these rulers engaged in the ritual smiting before burning their noisome victims. In the face of so much evidence, it is difficult to suppose that the Egyptians did not kill leaders who were captives. While most of the evidence presented has been from the New Kingdom, the two examples just cited demonstrate that the practice was not confined to this time period.

Furthermore, this preponderance of evidence casts new light on the smiting scenes pictured on the kiosks of royal barques. We know of such depictions for Akhenaten, Nefertiti, Ramesses III, and Herihor.[78] We also know that Amenhotep II carried prisoners on the prow of his ship before ritually smiting them. Tuthankhamun is pictured with both live and dead prisoners on his vessel. Tuthmosis I is described as carrying a dead prisoner on the prow of his barque. The Giza cage suggests that Khufu also carried prisoners aboard his boat. Taken together, these incidents strongly suggest that Grimm was correct in positing the existence of a festival of triumph as a lasting Egyptian practice.[79] While some prisoners were slain before the boat ride and some were slain after, and while the smiting scene kiosks are chronologically indeterminate, all cases possess the same associations. It seems that no matter when prisoners were slain—before, after, or during the boat procession—the key element was the transportation of the ritual victim on the Nile aboard the royal barque.[80]

If a festival of triumph were a common practice, one would expect a ritual of conquest to be an element of the festival. Such a ritual may have been carried out on an inanimate object. There is some evidence for this, such as a later relief at Edfu depicting nine statuettes being executed.[81] Nevertheless, the inclusion of destroying inanimate objects in a festival does not exclude the destruction of animate beings. As with the insistence that curses belong either to this world or to the next, an argument that triumph rituals could only employ animate or inanimate beings imposes a false dichotomy. A few examples will illustrate.

At Edfu the king is depicted as ritually slaying a hippopotamus. The same argument which suggests that the ideological representation of smiting enemies cannot have a real referent, if applied to hippopotamus hunting, would mean that since it was depicted in art it never really happened. Yet we know that kings actually hunted hippopotami[82] and that the ritual also took the form of cutting up a hippo-shaped cake.[83]

Likewise, no Egyptologists would make the argument that since reliefs depict offerings for the deceased, actual food items were never presented at the tomb. Again, the system of redundancy in Egyptian religious practice must be stressed. The depiction of a rite makes it likely that the rite actually took place. The obvious examples of copying smiting reliefs, and a general sense that Egyptians did not ritually slay people, cannot offset the mounting evidence that such a rite frequently involved actual humans.

Such an interrelation of potent artistic representation and kinetic actualization is just the type of sacramental overlapping that Assmann posits for the rite of smashing the red pots.[84] This rite was similar to the execration rite, which we know sometimes involved humans. The smiting of real people is to the smiting scene what the Mirgissa and Avaris slayings are to execration rites.

---

[77] *KRI* 5, 173, heading.

[78] Hall, *The Pharaoh Smites His Enemies*, pp. 25–6, 36, figs. 39, 40, 66, and 82.

[79] Alfred Grimm, "Ein Käfig für einen Gefangenen in einem Ritual zur Vernichtung von Feinden", *JEA* 73, 1987, 203 and addendum.

[80] See Kerry Muhlestein, "Death by Water: The Role of Water in Ancient Egypt's Treatment of Enemies and Juridical Process", in Alessia Amenta, Michela Luiselli, and Maria Novella Sordi (eds.), *L'Acqua Nell'antico Egitto: Vita, Rigenerazione, Incantesimo, Medicamento*, Rome: L'Erma di Bretschneider, 2005.

[81] See Raphael Giveon, "Remarks on the Transmission of Egyptian Lists of Asiatic Toponyms", Jan Assman, Erika Feucht, and Reinhard Grieshammer (eds.), in *Fragen an die altägyptische Literatur*, Wiesbaden: Dr. Ludwig Reichert Verlag, 1997, p. 172. See also Robert Ritner, *The Mechanics of Ancient Egyptian Magical Practice*, Studies in Ancient Oriental Civilization, Chicago: The University of Chicago, 1993, vol. 54, the section on manipulation of objects.

[82] Hartwig Altenmüller, *Darstellungen der Jagd im alten Ägypten*, Berlin: Parey, 1967, pp. 20–40; Wolfgang Decker, *Sports and Games of Ancient Egypt*, Allen Guttmann (trans.), London: Yale University Press, 1992, pp. 148–50; and Toby A.H. Wilkinson, *Early Dynastic Egypt*, New York: Routledge, 1999, p. 216.

[83] Pascal Vernus, "Les jeux d' écriture et Les graphies du nom d' Amon-Rê dans un papyrus funéraire", in Jean-Paul Boulanger and Geneviève Renisio (eds.), *Naissance de l'écriture: cunéiformes et hiéroglyphes: [exposition]*, Galeries nationales du Grand Palais, Paris: Ministère de la culture Editions de la Réunion des musées nationaux, 1982, pp. 131–5; Richard H. Wilkinson, *Symbol & Magic in Egyptian Art*, New York: Thames and Hudson, 1994, pp. 178–9.

[84] Jan Assmann, "Spruch 23 der Pyramidentexte und die Ächtung der Feinde Pharos", in Catherine Berger, Gisèle Clerc, and Nicolas-Christophe Grimal (eds.), *Hommages à Jean Leclant*, Le Caire: Institut français d'archéologie orientale, 1994, pp. 53–4. See also Christopher Eyre, *The Cannibal Hymn: A Cultural and Literary Study*, Bolton: Liverpool University Press, 2002, p. 34, who writes that in ceremony the literal and symbolic were intertwined. Additionally, Schulman, "Narmer and the Unification", p. 83, points out that these scenes may have also fulfilled a psychological propagandistic role.

Eyre has argued along these same lines, saying: "Standard iconography shows the king slaughtering the helpless enemy, often bound as a captive. There is then a direct thematic connection between the normal butchery of enemies in the aftermath of victory, indeed as the purpose of campaigning, a focus on such slaughter as public propaganda, and its enactment in a great many rituals. It is not unlikely that actual ritual occasionally—exceptionally—included the slaughter of a real prisoner, beyond the normal enactment of ritual over a statue or model of a captive."[85]

As Shaw has pointed out, an analysis of this type of scene "is complicated by our modern need to be able to distinguish between event and ritual. But the ancient Egyptians show little inclination to distinguish consistently between the two."[86] Wilkinson writes that images associated with maintaining order involve an "interplay of the real, mythical, and iconographic spheres."[87] It seems likely that it is just this type of interplay we witness in the smiting scene. It is possible that the iconographic representation of smiting and the representation of any real referent were intended to have an effect in different spheres. As was mentioned above, Schulman postulated that ritual smitings took place as a type of thank-offering to the gods for victory in battle. I believe there is a more probable explanation.

The ideological iconographic representation of smiting presumably served several purposes. In its fugacious context, the smiting scene may have sometimes commemorated actual victories. It may have displayed, and thus politically and magically reinforced, the power of the king. It probably also made the king's victory over enemies, and hence over chaos, a victory in perpetuity.[88]

As was discussed above, and will be further discussed below, rituals are acts that are efficacious in other spheres and times. Thus, if Egyptian kings desired to defeat enemies on a mythological level, such as defeating chaos, they would have to do so via ritual. Much of Egyptian ritual was concerned with returning things to the state of *sp tpi*, or the pristine state of the creation.[89] It seems plausible, then, that the defeat of enemies and chaos needed to take place in three spheres, or times: the past (*sp tpi*), the present, and the future. While this may be a Western conception of chronology, it is clear that the ancient Egyptians thought of the "first time," the mortal realm, and that which was yet to happen as three realms that had to be dealt with. The actual conquering of enemies in battle would have effected the destruction of Isfet in the present. The iconography of smiting would have been effectual for the future, conquering Isfet in perpetuity. A ritual of smiting would have been efficacious in the past, presenting the opportunity to return to *sp tpi*. This tripartite program of victory over chaos is both plausible and appealing, but it can be neither proved nor disproved.

Certainly there are smiting scenes that are purely iconographic and some that were both iconographic and commemorative without representing an actual ritual. Concurrently, evidence indicates that actual ritual smitings did take place. It is less important to discern which depictions possess actual referents than it is to realize that *some did*. The investigation does not yield an irrefutable argument. Yet the known examples, the sheer volume of evidence, and the ideology of ritual just presented lead to the conclusion that ritual smitings were likely a regular feature throughout Egyptian history.

---

[85] Eyre, *The Cannibal Hymn*, pp. 163–4.
[86] Ian Shaw, "Introduction: Chronologies and Cultural Change in Egypt", in Ian Shaw (ed.), *The Oxford History of Ancient Egypt*, Oxford: Oxford University Press, 2000, p. 3.
[87] Wilkinson, *Symbol and Magic*, p. 173.
[88] See, for example, the view expressed in Jean Yoyotte, "Héra d' Héliopolis et le Sacrifice Humain", *Annuaire—Ecole pratique des hautes études, Section-sciences religieuses* 89, 1980–81, 36.

[89] See chapter 11, the section on The Egyptian Return.

Chapter 11

VIOLENT MYTH IN THE RITUAL OF RETURN

Pepi was born in Nun; Before there was sky; Before there was earth; Before there were mountains; Before there was strife.

—*Pyramid Text 486*

Ritual and Return

Much of the sanctioned killing explored in this study involves elements of ritual. Therefore, to more fully understand this phenomenon, we must understand something of the place of ritual in ancient society. In the recent past, discussion has centered on the theory and meaning of rituals.[1] The purpose of the current study is certainly not to define ritual theory or practice, and a discussion on recent movements and debates in ritual theory would only serve to distract from the topic at hand. For our purposes, it suffices to say that despite diverging views on many aspects of ritual, ritual theorists largely agree on some concepts, one of which is that rituals express beliefs.[2]

For example, Durkheim writes that "in all these formulae [rituals] it is the nature of religion as a whole that they seek to express."[3] Likewise, Bell expands on the idea that rites express the nature of religion, observing that some theorists believe that ritual is the place where belief is most easily studied due "to ritual's public nature, whereby rituals are 'analogous to culturally produced texts' that can be systematically read to endow 'meaning upon experience.'"[4] Bell further states that "beliefs, creeds, symbols, and myths emerge as forms of mental content or conceptual blueprints: they direct, inspire, or promote activity, but they themselves are not activities. Ritual, like action, will act out, express, or perform these conceptual orientations."[5]

Ritual is symbolic action that is not only a "conceptual blueprint" of a belief but also an "expression" or "performance" of that blueprint. This concept impinges greatly on the current study. Because many forms of attested sanctioned killing are bereft of religious explanation, our hope for determining the beliefs that led to such action lies in examining the rituals connected with them.[6] Furthermore, our understanding of Egyptian culture will enhance an examination of these rituals. In turn, examining these rituals will enhance our understanding of Egyptian culture: "The ritualized social body, therefore, is one that comes to possess, to various degrees, a cultural 'sense of ritual.'"[7] Thus, examining the rituals of sanctioned killing will allow us to better understand Egypt's cultural concerns, along with cultural changes over time because "ultimately, the notion of ritual is constructed in the image of the concerns of a particular cultural era."[8] As E.O. James notes, "The function of myth and ritual, however, is not to chronicle past events so much as to enable a community to deal effectively with the practical issues which

---

[1] For a good summary of discourse on ritual and a large, though now somewhat dated, bibliography of ritual studies, see Ronald L. Grimes, *Research in Ritual Studies: A Programmatic Essay and Bibliography*, Chicago: Scarecrow Press, 1985. For more recent works, see *Religion in Mind: Cognitive Perspectives on Religious Belief, Ritual, and Experience*, Jensine Andresen (ed.), New York: Cambridge University Press, 2001; Catherine Bell, *Ritual: Perspectives and Dimensions*, New York: Oxford University Press, 1997; *Ecology and the Sacred: Engaging the Anthropology of Roy A. Rappaport*, Ellen Messer and Michael Lambek (eds.), Ann Arbor, University of Michigan Press, 2001; and Michael Chuk-Young Chwe, *Rational Ritual: Culture, Coordination, and Common Knowledge*, Princeton: Princeton University Press, 2001. See also Kerry Muhlestein, "Ritual and Meaning", in *The Use of the Palm of the Hand in the Tabernacle and Temple of Solomon*, Master's thesis, Brigham Young University, 1997.

[2] Emile Durkheim, *Elementary Forms of Religious Life*, New York: The Free Press, 1915, p. 51, believes that one of the characteristics of ritual is that it is always associated with beliefs.

[3] Durkheim, *Elementary Forms of Religious Life*, p. 51. In fact, Durkheim, pp. 51–6, believes that religion consists of belief combined with ritual.

[4] Durkheim, *Elementary Forms of Religious Life*, p. 19.
[5] Durkheim, *Elementary Forms of Religious Life*, p. 19.
[6] Christopher Eyre, *The Cannibal Hymn: A Cultural and Literary Study*, Bolton: The University of Liverpool Press, 2002, p. 25, writes of the importance of understanding the performative context of ritual.
[7] Bell, *Ritual*, p. 107.
[8] Bell, *Ritual*, p. 222.

press upon it daily in the serious business of living, often in a precarious and unpredictable environment."[9]

Moreover, ancient Egyptian ritual helps us perceive those things that were culturally feared and those that were culturally desired. This is so because of ritual's tendency to attempt to align current reality with ideal reality. Wright has written:

> Ritual seeks to define the world, to put people and things in their proper places. This is chiefly so when they need to be assigned spheres of existence (e.g., in *rites de passage*) or when they appear to have gotten out of place and need to be restored to order (e.g., in healing or purification rituals). To reorganize reality, ritual often resorts to means of expression beyond the literal. This is particularly necessary when the state of affairs needing transformation is strange, inexplicable, uncontrollable, and threatening. Analogy in all its forms allows the unknown, unexpressible, or overwhelming to be concretized, comprehended, grasped, and, as a result, brought conceptually under one's power.[10]

This idea is furthered by Smith, who writes: "I would suggest that, among other things, *ritual represents the creation of a controlled environment* where the variables (i.e., the accidents) of ordinary life may be displaced *precisely* because they are felt to be so overwhelmingly present and powerful. *Ritual is a means of performing the way things ought to be in conscious tension to the way things are in such a way that this ritualized perfection is recollected in the ordinary, uncontrolled, course of things.*"[11]

Ritual accomplishes this task for at least two reasons: ritual connects different spheres, and ritual connects different times. James describes ritual as "traffic with the supernatural," believing that ritual was the one way through which a person could voluntarily interact with the supernatural in a controlled manner.[12] Paul Jones states that ritual addresses a "transcendent," a deity, force, or power structure. He believes that ritual is a symbol designed both to reflect the transcendent and to communicate with it.[13] The ability to interact with this "other," or "sacred," sphere is important because the sacred represents the "ultimate reality."[14] It is only through contact with this sphere that current reality can be aligned with the ideal reality, which still exists, uncorrupted, in the sacred sphere.

Ritual also has a divine archetype; it is a reenactment of what the gods did.[15] This is particularly true of the Egyptian king, who received his degree of divinity via ritual. The king's actions were constrained into "accepted and acceptable patterns of behavior," by the rituals in which his life was enveloped, as he acted in behalf of the gods whose actions he iterated.[16] This reenacting quality of ritual creates a juxtaposition of two times: the point in time in which it is performed and the perpetual existence of sacred time, or the atemporal point before time began. Every religious festival or rite is a reactualization of a sacred event of the mythical past.[17] Thus, ritual projects man to the beginning of the world.[18] In this way, mankind can live in sacred time, which is periodically recovered via ritual.[19]

Eliade sums up these two aspects of ritual:

> Through the paradox of rite, every consecrated space coincides with the center of the world, just as the time of any ritual coincides with the mythical time of the "beginning." Through repetition of the cosmogonic act, concrete time, in which the construction takes place, is projected into mythical time, *in illo tempore* when the foundation of the world occurred. . . . Any ritual whatever, as we shall see later, unfolds not only in a consecrated space (i.e., one different in essence from profane space) but also in a "sacred time," "once upon a time" (*in illo tempore, ab origine*), that is, when the ritual was performed for the first time by a god, an ancestor, or a hero.[20]

Specific to this study, in *illo tempore* deity has slain chaos monster/rebels, and via violent means—often enacted in a sacred place—man repeats this act and thus returns to the time and space of the god or gods, wherein a pristine world still existed.[21]

---

[9] E.O. James, *Myth and Ritual in the Ancient Near East*, London: Thames and Hudson, 1958, p. 304. He writes at some length on this subject, in pp. 304–9. As will be seen, not everyone agrees completely with this view.

[10] David P. Wright, "Ritual Analogy in Psalm 109", *The Journal of Biblical Literature* 113, 1994, 403. See also Wagner's discussion of ritual seeking to deal with paradoxes in the perceived world in Roy Wagner, *The Invention of Culture*, Chicago: University of Chicago Press, 1981, p.10.

[11] Jonathan Zittell Smith, "The Bare Facts of Ritual", in *Readings in Ritual Studies*, Ronald L. Grimes (ed.), Upper Saddle River, New Jersey: Prentice-Hall, 1996, p. 480.

[12] James, *Myth and Ritual*, p. 293. Similarly John M. Lundquist, *The Temple, Meeting Place of Heaven and Earth*, London: Thames and Hudson, 1993, p. 20, writes, "Ritual is the primary means that makes communication possible between humans and the powers beyond immediate human life—the transcendent. Ritual is the process through which contact with the world of the numinous powers is activated. It is not something dry, ossified, or meaningless, as it is widely thought to be in the Western world (cf. The word 'ritualistic'). It is a means of access to spiritual power."

[13] Paul D. Jones, *Rediscovering Ritual*, New York: Paulist Press, 1973, pp. 4–5.

[14] R. Scott Appleby, *The Ambivalence of the Sacred*, New York: Rowman & Littlefield Publisher, 2000, p. 28.

[15] Mircea Eliade, "Ritual and Myth", in *Readings in Ritual Studies*, Ronald L. Grimes (ed.), Upper Saddle River, New Jersey: Prentice-Hall, 1996, p. 198.

[16] John Baines, "Kingship, Definition of Culture, and Legitimation", in *Ancient Egyptian Kingship*, David O'Connor and David P. Silverman (eds.), New York: E.J. Brill, 1995, p. 4; and John Baines, "Origins of Egyptian Kingship", in *Ancient Egyptian Kingship*, David O'Connor and David P. Silverman (eds.), New York: E.J. Brill, 1995, p. 129.

[17] Mircea Eliade, *The Sacred and the Profane: The Nature of Religion*, New York: Harcourt Brace, 1959, pp. 68–9, 85, and 105.

[18] Eliade, *The Sacred and the Profane*, p. 82.

[19] Eliade, *The Sacred and the Profane*, p. 104.

[20] Eliade, *Ritual and Myth*, pp. 197–8.

[21] Eliade, *Sacred and Profane*, p. 100.

Sacred time and sacred space are inextricably interrelated. It is often in sacred space that one can reach sacred time. Yet, since sacred time is a reflection of *illud tempus*, when one becomes part of sacred time, one is intrinsically in sacred space. The concept of sacred space is important for the current study. Yet, we know little of the space in which many of the acts discussed thus far took place, though we are certain that many others did indeed occur in sacred space. Such knowledge will continue to be noted. Nevertheless, since the rest of the chapter discusses acts that were mythologized (and how they were mythologized), the important element in this discussion is sacred time.

The Egyptian *Illud Tempus*

In order for any of this ritual theory to have relevance to the current study, we must determine if the hypothesized conditions of an ideal reality reflected in an "original time," or *illud tempus*, existed in Egyptian thought. We must also determine if there is evidence of a desire to return to such a time. Specifically, we must determine if there was an Egyptian idea of violently ending *Isfet* and regaining *Ma'at* in sacred time and if such violence was reiterated in an effort to return to this sacred time.

There is abundant evidence that the Egyptians conceived of a sacred cosmogonic time. The Egyptian phrase *sp tpi* is literally the "top" or "head time" but is best translated as the "first time." This is an almost exact semantic equivalent of *illud tempus*. This is the time before the gods separated the earth and themselves from the earth.[22] It is also the time before strife came about.[23] It is clear that the creator intended for creation to remain in this pristine state but that instead it was foiled by the actions of mankind. He said, "I made every man like his fellow. I did not ordain that they do Isfet. It was their desires that injured what I had said."[24]

This statement highlights one of the main motifs of the cosmogonic introduction of Isfet, the motif of the rebellion of mankind against the original order of creation and the gap it created between the human and divine spheres.[25] While the Pyramid Texts quoted above refer to this theme, it is only through later narrative that we understand the references. This is typical of the evolution of Egyptian myth and mythology. The narrative mythology that relates to these mythical elements is the first narrative myth about which we know: the Myth of the Heavenly Cow.[26] We may not completely understand the relation between earlier mythical references, its later narrative sequence, or the reinterpretation that was doubtlessly part of this process,[27] yet the essential elements are clear enough for our purposes. While the text may have been originally composed in the Middle Kingdom, our earliest manuscripts come from the New Kingdom.[28]

In this tale, we are presented with Re—the self-created one—as the ruler of the earth, while "mankind plotted against him."[29] In consultation with other gods, Re decided the appropriate course of action was to slay rebellious mankind. As his eye (in the form of Hathor, or Sakhmet) set about this task, Re had a change of heart and stopped the destruction of mankind when it was halfway completed. Even with this change of heart, Re still decided he could no longer live on earth with mankind. When men saw Re leaving, in an attempt to convince him to stay they slew his enemies. While this greatly pleased Re, he did not stay.

This story is corroborated by an allusion in the Instructions for Merikare. Toward the end of this text, the Ma'at-establishing actions of deity are laid out. Among these it is recorded that:

> He [god] defeated the water monster
> He gave the breath of life for their noses[30]
> ...
> He slew his enemies, he destroyed his children
> When they thought of making rebellions (*irit sbiwt*)[31]
> ...
> He made for them rulers in the egg
> Governors to uplift the back of the weak
> He made for them magic as weapons
> To protect from the blow of happenings
> Guarding against it day and night
> He slew the malcontents among them[32]

In this stanza it is repeatedly made clear that in *illo tempore* god had slain the chaos monster, specifically by slaying his rebellious children. This mythical reference

---

[22] Pyr. 1208 speaks of the time "when heaven was separated from earth, indeed, when the gods went to heaven" (*m wpt pt ir t3 m prt r=f ntr.w ir pt*). Pyr. 1778 speaks of one who "keeps assuming the office of Atum of separating heaven from earth and the primeval waters" (*itt hrt itm n dsr pt ir t3 nmw*).
[23] Pyr. 1040 speaks of the time "before strife existed, before fear came about through the Horus Eye" (*n(i) hprt hnnw n(i) hprt snd pw hpr hr irt hrw*).
[24] CT VII:464a–b.
[25] See Antonio Loprieno, "Der demotische Mythos vom Sonnenauge", in *Texte aus der Umwelt zum Alten Testament. III, 5: Mythen und Epen*, Otto Kaiser, Mohn: Gütersloher (ed.), 1995, p. 1038.
[26] John Baines, "Myth and Literature", in *Ancient Egyptian Literature: History and Forms*, Antonio Loprieno (ed.), New York: E.J. Brill, 1996, p. 363; and Antonio Loprieno, "Defining Egyptian Literature: Ancient Texts and Modern Theories", in *Ancient Egyptian Literature: History and Forms*, Antonio Loprieno (ed.), Leiden: E.J. Brill, 1996, pp. 49–50.
[27] See John Baines, "Egyptian Myth and Discourse: Myth, Gods, and the Early Written and Iconographic Record", *JNES* 50, 1991, no. 2, for a discussion of this complicated issue.
[28] Miriam Lichtheim, *Ancient Egyptian Literature: A Book of Readings. Volume II: The New Kingdom*, Berkeley: University of California Press, 1975, pp. 197–8.
[29] Myth of the Heavenly Cow as in Erik Hornung, *Der Ägyptische Mythos von der Himmelskuh. Eine Ätiologie des Unvollkommen*, Orbis Biblicus et Orientalis, Göttingen: Universitätverlag Freiburg Schweiz Vandenhoeck & Ruprecht, 1982, p. 1.
[30] P. Leningrad 1116A, 131–2.
[31] P. Leningrad 1116A, 133–4; supplemented by P. Carlsberg VI, 5, 8–9.
[32] P. Leningrad 1116A, 135–37.

matches well with the picture painted by the narrative myth presented in the Myth of the Heavenly Cow. Thus, we can see that in one version of ancient Egypt's *illud tempus* mankind rebelled against god, in response to which mankind was slain by both deity and men.[33] Assmann argues that it is the theology of the rebellion outlined in this narrative that leads to a world in which Ma'at competes with Isfet for dominance; it is this split condition that leads to the need for a ruler to enforce Ma'at and destroy Isfet with a white-hot fury.[34]

This is not, however, the only narrative myth in ancient Egypt that contains an *illud tempus* rebellion. The well-known story of Horus and Seth presents in narrative form part of a myth that is alluded to in the earliest theological texts. According to this theology, the original rebel was Seth, who slew his brother Osiris and sought to gain the throne for himself. Horus, Osiris's son, was eventually able to win the crown and thus vanquish his rebellious uncle. While Seth is a complicated figure who sometimes fights against chaos,[35] he became a symbol of chaos, the antagonist to order.[36] Hearkening to the Pyramid Text reference from the New Kingdom quoted above, which mentions the time "before strife,"[37] Seth's birth was referred to as the beginning of strife.[38] Because of his role as the first human to confront and disturb the pristine order of things, Seth became an archetypal rebel.

These two crises form the backbone of *illud tempus* rebellion in ancient Egypt. In each case the disturbance to the pristine state was put right, though not without lasting consequences: in the Myth of the Heavenly Cow, Re left the earth, and in the myth of Horus and Seth, Osiris was perpetually the dead king with Horus serving as the living ruler. These parallel disturbances had both happened in *sp tpi* or *hrw*[39] *tpi*, or mythical time. By the time any historical events occurred, the disturbances had already been overcome, bringing the world to its new ideal state.[40]

There is, however, another prototype of rebellion and chaos that impinged upon ideal reality. Apophis, usually represented as a giant snake, was chaos incarnate. Apophis, in the Neith cosmogony, was created from divine saliva and began at the very beginning to conceive of rebellion.[41] Hornung infers from the defeat of Apophis's creatures, who are destroyed at the primeval hill, that Apophis "is already there at the creation of the world and must be defeated for the first time by the creator god and driven out of the ordered world of existence."[42] Thus, Apophis takes his place as a force of chaos in *illo tempore*. Apophis is identified with those who rebel because he is a rebel himself. In the Book of Overthrowing Apophis, both Apophis and the children of vice are described as rebellious, and the king overthrows both Apophis and these defective, rebellious men as a result of their rebellion.[43] In one line, Apophis is specifically called the rebel (*sbi*).[44] Apophis, rebellious mankind, and Seth form a triumvirate of rebels who disturb order in *illo tempore*.

As stated above, in order to determine the relevance of ritual theory—especially its ideas of mankind attempting to return to *illo tempore* via ritual—for this study we need to determine if the concept of an ideal reality, pre-chaotic intrusion, existed in ancient Egypt, and if there is a manifest desire to return to such a state. It is now abundantly apparent that the Egyptians conceived of a time in which there was no strife, a hyper-reality that was disturbed by the intrusion of rebellion. Hence, we turn our attention to texts that demonstrate a clear desire to return to the pristine state of *illud tempus*, or *sp tpi*.

The Egyptian Return

A number of texts are explicit about desiring to return to *illud tempus*. Amenemhet I claimed to have appeared "as Atum himself, setting in order that which he found decaying."[45] Thutmosis III was described as one who "transforms Egypt into the condition of the past, as when Re was king."[46] In addition, he was described as one who was "violent before the first generation of men."[47] The implication is that the violent acts in which Thutmosis III appropriately engaged were acts that really took place in *sp tpi*, before the generations of men, and not in current time. As with his predecessors, Tutankhamun had made it so that "the land is as it was in its first time."[48] Horemheb had "set this land in order and ordained it as it was in the time of Re."[49] The Twenty-first Dynasty high priest Menkhepere expelled enemies so that things might be as they were in the time of Re.[50]

---

[33] In the Merikare text, men seem to be represented by the king.

[34] Jan Assmann, *Ma'at. Gerechtigkeit und Unsterblichkeit im Alten Ägypten*, München: C.H. Beck, 1995, pp. 221–2.

[35] See Herman te-Velde, *Seth, God of Confusion*, Leiden, Netherlands: E.J. Brill, 1967.

[36] For example, Barry J. Kemp, *Ancient Egypt: Anatomy of a Civilization*, New York: Routledge, 1989, p. 52, writes, "Seth becomes the loser, and the antagonist to Horus. He becomes the antagonist to order on a grand scale."

[37] Pyr. P. 1040.

[38] See te-Velde, 27–8; and Erik Hornung, *Conceptions of God in Ancient Egypt. The One and the Many*, John Baines (trans.), Ithaca: Cornell University Press, 1996, p. 158 and n. 56. See also Linda J. Tessier, "Boundary Crossing: The Chaos-Cosmos Dynamic in Cosmogonic Myth", Ph.D. diss., Claremont Graduate School, 1987, p. 245.

[39] The word *hrw* means day. In narrative, the "first time" becomes a "first day," probably to accommodate the narrative. I am grateful to Dr. Antonio Loprieno for insight into this term.

[40] See Loprieno, "Mythos vom Sonnenauge", p. 1038.

[41] Mpay Kemboly, *Violence and Protection in Early Egyptian Funerary Texts*, Master's thesis, Oxford University, 2000, pp. 17–18.

[42] Hornung, *Conceptions of God*, p. 159.

[43] P. Bremner-Rhind, 25, 18–21, as in Raymond O. Faulkner, *The Papyrus Bremner-Rhind (British Museum No. 10188)*, Bruxelles: Édition de la Fondation Égyptologique Reine Élisabeth, 1933. See also Raymond O. Faulkner, "The Bremner-Rhind Papyrus-III", JEA 23, 1937, no. 2, 171.

[44] Bremner-Rhind, *The Papyrus Bremner-Rhind*, p. 19.

[45] *Urk.* 7, 27.

[46] *Urk.* 4, 1246.

[47] Armant Stele of Thutmosis III, line 2, as in Robert Mond and Oliver Humphrys Myers, *Temples of Armant: A Preliminary Survey*, London: The Egypt Exploration Society, 1940.

[48] *Urk.* 4, 2026.

[49] *Urk.* 4, 2119.

[50] Heinrich Karl Brugsch, *Reise nach der grossen Oase El Khargeh in der libyschen Wüste; Beschreibung ihrer Denkmäler und wissenschaft-*

Other Egyptologists have recognized this desire among the ancient Egyptians. Assmann writes that each king is charged with the pathos of again bringing about the condition of the first time.[51] Wilkinson states that Egyptian ritual was a "magical means of effecting the required 'transformation of state'" that brought Egypt back to the pattern of creation.[52] It is evident that there was a demonstrable desire to return to the state of *sp tpi*.[53]

The Egyptian texts make it equally conspicuous that part of returning to *sp* or *hrw tpi* was the destruction of Isfet and the upholding of Ma'at and that the latter was contingent on the former. One Pyramid Text states that "Ma'at is in the presence of Re, on the festival of the first day of the year. The sky is content, the earth is in joy, because they have heard that the King put Ma'at in the place of Isfet."[54] In another Pyramid Text, the king describes part of the reason that he can be with Re and receive a renewal of life as the fact that he has "put Ma'at in the place of Isfet."[55] Of Amenemhet I, Khnumhotep writes, "His majesty came to drive out, Isfet appearing as Atum himself, setting in order that which he found decaying . . . since he loves Ma'at so much."[56] In the context of describing the king bringing about a renewal and restoration, the prophecies of Neferti state that "Ma'at will return to its seat, Isfet is driven out."[57]

Texts of the New Kingdom and later continue this trend. Tutankhamun is described as having "driven Isfet out of both lands, and Ma'at is fixed in its place; he has made it so that falsehood is abhorred and the land is as it was in its first time."[58] Taharqa was one of whom it was said, "The land was inundated in his time as it was in the time of the lord of all. Each man sleeps until the shining of day and none say 'that I had!' Ma'at is spread throughout the land, Isfet is transfixed to the ground."[59]

These texts are explicit and intentional in demonstrating both the desire to return to *sp tpi* and the need to re-create those conditions by again forcing Isfet out and bringing Ma'at back.[60] This pattern being established, we must ascertain whether the violent events depicted in this study constitute an attempted destruction of Isfet as part of a ritual return. If this is the case, we can expect that foreigners (as representatives of chaos) and rebels were identified with Seth, Apophis, and the mythical rebellious mankind.

That such was the case is inescapable. One inscription we have already encountered dictates that any who misappropriated tomb personnel would go "to the fire of the king on the day of his fury. His Uraeus shall spit fire on their heads, annihilating their bodies and devouring their flesh, having become like Apophis on the morn of the New Year."[61] A hymn to Amun likens Apophis to those who rebel: "The weapon is in Apophis the injurer, felled by his sword. Our rebels, they are cut down."[62] In the book of Felling Apophis, we read that Apophis and the children of revolt are rebellious, and thus the king fells them both.[63] Posener has illustrated that the condemned were specifically associated with, or even named, Apophis.[64] In a ritual designed to thwart foreign rulers and incursions, Seth and Apophis are told they can no longer enter Egypt and are called "rebel vile of character."[65] Hornung notes a Ptolemaic tomb inscription that identifies potential violators with Apophis, making them "not exist."[66] Assmann has summed it up saying that the task was "to thwart the evil designs of Apophis and so ensure the course of the sun and the continuation of creation." He then goes on to note how this sometimes was manifest in the annihilation of political enemies.[67]

Equally attested are identifications with mankind rebelling against Re. Ramesses II had his actions in the battle of Qadesh described as:

> On my brow my serpent was felling my foes for me
> Casting her blast of flame in the faces of my enemies
> I was like Re when he rises at dawn
> My rays burned the flesh of the rebels.[68]

Understanding the parallelism of these couplets highlights the comparison. The serpent felling foes is

---

liche Untersuchungen über das Vorkommen der Oasen in den altägyptischen Inschriften auf Stein und Papyrus, Leipzig: J.C. Hinrichs, 1878, pl. 21, line 7. Jürgen Von Beckerath, "Die 'Stele der Verbannten,'" RdE 20 (1968): 7-36.

[51] Assmann, *Ma'at*, p. 224. See also James P. Allen, *Genesis in Egypt: The Philosophy of Ancient Egyptian Creation Accounts*, William Kelly Simpson (ed.), Yale Egyptological Studies, New Haven: Yale University, 1988, p. 26, who writes of the eternal recurrence in ancient Egypt which maintains the undisturbed Ma'at of creation. See also Jan Assmann, *The Mind of Egypt: History and Meaning in the Time of the Pharaohs*, Andrew Jenkins (trans.), New York: Metropolitan Books, 2002, p. 206.

[52] Richard H. Wilkinson, *Symbol & Magic in Egyptian Art*, New York: Thames and Hudson, 1994, p. 180.

[53] See Jeremy Naydler, *Temple of the Cosmos: The Ancient Egyptian Experience of the Sacred*, Rochester, Vermont: Inner Traditions, 1996, pp. 91-3, for a philosophical argument as to the necessity of the Egyptian Return.

[54] Pyr. 1774-6.

[55] Pyr. 265.

[56] *Urk.* 7, 27.

[57] P. Leningrad 1116B, 69, as in Wolfgang Helck, *Die Prophezeihung des Nfr.tj*, Wiesbaden: O. Harrassowitz, 1970, p. 57.

[58] *Urk.* 4, 2026.

[59] Stela of Taharqa year 6, lines 3-5 (Kawa version), as in M.F. Laming Macadam, *The Temples of Kawa I*, London: Oxford University Press, 1949.

[60] See also Naydler, *Temple of the Cosmos*, pp. 93-7.

[61] C. Robichon and A. Varille, *Le temple du scribe royal Amenhotep, fils de Hapou*, Cairo: Imprimerie de l'institut français d'archéologie orientale, 1936, line 8. See also Jan Assmann, "Inscriptional Violence and the Art of Cursing: A Study of Performative Writing", *Stanford Literature Review*, 1992, vol. 9, no. 1, 62.

[62] Leiden hymn 30, as in J. Zandee, *De Hymnen aan Amon van Papyrus Leiden I 350*, Leiden: Rijksmuseum van Oudheden, 1947, pl. 2, lines 20-1. John L. Foster, *Echoes of Egyptian Voices: An Anthology of Ancient Egyptian Poetry*, Norman, Oklahoma: University of Oklahoma Press, 1992, p. 67, ammends the "Apophis" I have included here.

[63] P. Bremner-Rhind, pp. 25, 18-19.

[64] Georges Posener, "Les Criminels Débaptisés et les Morts sans Noms", *RdE* 5, 1946, 53.

[65] *Urk.* 4, 17.

[66] Erik Hornung, *Conceptions of God*, John Baines (trans.), Ithaca: Cornell University Press, 1996, p. 158n57.

[67] Assmann, *Mind of Egypt*, p. 147.

[68] *KRI* 2, 887, lines 280-4.

parallel with fiery breath in the enemies' faces. Ramesses being like Re when he rises is parallel with Ramesses' rays burning rebels. This harks back to Re having those who rebelled against him killed by his eye at the beginning of a new day. This idea is strengthened in the next four lines of the poem, wherein Ramesses' enemies describe him as Sakhmet the Great. In the Myth of the Heavenly Cow, it was Sakhmet who destroyed rebellious mankind for Re. Additionally, as Willems has pointed out, the sacred space of the altar at the Temple of Tod, the same temple in which Senusret I claimed to have burned humans, contains numerous references to the destruction of mankind as presented in the Myth of the Heavenly Cow.[69] Moreover, as outlined in Chapter Eight, when commanding the execution of Theban rebels, Osorkon specifically likened the situation to bringing the eye of Re, an allusion to the Myth of the Heavenly Cow.[70]

Seth is also equated with chaos in various texts. Pyramid Text 231 describes Nubians being slain by harpoons. Seth has argued that this spell was recited during a ritual hippopotamus slaying, and both he and Willems argue convincingly that this ritual was tied into defeating Seth and chaos.[71] Execration texts, which were explicitly tied to rebels, also dealt with Seth and Apophis.[72] It has been proposed that slaying the *tekenu* was a Sethian rite.[73] A stela from Dakhla states that those who disregarded its inscription would be killed by Amun-Re and Sakhmet and were "an enemy of Osiris, lord of Abydos."[74] The enemy of Osiris is Seth; also, Amun-Re and Sakhmet jointly killing is reminiscent of the narrative of Sakhmet killing rebellious mankind for Re. Evocative of the incidents of tying prisoners to boats, a magical papyrus describes Seth as being tied to the bow of Re or Osiris's boat.[75] A Ramesseum papyrus equates rebels (*sbiw*) with the son of Nut, which is a clear reference to Seth.[76] Later sources speak of red foreigners being killed to represent eradicating Seth and all the enemies of Osiris.[77] Assmann has identified rites in which the sacrificial animals were identified with he who slew Osiris.[78] Indeed, throughout Egyptian history many sacrifices were equated with Seth, most of these being offered to Horus.[79] The principle of humans serving as or being equated with destructive or wild elements continued at least through Ptolemaic times, as is evidenced by depictions at Dendera of a human wearing a jackal mask being sacrificed at a stake before Osiris Khentiamentiu.[80] Other depictions in the temple make it clear that there were indeed people behind the animal masks.[81]

Modern scholarship has also articulately demonstrated the theological inferences that identify human rebels with mythical counterparts.[82] Willems has argued convincingly that those who damaged inscriptions were manifestations of Seth and Apophis.[83] Leahy explains that rebellion echoed mythical assaults on Ma'at and the rebellion of Seth against Osiris.[84] Garthoff writes that enemies of the king were always seen as chaotic forces, personified by Apophis, and that this connection was made explicit beginning with Merneptah.[85] He also demonstrates that Merneptah associated his battle against the Libyans with Seth's contentions against Horus.[86] Yoyotte believes that certain Heliopolitan rites that possibly involved ritual slaying in a sacred space were associated with fighting off the enemies of Re or Osiris.[87] Hornung discusses the blurring that occurs between mythical and political or juridical spheres due to the tendency to identify chaotic events with myth.[88] He believes that any who were slain by the fire of the royal snake (as is described in many of the texts presented in this study) were seen as mythical enemies of Order.[89]

In summary, the ancient Egyptians associated rebels, including the archetypal foreigner, with mythical rebels;

---

[69] *Urk.* 4, 17. See also Harco Willems, "Crime, Cult and Capital Punishment (Mo'alla Inscription 8)", *JEA* 76, 1990, 43; Jean Yoyotte, "Héra d' Héliopolis et le Sacrifice Humain", *Annuaire—Ecole pratique des hautes études, Section-sciences religieuses* 89, 1980–1, 35.

[70] Bubastite Portal, Annals of the High Priest Osorkon, inscription of Year 11 of Takelot II, cols. 35–6, as in Harold Hayden Nelson and University of Chicago Oriental Institute. Epigraphic Survey, *Reliefs and Inscriptions at Karnak*, Chicago: University of Chicago Press, 1936, pp. 16, 18–19. See also Ricardo Caminos, *The Chronicle of Prince Osorkon*, Rome: Pontificium Institutum Biblicum, 1958, p. 48; chapter 8, the section on Dynasty 22.

[71] Kurt Sethe, *Ubersetzung und Kommentar zu den altägyptischen Pyramidentexte*, vol. I (Glückstadt), pp. 205–6; Willems, "Crime, Cult and Capital Punishment", pp. 44–5.

[72] See *Urk.* 7, 17; Willems, "Crime, Cult and Capital Punishment", 48, esp. n. 111; see also Posener, "Les Criminels Débaptisés", p. 53.

[73] J. Gwyn Griffiths, "The Tekenu, the Nubians and the Butic Burial", *Kush* 6, 1958, 114.

[74] Jac. Jansen, "The Smaller Dakhla Stela", *JEA* 54, pl. 25a, line 14.

[75] H.O. Lange, *Der Magische Papyrus Harris*, Copenhagen: Andr. Fred. Høst, 1927, pp. 50–2.

[76] P. Ram. IX, 2, 2–5 as in Alan H. Gardiner, *The Ramesseum Papyri: Plates*, Oxford: Oxford University Press, 1955, p. 41.

[77] J. Gwyn Griffiths, "Human Sacrifices in Egypt: The Classical Evidence", *ASAE* 48, 1948, 417.

[78] Jan Assmann, "Spruch 23 der Pyramidentexte und die Ächtung der Feinde Pharos", in *Hommages à Jean Leclant*, Catherine Berger (ed.), Gisèle Clerc, and Nicolas-Christophe Grimal, Cairo: Institut français d'archéologie orientale, 1994, p. 52.

[79] See for example, Pyr. 1544a–1545d; Pyr. 1976a-1977d; or J. Gwyn Griffiths, *The Origins of Osiris and His Cult*, Leiden: E.J. Brill, 1980, pp. 211–15.

[80] Auguste Mariette, *Dendérah: description générale du grand temple de cette ville, vol. iv*, Paris: A. Franck, 1873, pl. lvi.

[81] Margaret A. Murray, *The Osireion at Abydos*, London: Gilbert and Rivington, 1904, p. 30.

[82] For a discussion on the general use of sanctioned violence in the mythologization process, see Mark Edward Lewis, *Sanctioned Violence in Early China*, Albany: State University of New York Press, 1991, pp. 4, 205.

[83] Willems, "Crime, Cult and Capital Punishment", p. 52.

[84] A. Leahy, "Death by Fire in Ancient Egypt", *Journal of the Economic and Social History of the Orient* 27, 1984, 201.

[85] B.W.B. Garthoff, "Merenptah's Israel Stela: A curious case of Rites de Passage?", in *Funerary Symbols and Religion: Essays Dedicated to Professor M.S.H.G. Heerma van Voss on the Occasion of His Retirement from the Chair of the History of Ancient Religions at the University of Amsterdam*, Jacques H. Kamstra, H. Milde, and K. Wagtendonk (ed.), Kampen, the Netherlands: J.H. Kok, 1988, p. 23.

[86] Garthoff, "Merenptah's Israel Stela", p. 25.

[87] Yoyotte, "Héra d'Héliopolis", pp. 43, 102.

[88] Erik Hornung, *Altägyptische Höllenvorstellungen. Mit 7 Lichtdrucktafeln und 6 Abbildungen im Text*, Abhandlungen der Sächsischen Akademie der Wissenschaften zu Leipzig, Philologisch-historische Klasse Bd. 59, Heft 3, Berlin: Akademie-Verlag, 1968, p. 27.

[89] Hornung, *Altägyptische Höllenvorstellungen*, p. 28.

they perceived a homology between mundane and mythical events. Since most of the violence outlined in this study is aimed at rebels, we can conclude that this violence was aimed at mythical rebels. The sanctioned killing of mortals on earth was equivalent to the annihilation of chaotic, rebellious elements in the mythological and divine sphere.[90] This congruence not only created a richness of meaning in the sanctioned killing of criminals and hostile foreigners—the two faces of rebellion—but also imbued it with a greater sense of urgency. Since the need to destroy chaotic characters on the mythical plane was absolute and insistent, the similar demand in the mortal sphere could be no less so.

---

[90] David O'Connor, "Egypt's View of 'Others'", in *Never Had the Like Occurred: Egypt's View of Its Past*, John Tait (ed.), Portland: Cavendish Publishing, 2003, p. 176, concludes similarly.

Chapter 12

THOSE WHO ARE ABOUT TO DIE, WE ABHOR YOU

Do not be enraged toward a man unjustly, but be enraged regarding that about which you should be enraged.

—*Tomb of Rekhmire*

Thus far in this disquisition, each chronological chapter has contained a summary of the data presented therein. Additionally, chapter 9 presented a synopsis of the entirety of the data communicated up to that point and an analysis thereof. Hence, the need here is not for yet another summarization of the data but instead for a discussion of how the data relates to the theories of mythologization presented in the previous chapter.

As Eliade has opined, life is lived on two planes: the human plane and the transhuman, or cosmic, plane.[1] Our evidence concludes that for the ancient Egyptians this was especially true of those who engaged in rebellious acts and of he whose primary duty was to counteract these acts—the King. Apparently certain acts constituted an identification with mythical rebellion and thus demanded eradication.[2] The specific acts that created this identification may have changed over time. For example, it seems to be a late phenomenon that historical murder came to be associated with mythical murder, e.g. the murder of Osiris by Seth. Likewise, associating being false in office with mythical rebellion seems to be a later tendency. It could be that as personal piety increased, so did the tendency to equate more personal acts with another realm. Still, while the nature of offenses that crossed spheres may have changed over time, the principle of rebellion across planes seems to have remained constant. Throughout time, some acts lifted their perpetrators from the plateau of daily imprudence to the pinnacle of mythical rebellion. These actors' role in the temporal realm was eclipsed by their newfound role in the mythical sphere. Acting in *illo tempore*, they soon found themselves responded to in a manner congruent to the actions of that sacred time. Often this response took place in a sacred space, making the correspondence all the greater and more obvious.

Ritual slaying, because of its nature, is a reenactment of *sp tpi*, or the pristine state before the mythical creation, and thus intrinsically mythologizes its actors and actions. As has been noted, a host of sacrifices were Sethian in nature,[3] and some ritual slayings would have inevitably taken on this characteristic. Many types of violence discussed in this study do not contain enough information for us to know if they were conducted in a ritual context. Can non-ritualized sanctioned killing constitute the type of mythologization discussed in the previous chapter? It is clear that much of the mythologization presented there was not exclusive to explicitly ritual activities. A brief recitation of some of the crucial texts will demonstrate this. A punishment for misappropriating tomb personnel reads that the offender would go "to the fire of the king on the day of his fury. His Uraeus shall spit fire on their heads, annihilating their bodies and devouring their flesh, having become like Apophis on the morn of the New Year."[4] It is explicit that the action had been mythologized and would be dealt with on a mythical level, but it is not clear that such would take place in a ritual setting. The account of Ramesses II slaying enemies in battle mythologized the event, though such a battle clearly did not take place as a ritual. The Dakhla stela quoted above warns that any who disregarded its inscription would be killed by Amun-Re and Sakhmet and was "an enemy of Osiris, lord of Abydos."[5] Again,

---

[1] Mircea Eliade, *The Sacred and the Profane: The Nature of Religion*, New York: Harcourt Brace, 1959, p. 167.

[2] Those who represented "rebellious" groups, whether specifically guilty or not, could become mythologically guilty, regardless of temporal guilt. See René Girard, "Generative Scapegoating", in *Violent Origins: Ritual Killing and Cultural Formation*, Walter Burkert, Rene Girard, and Johnathan Z. Smith (ed.), Stanford: Stanford University Press, 1987, p. 79.

[3] J. Gwyn Griffiths, *The Origins of Osiris and His Cult*, Leiden: E.J. Brill, 1980, pp. 211–15.

[4] C. Robichon and A. Varille, *Le temple du scribe royal Amenhotep, fils de Hapou*, Cairo: Imprimerie de l'institut français d'archéologie orientale, 1936, line 8. See also Jan Assmann, "Inscriptional Violence and the Art of Cursing: A Study of Performative Writing", *Stanford Literature Review* 9, 1992, no. 1, 62.

[5] Jac. Jansen, "The Smaller Dakhla Stela", *JEA*, 54, pl. XXVa, line 14.

the mythologization of the acts is evident, yet ritual is likely uninvolved. The identification of tomb desecrators with mythical rebels was probably bereft of ritual. The equation of foreigners with mythical rebels did not always involve ritual, such as Merneptah likening his Libyan foes to Apophis or Seth. It is clear that fugacious actions were capable of greatly altering the actor into a grotesque *illud tempus* character.

This tendency to raise certain mundane events to the mythological level results in a dual sphere existence of humans, which leads to confusion about inscriptional curses. As has been noted, curses may have been intended as a consequence in the mortal life and may also have appealed to the post-mortal realm for punishment in case perfect justice was not enacted in the mortal realm. Concomitantly, these inscriptions used mythological language because the acts they were dealing with were perceived as taking place in both spheres. Crimes against tombs and memorial inscriptions simultaneously affected a person's existence in both realms and were the repetition of rebellious acts that had happened in the mythological sphere, thus demanding appeals to myth. The authors of these inscriptions were well aware of the many layers of "reality" in which they were attempting to be efficacious; hence they used language that is confusing to those who try to compartmentalize the threats' spheres of influence. When we allow the Egyptians to operate in all of the planes they intended, we are able to make much more sense of tomb threats, allowing us to realize their viability and applicability in the mortal realm. This is not only true of curses but also of much of the juridical and political terminology and procedure encountered in this study. They were designed to operate in a multivalent manner that allowed sanctioned killing to deal with problems which, by their nature, had ramifications in multiple spheres; sanctioned killing expurgated *Isfet* on both a daily and a mythological level.

This need to eradicate such Isfet-saturated elements in two spheres also explains the heavy reliance on punishments, which brought about a complete destruction of a person. Burning, drowning, and beheading were all punishments that annihilated a person's chance to live in both the mortal and post-mortal realm. This was necessary, for if the rebel had raised himself to acting on the mythical level, it was no longer enough to merely remove him from the mortal sphere; such monsters had to be removed from any existence, lest they continue to be a threat in the afterlife or in the mythical realm. Ritual slaying, because of its position in sacred time and space, would also have this effect. It has been argued that even impaling may have been conceived of as a way of fixing the *b3* and shadow (parts of a person's non-physical existence) of a person to the ground, thus preventing their ability to move and cause mischief in the afterlife.[6]

The efficacy of sanctioned killing in the mythical sphere does not mean that such acts were not also prudent in the temporal sphere. Assmann states that ritual repetition "generates *cultural* order with a view to sustaining *cosmic* order; *memoria* is raised to the rank of cosmogony."[7] As noted above, "The function of myth and ritual, however, is not to chronicle past events so much as to enable a community to deal effectively with the practical issues which press upon it daily in the serious business of living, often in a precarious and unpredictable environment."[8] Mundane ramifications—such as maintaining political power, increasing military or economic control, or removing unruly elements from society—were neither unexpected nor undesired effects. Indeed, these consequences may have been the driving force behind decisions to enact sanctioned killing. Political and cosmic motivations were by no means mutually exclusive. To the contrary, the Egyptians considered the two realms intertwined, and thus that which was seen as politically expedient was cosmically expedient and was hence conceived of as being played out to some degree in the mythical realm.[9] In this realm the king had to act as one who killed the enemies of Osiris, or who slew Apophis, or as one of the loyal men who slew Re's enemies after Re removed himself from the earth. Thus, it is unsurprising that sanctioned killing was conceived of as an event that took place because of actions which, by their nature, moved rebels into a mythical sphere, where they met mythical consequences. This sanctioned violence was thus able to fulfill the primary duty of the king: to uphold *Ma'at* in the mortal and immortal realms. The need for upholding Ma'at actually drove those in power unrelentingly toward killing in the appropriate context.

This study has demonstrated that sanctioned killing was a part of Egyptian society. Its persistence and longevity are amply apparent. Burning and decapitation were methods regularly employed over the span of Egyptian history. Impalement became popular in the Ramesside era. Sacrificial servant burial in an effort to maintain order was common in the earliest periods and sporadic thereafter.

The argument that ritual slaying was not part of ancient Egypt is no longer sustainable. Nevertheless, the evidence we have for ritual slaying leaves many unanswered questions. It does seem that there were some regular programs of ritual slaying. Certainly the sacrificial servant burials of the early dynasties, and probably the *tekenu* rites of later periods, were such. Ritual slaughter of enemies, as evidenced by the smiting scene and victory boat parades, were probably also somewhat systematized. The Eighteenth Dynasty exhibits some evidence that coronation rites may have regularly included ritual slaying.

---

[6] Wolfgang Boochs, "Über den strafzweck des Pfählens", *GM* 69, 1983, 7–10.

[7] Jan Assmann, *The Mind of Egypt: History and Meaning in the Time of the Pharaohs*, Andrew Jenkins (trans.), New York: Metropolitan Books, 2002, p. 72.

[8] E.O. James, *Myth and Ritual In the Ancient Near East*, London: Thames and Hudson, 1958, p. 304.

[9] Christopher Eyre, *The Cannibal Hymn: A Cultural and Literary Study*, Bolton: The University of Liverpool Press, 2002, p. 50, writes that the Cannibal Hymn is a mythologizing of practical actions. This is representative of what many of the ritualized slaying presented in this study would be.

There is slight evidence for other forms of a regular program of ritual slaughter, such as the festival commemorated on the ivory labels of Aha and Djer's, or the possibility of ritual slayings at Hekaib. On the other hand, some ritual slayings seem to have been a response to certain stimuli, for example, Senusret I's ritual slaughters at Tod or Prince Osorkon's at Karnak. Yet other cases may be either part of a regular system or a response to a situation. For example, sacrifices associated with execration rites may have been in response to a certain dangerous situation, as some execration rites certainly were. Yet other execration rites seem to have been part of a regular prophylactic practice, warding off all potential rebels before they had begun any of their minatory acts. Similarly, the repeated possibility that criminals were ritually slain may have taken place whenever certain types of criminals were apprehended, or the slayings may have been a regular ritual for which some criminals were chosen as participants. These ambiguous cases do not take away from the safe conclusion that ritual slaying was a feature of regular systematization in ancient Egypt, and it took place as a response to certain stimuli.

As has been briefly mentioned, we do not know how much sanctioned killing took place outside the ritual setting. It is possible that all killing, because of its links to mythology, took on ritual aspects in one form or another. Nevertheless, many acts of sanctioned killing examined in this study display no notion of ritualization in the sources available to us. Moreover, the presence of a few bits of ritual trappings that may have occurred in some situations would not necessarily qualify the event for meeting the criteria set for ritual slaying. These non-ritual slayings seem to be largely a response to a stimulus. If conspirators attempted a royal assassination, they identified themselves with mythical rebels, and in response they were killed. If thieves accomplished such an identification by plundering tombs and temples, they met the same response. The same can be said for murder, embezzlement, and a host of other acts identified within this disquisition as bringing about sanctioned killing. These deaths were brought about because the specific situation demanded it. In both the case of demonstrably ritual slaughters and killings that do not seem to exhibit rituality, the bloodshed brought about a restoration of order. The actions that qualified a person for sanctioned killing, whether in a ritual context or not, likely changed over time, but the mythical context of sanctioned killing did not. For over two millennia, Egypt steadily witnessed sanctioned killing that served order.

www.ingramcontent.com/pod-product-compliance
Lightning Source LLC
Chambersburg PA
CBHW041707290426
44108CB00027B/2889